# 1 MONTH OF
# FREE
# READING

## at
## www.ForgottenBooks.com

By purchasing this book you are eligible for one month membership to ForgottenBooks.com, giving you unlimited access to our entire collection of over 1,000,000 titles via our web site and mobile apps.

To claim your free month visit:
www.forgottenbooks.com/free897779

ISBN 978-0-265-84285-0
PIBN 10897779

This book is a reproduction of an important historical work. Forgotten Books uses
state-of-the-art technology to digitally reconstruct the work, preserving the original format
whilst repairing imperfections present in the aged copy. In rare cases, an imperfection in
the original, such as a blemish or missing page, may be replicated in our edition. We do,
however, repair the vast majority of imperfections successfully; any imperfections that
remain are intentionally left to preserve the state of such historical works.

*I* EXPECTED a good year in 1890, believing that 1889 was near bottom, and I have to thank my friends most gratefully for a year whose prosperity has never been surpassed but once in my business career. For 1891 I expect to excel all previous records, and with this end in view hand you herewith the best seed catalogue I have ever published, filled to the very brim with good things you and your neighbors need. When it is considered, however, that this catalogue is eagerly looked for the first of every year in more than 175,000 homes, to deserve the esteem and favor of such an intelligent clientage it ought to be a good one.

Maule's seeds have now been supplied direct to customers at 33,631 post-offices in these United States. Further comment is scarcely necessary. I know of no other house, whether in the seed or any other line of business, that can make such a statement.

Now, it stands to reason that this immense business—which has been built up in little more than a dozen years—could only have been obtained in one way, namely: through the superior excellence of Maule's seeds. Every reader of this book knows it would be impossible to build up such a trade as this catalogue represents with poor seeds as a foundation.

All the signs point to a more active demand for everything relating to plant life than for years, and with this end in view I have made preparations for a large trade the coming spring;

**An Apology.** I have a confession to make to some of my customers, and might as well make it right here and be through with it. Last year, owing to an unusual demand, I ran out of my own stock of Stratagem Peas, and in the pressure of the busy season I procured ten bushels from what I considered the most reliable source. They were distributed in small quantities to over 200 of my customers. On making three separate tests of peas from this lot last summer I discovered, much to my chagrin, that only half of them grew. Now, it speaks a good word for Maule's seeds, that only two customers complained, and on inquiry I found that my friends had blamed the fact of their having a poor stand to the weather or other causes. Mistakes will sometimes occur in the best regulated families, and I am sorry to report one here ; but will, of course, take pleasure in refilling every one of my customers orders for Stratagems, who will notify me that they had a poor stand.

**MY 4 LEAF CLOVER GUARANTEE**

I. SAFE ARRIVAL.—I guarantee that all goods sold by me shall reach my customers in good order.
II. MONEY INSURED.—I guarantee to hold myself responsible for the safe arrival of all remittances sent me by post-office order, draft, check or registered letter.
III. FREE BY MAIL.—I guarantee to deliver all garden and flower seeds, except where quoted by peck, bus., bbl., or by the 100 lbs., free of all charges.
IV. AS REPRESENTED.—I guarantee my seeds to be just as represented. If they prove otherwise, I will refill the order free of charge ; but it must be understood I do not guarantee the crop any further than to refill the order.

and am glad to be able to inform my friends that my supply of everything in this book was never so complete, never of better quality, nor has my organization for filling orders promptly and effectively ever been in better shape. Few who read this catalogue can appreciate what this last statement means, on account of the mammoth proportions of the business now annually done in Maule's seeds. Nothing I can think of more pointedly shows its growth than the statement that in a single registered mail I have received orders, with cash enclosed, amounting to more than $2,200 ; or the fact that the Assistant Postmaster of Philadelphia, as long ago as 1888, informed me that I had received more registered letters in a single delivery than had come to any other business house in Philadelphia—the then second largest city in the Union. But I am glad to say that with my four separate and distinct departments for filling orders, I will be able to execute all the favors my friends see fit to send me in 1891 with quicker dispatch than ever.

To those into whose hands this book may come this year for the first time, I would only add that Maule's seeds are recognized as the American standard of excellence by more than 175,000 of the most successful gardeners in these United States, who have planted them for years, who consider them the best they have ever sown, and to whom alone I am indebted for a most generous patronage, and a business success that has been unprecedented in the annals of the American seed trade. To my customers I give the credit of building up what is to-day the largest mail order seed business in America, if not in the world, and with best wishes to each and every one of them for the coming year, I remain,

Yours to command, *Wm. Henry Maule*

**TERMS.** Cash with order, or satisfactory Philadelphia or New York references. Money can be sent by post-office or express order, draft, or check. If you don't remit in any of these ways, register the letter ; you can do this at any post-office in America. For expense of forwarding money, I will send seed as an equivalent. I will send C. O. D. by express, on orders exceeding $10, if 25 per cent. of the money is remitted with the order. I cannot ship C. O. D. by freight. I receive postage-stamps as cash.

**ARE YOU A MARKET GARDENER?**

*If you raise truck to sell, you ought to have my Special Price List. It will be mailed free to Market-Gardeners ; but as it is intended only for this particular trade, I cannot send it to private gardeners, even if they apply for it. For index of contents of this book see page 4.*

In 1884 I first offered **EARLIEST OF ALL**, as the **EARLIEST PEA** in cultivation. It has proved itself to be a remarkable addition, and if you desire to have peas **before your neighbors**, this is just the sort to plant. But extra earliness is not the only thing to recommend Earliest of All, for besides being earlier than any other, it is a **wonderful bearer**, producing an enormous number of fine pods, we'll filled with extra plump peas of the most **delicious flavor**. It is an even cropper, can almost always be **cleaned off with one or two pickings.** Market-gardeners will all appreciate this quality. Vines grow about two feet high, and are always **loaded down** with pods. Packet, 15c.; pint, 35c.; quart, 60c, postpaid.

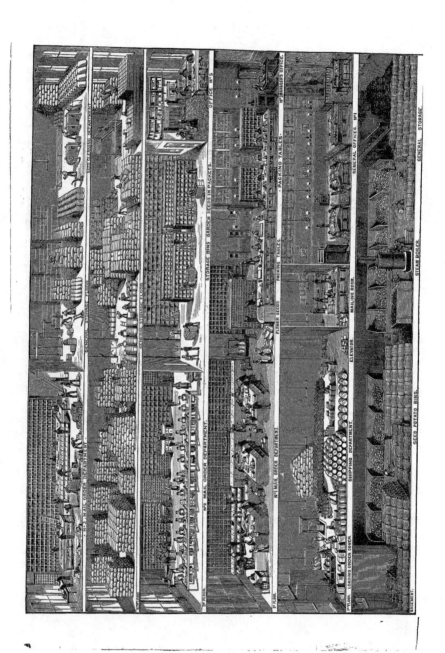

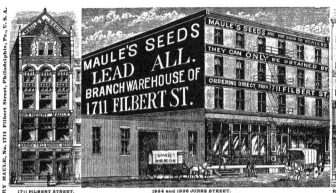

1711 FILBERT STREET.   1934 and 1936 JONES STREET.   Rear, 1711 FILBERT ST.

## The Illustrations

of my Philadelphia Warehouses, given on this and the preceding page, show much better than anything I could write the present dimensions of the business now annually done in Maule's Seeds. **Two such stores can not be found elsewhere in America, nor can the system under which the business is conducted in them be equaled by any other seed firm.**

New readers of this book must bear in mind that these stores are entirely occupied in a retail business. Maule's Seeds are not sold to dealers, **but every department herein illustrated is at all times at the call and service of any customer who sends an order from this book.** It was only five years ago that I had especially built for me, at 1711 Filbert Street, the finest warehouse in America, for conducting the mail order seed business. It was carefully planned and erected, from the basement to the fifth floor, with an idea of answering every requirement of my business for many years to come. A careful examination of cut on opposite page will give every one an excellent idea how really complete it is—the inside fixtures alone costing more than $10,000. What was the result? In three years' time the demand for Maule's Seeds had increased to such proportions as to make another warehouse necessary; hence the two stores in which my business is at present conducted. In both stores I carry a complete line of every thing in which I deal. If one of my warehouses should burn down, even in the height of the season, while I should of course suffer loss and inconvenience, still my customers would lose nothing, for my business would not be interrupted for an hour.

The above cuts are exact representations of the exterior of my Jones and Filbert Street Stores; that on opposite page an excellent illustration of the interior of the Filbert Street Warehouse, while that at the bottom of this page well illustrates Mail Order Department No. 4, which occupies the entire third floor of the Jones Street Warehouse. These are not fancy pictures, **but represent things just as they are.** It is needless to say that I am very proud to show any one of my customers through my warehouses. Frequently customers from a distance happen to be stopping in Philadelphia, and while here, come to see the place from which they obtain their seeds. I am always glad to see them, and after showing them through my stores, **all express the same opinion that the half had not been told,** and that they had no idea there was such a place in the country. As it is impossible for all my customers to go through my establishment in person, I will explain opposite illustration; beginning at the bottom.

**THE BASEMENT.**—This is entirely devoted to storing seed potatoes.

**FIRST FLOOR.**—To the right, will first be seen office No. 1. This is devoted entirely to booking orders. For this purpose I require 37 enormous ledgers, which if laid one on the top of the other, make a pile almost 8 feet high. **They contain 61,801 separate accounts,** or one for every P. O. in the country. Back of this office is the outgoing mail room; here, almost all day long, half a dozen clerks are busy placing the stamps on packages that go by mail, and packing them in Uncle Sam's mail sacks, which the post-office authorities furnish me for that purpose. Back of this is the shipping room. Here I have a drive-way right into the store into which wagons are backed, so that all my unloading and loading in the Filbert Street warehouse is done under cover.

**SECOND FLOOR.**—To the right will be seen the office of my manager. Back of his office is my private office. The balance of this floor is fitted up to fill the larger mail-orders.

**THIRD FLOOR.**—To the right will be seen office No. 5; here young women are kept busy addressing catalogue wrappers, and filing orders, according to number, in books of 500 orders each, after they have been filled. Back of this, and right over my private office, is the office for opening the mail. In the busy season my entire time, from 8 A. M. to 11 P. M., assisted by four or five trusty clerks, is taken up opening the thousands of letters brought me by every mail and in dictating to a stenographer such letters as require answering. In the middle of this floor will be seen part of my storage bins for seeds in packets; here I have stored away millions of papers which are done up as soon as new seeds come to hand in the fall, and are packed here for use in the rush of business. Back of this room is the Mail Order Department No. 2; here all mail-orders amounting to less than $2.00 are filled and this room is also used in December and January for mailing my catalogue.

**FOURTH FLOOR.**—Is devoted to storage purposes.

**FIFTH FLOOR.**—Forward part is devoted to storing onion sets and cleaning seeds. The rear contains Mail Order Department No. 3; in this department all orders amounting to more than $2.00 and less than $4.00 are filled.

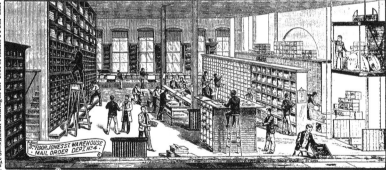

3rd FLOOR JONES ST. WAREHOUSE MAIL ORDER DEPT N? 4.

Page 4—Annual Catalogue for 1891 of Maule's Four-Leaf Clover GUARANTEED SEEDS. Address all Orders to WM. HENRY MAULE, No. 1711 Filbert Street, Philadelphia, Pa., U. S. A.

FOR THE 1891 CASH PRIZES SEE PAGE 68

$100.00 IN 1883 CASH CLUB PREMIUMS $1000.00 IN 1891.

From a very small beginning in 1883, the club orders sent me by my customers have grown to their present proportions. The outlook for 1891, as stated on page one, is certainly encouraging and my customers and their friends, I think, will be sure to want even more seeds this year than last; consequently, I am satisfied that every one of my old club raisers, as well as every one who may try this year for the first time, will have little trouble in sending me as large club orders, if indeed they are not larger, the coming season than ever before. I am always inclined to look on the bright side of everything, so that, while the top club order may not be as large as that which secured the prize last season, still I am very sure it will not be quite as small as in 1889, when the first club order securing the $250 premium only amounted to $105.70. (See last year's catalogue.) But no matter, if the club orders received do not amount to as much as the prizes themselves, the persons sending them in can depend on receiving that $1,000 July 1st, as promised. I consider one secret of my success in offering these club prizes is the fact that my customers know that every premium offered is paid promptly to the proper person at the time agreed upon, no matter what the amount of the order may be. I do not believe, as some others do, in offering premiums and then not publishing the names of those who secured the money. Below will be found the names and post office addresses of the 93 successful club raisers of 1890 :

**FIRST PRIZE** of $250 for club of $259.95.—C. A. HEAGY, Middletown, Md.

**SECOND PRIZE** of $100 for club of $189.35.—MRS. IDA. M. DAVISON, Athens, Ga.

**THIRD PRIZE** of $50 for club of $156.15.—J. POLK HEIVNER, Augusta, Ga.

FIVE PRIZES OF $25.00 EACH AWARDED TO THE
For Club    FOLLOWING:
$121.00—Mrs. Jas. A. Grant, Athens, Ga.
116.00—A. M. Stevens, Williamstown, Mass.
111.64—J. W. Delahoy, Conewango Val., N.Y.
91.17—J. N. Brown, Custer City, Pa.
80.45—Esther Seese, Wakarusa, Ind.

FIVE PRIZES OF $20.00 EACH AWARDED TO
For Club    FOLLOWING:
$74.65—Geo. W. Collier, Cleveland, N.Y.
73.55—C. E. Griffin, Kingsley, Iowa.
73.15—Jno. R. Tomlinson, Picture Rocks, Pa.
70.30—Dwight A. Mets, Strawberry Prat, Ia.
69.00—Jos. M. Michael, Anderson, Ind.

FIVE PRIZES OF $15.00 EACH AWARDED TO THE
For Club    FOLLOWING:
$65.75—Lot Pickering, Gambier, Ohio.
63.37—E. F. Hiley, Eastmanville, Mich.
53.40—Lizzie Miller, Pataskala, Ohio.
51.20—W. E. Barber, New Bridge, Oregon.
47.55—Jas. E. Gibson, Charlesville, Pa.

TEN PRIZES OF $10.00 EACH AWARDED TO THE
For Club    FOLLOWING:
$47.30—Allen S. Fields, So. Wabash, Ind.
38 38—J. A. Prizer, Boyertown, Pa.
37.55—R. F. Hoyt, Manchester, Iowa.
33.00—W. H. Harrell, Bellefonte, Ark.
29.70—Mrs. C. V. McLendon, Hatoff, Ga.
28.70—Jos. Kaufman, Syracuse, Ind.
27.85—Geo. E. Walker, Rumford, R. I.
26.67—A. W. Claypool, Nashport, Ohio.
25.65—P. F. Garrett, Roswell, N. Mexico.
25.00—Theo. M. Millen, Monmouth, Ill.

TEN PRIZES OF $5.00 EACH AWARDED TO THE
For Club    FOLLOWING:
$24.60—Peter M. Johnson, Dawson, Minn.
24.40—Mrs. N. D. Arnold, Sugar Run, Pa.
23.90—Albert G. Gass, Mexico, Mo.
23.40—C. A. Morgan, Gerald, Texas.
23.30—N. O. Baldwin, Pomeroy, Washing'n.
23.10—M. A. Howland, Manson, Iowa.
20.50—Wm. H. Gehman, Reading, Pa.
20.40—Benj. G. Rosenberger, No. Wales, Pa.
19.60—Isaac C. Ellis, Woodville, R.I.
19.35—B. M. Moyer, Hatfield, Pa.

TWENTY PRIZES OF $4.00 EACH AWARDED TO THE
For Club    FOLLOWING:
$18.95—E. F. Manning, Youngstown, Ohio.
18.25—John Warner, Keyesport, Ill.
18.20—L. C. Claprood, Herring, Ohio.
17.65—Mary L. Coe, Upper Penasco, N. Mex.
17.35—W. Vincent, Tekonsha, Mich.
17.05—S. D. Moore, St. Johns, Arizona.
16.75—John Y. Ellis, Muncy, Pa.
16.50—Geo. Cole, West Lebanon, Ind.
16.35—Mrs. M. Niles, Foster Brook, Pa.
16.10—A. G. McCleve, Taylor, Arizona.

TWENTY PRIZES OF $3.00 EACH AWARDED TO THE
For Club    FOLLOWING:
$15.80—H. Hofses, No. Waldoboro, Maine.
15.80—H. J. Wright, St. Clair, TeKuiti, Waikati, New Zealand.
15.80—McClean & Lisee, Meriden, Conn.,
15.35—Mrs. E. B. Dodder, Linden, Mich.
15.35—W. J. Alderman, Windsor, O.
15.15—Mrs. Frank Watson, Flagg Spr'g, Ky.
15.15—H. A. Irvine, Monticello, Minn.

15.00—Geo. G. Collier, Spurger, Texas.
15.00—D. Auretius Gardner, Hancock, Mass.
15.00—Alfred Thompson, Raw River, N. C.
14.75—Mrs. C. Lou Oates, Vicksburg, Miss.
14.50—G. Miller Wolfe, Clear Brook, Va.
14.40—W. B. Bennett, W. Jordan, Utah.
14.40—Jas. Green, Norwood, Wash.
14.40—H. W. Pickett, Wentworth's Loc'n, N.H.
14.00—Sam'l L. Earick, Horton's, Pa.
13.90—Edwin E. Allen, E. Stoneham, Maine.
13.90—A. G. Crocker, Finlayson, Minn.
13.75—Geo. W. Wood, Macy, Arks.
13.65—Mrs. Lena Ragland, Licking, Mo.
13.65—Mrs. M.H. Yost, Berkeley Sp'gs, W.Va.

TWENTY-FIVE PRIZES OF $2.00 EACH AWARDED TO
For Club    THE FOLLOWING:
$13.60—John Hinkle, Farwell, Mich.
13.55—R. L. Moore, Boonville, Mo.
13.50—J. F. Smith, Sterling, Iowa.
13.50—Walter J. Barnard, Doe Run, Pa.
13.45—John E. Wilkson, Seymour, Ind.
13.35—A. E. Rouillier, Paraje, N. Mexico.
13.30—E. A. Compton, Mt. Morris, Pa.
13.30—John B. Morton, Protection, Kan.
13.15—W. H. Nichols, Lyndell, Pa.
13.00—Geo. Morrow, American, Mo.
13.85—Levi Longcore, Benton, N.J.
12.85—H. B. Zimmerman, Martinsvi'le, N.J
12.50—Andrew C. Niewander, Broadw'y, Va.
13.70—Miles Ratcliff, Casey, Ill.
12.50—J. S. Brook, Evening Shade, Ark.
12.50—James F. Stedman, Marilla, N.Y.
12.50—Sam'l Reynolds, Mansfield, Austr'lia.
12.40—John W. Spencer, Sullivan, Ind.
12.25—James R. Shearer, Lock Haven, Pa.
12.15—David F. Morris, Ferndale, Ont.
11.90—Albert Kline, Sumption Prairie, Ind.
11.85—D. W. Neuhirter, Cedar Bluffs, Neb.
11.75—Mrs. E. Figgins, Jefferson, Md.

It will be noticed that the last club order amounts to $11.75. Now, on looking up my books, I found I had three customers who had sent to me for packets and ounces amounting to $11.75; so in addition to sending Mrs. E. Figgins the $2 prize, I also sent my check for $2 to Z. Matthews, Coldwater, Mich., and J. S. Ludington, Holmes, N.Y. Again, in the latter part of August, after all the club orders had been paid, Mr. J. L. Sanders, Schaefferstown, Pa., wrote me that he had been in hopes his club orders would have secured him a prize, and that, so far, he had failed to hear anything from me. On looking up my books I found that one of my clerks had overlooked Mr. S.'s orders entirely, and as he had sent me a club amounting to $70.15 he was entitled to a $20 premium. I then, of course, sent him my check for this amount.

**AS ALREADY STATED ABOVE,** this coming July 1, I will divide among the club raisers of Maule's Seeds, one thousand dollars for the 93 largest club orders, for packets and ounces only, sent me between now and July 1st, 1891. All will admit this is a large amount of money. Until you have once tried, you can have no idea how easy it is to have your neighbors join you in ordering their seeds. **IT IS SIMPLY ASTONISHING THAT MORE OF MY CUSTOMERS DON'T WORK FOR THESE PREMIUMS.** I know most of the prize-winning clubs during the past eight years have been secured with but little trouble. **One good afternoon's work has secured frequently a cash premium,** besides giving the club raiser the benefit of my largest discount on seeds in packets, **$15 for $10.** With the reputation Maule's Seeds has in all sections of the country for reliability and purity, and with this bright, new catalogue filled to overflowing with so many good things **you and your neighbors want,** will you not try it? Don't be discouraged if you do not get an order just at first. **The first two or three orders will be harder to secure than all the others.** Somebody is going to receive that $1,000 July 1st. **Why should you not receive part of it?** I have no secret terms to agents. I try to do everything open and above-board. Every reader of this Catalogue can go to work and raise a club for Maule's Seeds, knowing that no one has better terms than he. **Remember, all the orders you send, little or big, will be counted up July 1st.** Even if you should not be so successful as to secure a cash prize, you can, by making up a $10 club, secure my greatest discount on seed in packets. Always remember that for a **ten dollar bill you can select seeds in packets to the value of $15.** Should any one desire a few extra Catalogues to help them in canvassing, I will only be too glad to mail them. Let all enter this friendly competition determined to win. **Don't try for a small prize, GO FOR THAT $250.** It is worth an extra effort and any one who puts in a week or ten days of good solid work

has an excellent chance of securing it. Every one who makes even a small effort ought to, and can safely, I think, depend on being one of the 93 whose names will be published in my Annual Catalogue for 1892. **BEAR IN MIND** that every order you send me for packets or ounces of Maule's Seeds will be counted July 1st, 1891, when the Prizes will be awarded as announced below.

**FOR the Largest Club Order of Packets and Ounces of either Garden or Flower Seeds,**

| | |
|---|---|
| For the Largest Club Order | **$250.00** |
| For the Second Largest Club, | 100.00 |
| For the Third Largest Club, | 50.00 |
| For the next 5 Largest Clubs, each | 25.00 |
| For the next 5 Largest Clubs, " | 20.00 |
| For the next 5 Largest Clubs, " | 15.00 |
| For the next 10 Largest Clubs, " | 10.00 |
| For the next 10 Largest Clubs, " | 5.00 |
| For the next 20 Largest Clubs, " | 4.00 |
| For the next 20 Largest Clubs, " | 3.00 |
| For the next 25 Largest Clubs, " | 2.00 |
| **93 PRIZES,** | **Total, $1,000.00** |

# GENERAL LIST OF MAULE'S SEEDS FOR 1891.

☞ The following pages contain *The Cream* of all varieties known to the American Seed Trade. You will find no *Skimmed Milk* in this Catalogue.

TOOL HOUSE & GREENHOUSE AT BRIAR CREST

A PARTIAL VIEW OF THE TRIAL GROUNDS AT BRIAR CREST"

CONOVER'S COLOSSAL

MAULE'S MAMMOTH

I flatter myself that the following list of Garden Seeds is **unsurpassed by any other house in the United States**; not as large as that found in many other catalogues, **but I have winnowed the chaff from the wheat.** For years past I have culled out all the surplus varieties with an idea of offering **only the best**, and condensing the list to an extent that will not prove confusing to the market-gardener, let alone the private planter. It is rank injustice to offer the same variety of seed under half a dozen different names, and an absurdity to list a countless number of sorts for which there is no demand.

**All can rest assured, however, that I have omitted nothing worthy of a place in the following pages.**

## Special Discounts on Packets

It takes almost as much time, detail, etc., to fill an order for 20 or 25 cents, as it does one amounting to $1.00, consequently with an idea of increasing the size of our packet orders, and to offer my customers an inducement to have their neighbors send in their orders with them, I allow the following discount on seeds in packets: **Any one of my customers has the privilege of selecting seeds, in packets only, to the amount of $1.30 and sending me $1.00 for same; or, I will send seeds, in packets only, to the value of $2.75 for $2.00; or, purchasers remitting $3.00 can select seeds in packets to the value of $4.25.** Purchasers remitting

**$4.00 can select seeds in packets to the value of $5.70.** Purchasers remitting **$5.00 can select seeds in packets to the value of $7.25. PURCHASERS REMITTING $10.00 CAN SELECT SEEDS IN PACKETS ONLY, TO THE VALUE OF $15.00.**

When it is considered that I offer these discounts in addition to the liberal cash prizes given on the preceding page, I trust it will be appreciated by all of my customers. **It must be borne in mind, however, that this discount applies to seeds in packets only, and is not allowed on seeds by the ounce, pint, quarter pound, pound, etc.**

**ARTICHOKES. JERUSALEM.**—Over one thousand bushels have been produced on an acre. They are very hardy and resemble Potatoes in appearance; they should be planted in the same way and are very easily grown. If desired they need not be dug, but the hogs can be turned in the field to root them up; in this way one acre will keep 20 head in good condition until Spring, excepting when the ground is frozen too hard for the hogs to root them up. To destroy them the ground should be plowed when plants are a foot high. Pound, 40 cts.; 3 lbs., $1.00, by mail, postpaid. $3.00 per bushel, by express or freight, purchaser paying charges.

**GREEN GLOBE.**—A table variety largely grown abroad, but little known here. Edible portions are the flower heads, which should be used before they begin to open. Pkt., 10c.; oz., 30c.

JERUSALEM ARTICHOKE ROOTS

**ASPARAGUS CONOVER'S COLOSSAL.**—Known to all. Pkt., 5 cts.; oz., 10 cts.; ¼ lb., 20 cts.; lb., 50 cts. ROOTS, 1 year old, 100 by mail, $1.25; by express, 1 year old, $5.00 per 1000, 2 year old, $6.00 per 1000, purchaser paying charges.

**PALMETTO.**—It is claimed that this new variety is not only much earlier than Conover's, but is also a better yielder and of more even growth, while of a Southern origin it is well adapted for all sections both North and South. Pkt., 10 cts.; oz., 20 cts.; ¼ lb., 50 cts.; lb., $1.50.

**MAULE'S MAMMOTH.**—This variety, I consider, **excels all others**, not only in tenderness and flavor, but also in productiveness. It throws out an unusual number of strong, well-developed shoots the entire season, and it has sold in Philadelphia markets for **four times** the price of other sorts. At three years old has yielded crops valued at $500 per acre. Pkt., 10 cts.; oz., 20 cts.; ¼ lb., 50 cts.; lb., $1.50. ROOTS, 1 year old, 100 by mail, $1.50; by express, 1 year old, $6.00 per 1000, 2 year old, $7.50 per 1000, the purchaser paying charges.

MAULE'S BUTTER WAX

KING OF THE GARDEN

MAULE'S BUTTER WAX

NONPAREIL GREEN POD

**MAULE'S BUTTER WAX.**—During the last few years there has been quite a number of Wax Beans brought before the notice of the American public, so many varieties, in fact, that I certainly would have hesitated about adding another to the already long list, unless I was perfectly confident that I had a sort that would lay all others on the shelf. Butter Wax is unquestionably **the earliest** Wax Bean, while its beautiful, transparent golden-yellow pods **absolutely contain more meat** than any other variety. The dry beans are white with an irregular brown eye, and as it comes from an accidental cross between the Golden Wax and Dwarf Black Wax, it will be seen that it is very similar to that very fine variety recently introduced, called the Black Eyed Wax. Being **entirely** stringless. Maule's Butter Beans can be used as a String Bean until nearly ripe; in fact, **longer than any other sort.** It is also one of the hardiest varieties, and is **less liable to spot** than any other. Four cardinal points may be given why it should head the list of all other wax varieties. First, **quality,** which is unexcelled. Second, **stringlessness,** as they are absolutely without strings. Third, **earliness,** for in this respect they are not surpassed by any other wax bean in cultivation. Fourth, **solid meat,** for a pithy or hollow pod cannot be found. Maule's Butter Beans, as soon as their superior qualities are known, **will lead all other wax sorts.** Packet, 15 cents; pint, 35 cents; quart, 60 cents.

**NONPAREIL GREEN POD.**—**No garden will be complete without Nonpareil.** It is about the very last Bean to mature, and comes in at the time when almost all other varieties are hard and stringy. This one point, will recommend Nonpareil, but at the same time is only one of the many qualifications. On the grounds of the New York Experimental Station in 1888 and everywhere else where grown, it was by all odds **the most vigorous and hardy of all,** so I have no hesitancy in saying it **will withstand dry weather better than any other.** In productiveness it is certainly remarkable, the vines being fairly loaded with numbers of long, dark green pods, that, when pulled before maturity, are of most excellent quality, and if allowed to mature they will be found one of the most productive to grow for shell beans, as the crop is matured all at once, and the pods are always full of large, red speckled, kidney-shaped Beans, which cook tender and mealy. Pkt., 10 cents; pint, 30 cents; quart, 50 cents.

**KING OF THE GARDEN LIMA.**—"The vines grow luxuriantly, and furnish a bountiful supply of enormous pods, many specimens measuring from 5 to 8 inches and often producing 5 and 6 beans to the pod, all perfectly formed and possessing superb qualities, unexcelled by any that have come to my notice during a practical experience in bean culture of 20 years." Packet, 10 cents; pint, 35 cents; quart, 60 cents.

I will send one packet of each of the above Beans for 30 cents, or one pint of each of the above varieties for 75 cents.

7

# My Colored Plate Specialties. ✳

**MARKET-GARDENERS' BEET.**—This new variety was discovered eleven years ago in a field of Pineapple Beets. Ever since, by constant selection, and keeping in mind at all times its ideal shape, color and size, it has been perfected, **until now I consider it the best general purpose beet in cultivation.** As will be noticed from illustration on opposite page, which is an exact representation of this desirable variety reduced in size, it is very symmetrical, has but few fibrous roots and has unusually small top. At age of Egyptian it is larger, and continues to grow until late in fall, attaining large size, and making a good selling and eating Beet for winter. By 1st of Oct. they measure 8 in. in diameter, and average 4 lbs. in weight. One sowing only is necessary to produce early beets for market and main crop for winter use, which is not the case with any other variety. Color outside is deep blood red; inside layers blood red and light red alternately. When cooked they are a beautiful dark red throughout, fine grained and unsurpassed quality. Summing all up we find it **the Best Beet** for early market as well as **the Best Beet** for summer and winter use. Owing to small top, which permits them to be grown close together and peculiar shape of bulb, it is also the most profitable beet for market as well as family garden of any I know of. Packet, 10 cts.; oz. 25 cts.; ¼ lb. 60 cts.; lb. $2.00.

**NEW GIANT PASCAL CELERY.**—This new Celery which I took pleasure in introducing to my customers last year for the first time, promise to be as great an addition to our list of varieties of this delicious vegetable as the Golden Self Blanching. As it is an offspring of the latter, it partakes of its nutty flavor, and has no bitter taste at all; while being a wonderful keeper it can be sold and shipped after Golden Self Blanching is sold out. The height is about two feet; stalks are very large, thick, solid and not stringy. In fact, it is the largest celery ever known as to width of stalk. It is the celery for January and February use, as well as most excellent for shipping purposes, as it keeps crisp very long without flagging. The stalks are unusually tender and crisp, snapping like glass, and when desired can be sliced lengthwise. When fully grown the outer stalks will average two inches in width, and are fully as thick as a man's finger, and is well shown on the opposite page in the illustration of a stalk of Giant Pascal reduced in size. It blanches very easily, and after a very few days' earthing up, the outer stalks present a beautiful white appearance. Even without blanching, while the outer stalks are green, the heart will be a rich, bright yellow. Unlike most other celeries, it never becomes watery, and can be eaten when quite small. Last year, on account of the scarcity of the seed, I was not able to give Pascal as large a notice in my catalogue as I desired, but, nevertheless, the demand was simply remarkable, and every lover of good celery was delighted last fall with Giant Pascal. This year I am glad to say I have secured a large supply of seed direct from the originator, which I am able to offer my customers at the following reasonable figures, considering this is only the second year of its introduction. Pkt., 15c.; oz., 75c.

**IGNOTUM TOMATO.**—Last year I catalogued this magnificent variety for the first time, from the fact that I was very well pleased with the specimens I saw grown in 1889; but last season, growing it in a much larger way, my previous good opinion was not only confirmed but strengthened so much that I determined it was worthy of one of the most prominent places in my catalogue, as it is certainly one of the very finest tomatoes ever introduced. It was discovered by Prof. L. H. Bailey of the Michigan Agricultural College in 1887, as a sport of Eiformige Dauer. There have been many varieties introduced of late years, but no sort, in my opinion, ripens so regularly and produces so much fruit identical in shape and color. In fact, if I may be allowed the expression, on a single plant will be found dozens of specimens as nearly alike as peas in a pod. Ignotum grows to a good size; always a rich color, nearly round and very solid. It keeps its good flavor later in the season than most other varieties, and will be found not so liable to crack as the average. It is very productive; Prof. Taft, of the Michigan College, stating that in dry seasons it produced double the crop and very much more solid fruit than the Turner Hybrid or Mikado. This is saying a great deal, for, as my customers well know, Turner Hybrid is hard to beat, both in regard to prolificness and solidity. While I have a large supply of seed and expect to be able to fill all orders, still I would advise all my customers who desire to plant this magnificent variety in 1891, and who wish larger quantities than packets, to favor me with early orders. Pkt., 10 cts.; oz., 50 cts.; ¼ lb., $1.50.

ENGRAVED FROM A PHOTOGRAPH

HENDERSONS' **BUSH LIMA** The **PRIZE PLANT** OF 1889 323 PODS A DUPLICATE OF THE ORIGINAL PHOTOGRAPH 6 by 8 in. 10 CTS POSTPAID.

**THE NEW BUSH LIMA.**—In 1888, in connection with Messrs. Peter Henderson & Co., of New York, I took pleasure in offering my customers for the first time this, **the most valuable vegetable novelty that has been introduced in many years.** Thousands have been deterred from cultivating the most delicious of vegetables—the Lima Bean—from the great trouble and expense of procuring the unsightly poles on which to grow them. This is now a thing of the past, as the new Bush Lima grows **without the aid of stakes or poles.** In compact bush form, from fifteen to eighteen inches high, and produces enormous crops of delicious Lima Beans, which can be as easily gathered as the common garden bush bean. In competition for the $150 in prizes offered on this bean in my 1888 catalogue, the **first prize bush of Bush Lima, a plant less than 24 inches high, contained the enormous quantity of 323 well-developed pods, and was raised by J. Polk Heivner, of Augusta, Iowa.** This will give some idea of the enormous productiveness of this remarkable bean. The new Bush Lima is at least two weeks earlier than any of the climbing sorts. This fact alone would stamp it as the most valued novelty of recent years; but when in addition to this we realize that it is a true bush bean, requiring no supports, some idea of its great value can be realized. The New Bush Lima produces a continuous crop from the time it comes into bearing (it is fit for the table in the latitude of New York by the middle of July) until frost, and being enormously productive, a very small patch will keep a family supplied with this splendid vegetable throughout the season. A pint of seed will plant five rows, each fifty feet long, which is ample for an ordinary family. The beans are of the size of the Sieva or Southern Lima, and, as before stated, of delicious quality. The size of the dry bean will hinder the Bush Lima from becoming popular with market gardeners; but for private gardeners **I know of nothing that will prove more satisfactory.** Its habit of growth, delicious flavor, and wonderful productiveness recommending it to all. Pkt., 15 cts.; 2 pkts., 25 cts.; pint, 50 cts.; quart, 80 cts.; two quarts, $1.50; postpaid.

8

Free & Liberal Catalogue for 1891 of Maule's Four-Leaf-Clover GUARANTEED SEEDS. Address all Orders to WM. HENRY MAULE, No. 1711 Filbert Street, Philadelphia, Pa., U. S. A.

THE MARKET GARDENERS BEET. PACKET 10 CTS.

NEW GIANT PASCAL CELERY PACKET 15 CTS.

ONE PACKET OF EACH OF THESE THREE CHOICE VEGETABLES FOR 25 CENTS BY MAIL POST PAID.

WM. HENRY MAULE Philadelphia

NEW IGNOTUM TOMATO PACKET 10 CTS.

PRICE $ 2.00 POST PAID.
A COPY WILL BE MAILED FREE TO EVERY CUSTOMER ORDERING SEEDS FROM THIS CATALOGUE TO THE AMOUNT OF $7.50 OR OVER.

HOW TO MAKE
THE
GARDEN PAY
Presentation Edition
COMPLIMENTS OF
WM HENRY MAULE

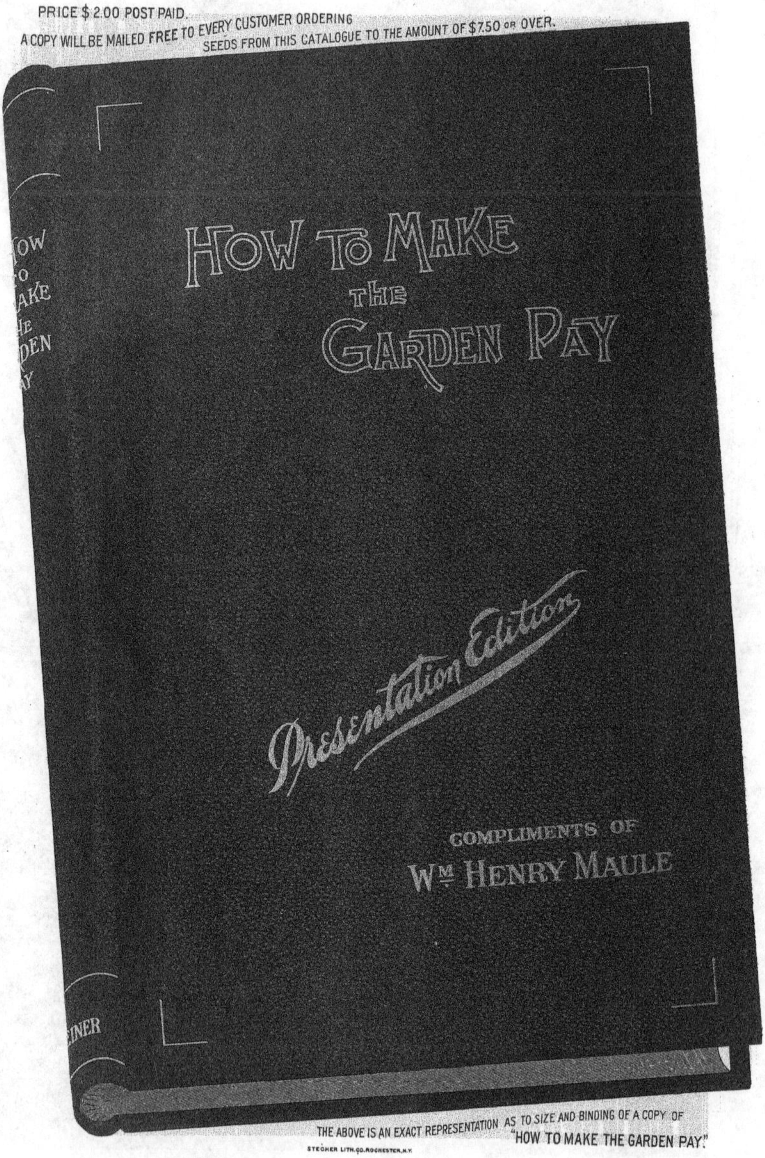

THE ABOVE IS AN EXACT REPRESENTATION AS TO SIZE AND BINDING OF A COPY OF "HOW TO MAKE THE GARDEN PAY."

STECHER LITH. CO. ROCHESTER, N.Y.

# A PAGE OF DWARF GREEN POD BEANS

**A SECTION OF MY TRIAL GROUNDS.**

**BEST OF ALL "GREEN POD"**

**MAULE'S FIRST OF ALL.**—Absolutely the earliest bean in cultivation. I regret I have no seed to offer this year, as my crop is an entire failure.

**EXTRA EARLY ROUND POD VALENTINE.**—A week to ten days earlier than the old Red Valentine, and in it we have probably the best green podded variety for market gardeners, as it combines earliness, productiveness, hardiness, together with a desirable size and shape. It is remarkably prolific; pods being tender and fleshy and remaining on the plants a long time before becoming hard; in fact, in this respect it is superior to almost every other sort. Pkt., 10 cts.; pint, 25 cts.; quart, 45 cts., post-paid.

**IMPROVED EARLY YELLOW SIX WEEKS.**—After the Valentine, I believe this Bean is the next best extra early green pod. It is absolutely stringless until it attains full size. It is extra early, very productive, and always makes a good, thick, meaty pod. Pkt.,10c.; pt., 25c.; qt.,45c.,postpaid.

**ROUND PODDED REFUGEE.**—This old well-known variety has lately been greatly improved by one of our most celebrated bean growers. It is somewhat later than either of the above, but still it is wonderfully prolific, of excellent shape, and in every way desirable; has always been largely grown for pickling. Pkt., 10 cts.; pint, 25 cts.; quart, 45 cts., post-paid.

**EARLY MOHAWK.**—A hardy, early sort, of old-established reputation. Pkt., 10 cts.; pint, 25 cts.; quart, 45 cts.

**BEST OF ALL.**—Pods are long, very fleshy, succulent and stringless, of good flavor. They are produced medium early and abundantly. Market gardeners in the neighborhood of New Orleans have long considered them the best of all. Although only known in the North to a limited extent, all planting them agree they well deserve the name. Pkt., 10c.; pt., 25c.; qt., 45c.

**WHITE KIDNEY.**—Popular either green or ripe, and is one of the very best for Winter use. Pkt., 10 cts.; pt., 25 cts.; qt., 45 cts.

**LARGE WHITE MARROWFAT.**—This has always been a popular variety in field culture, and a most profitable market sort. Pkt., 10c.; pt., 25c.; qt., 45c.

**PROLIFIC TREE.**—This is a small, very white bean, resembling the old-fashioned Navy Bean, but cooks in less time and is of better flavor. They should be planted in rows 2½ feet apart, and 20 inches apart in the rows, so as to secure a large yield; they should not be allowed to crowd each other. In competition for a $25 premium, M. B. Puryear, Linwood, Ark., raised a vine containing 711 pods. Mr. Thompson, of North Andover, Mass., a plant containing 612 pods. From this statement some idea can be had of their wonderful productiveness. Pkt. 10 cts.; pint, 25 cts.; quart, 45 cts., postpaid.

**EXTRA EARLY ROUND POD VALENTINE. Pkt. 10 cts.**

**EARLY MOHAWK. Pkt. 10 cts.**

**IMPROVED TREE BEAN**

**BURLINGAME MEDIUMS.**—In the Burlingame Mediums I consider I offer my customers the earliest, hardiest and most productive Field Bean in America. At present only known to a limited extent in western New York, it still, however, has increased in popularity to such an extent during the last few years, that wherever grown it is planted to

**BURLINGAME MEDIUMS AS GROWN ON THE GENESEE FLATS, N.Y.**

the exclusion of all other sorts. While riding through the Genesee Flats, above Rochester, in New York State, it was the only Field Bean I saw growing in that great Bean growing district, and fields of them, containing 20 to 40 acres were not uncommon. On inquiring, I found 40 bushels to the acre, not an unusual yield, and they have frequently, under favorable circumstances, made a much larger return. They ripen several days earlier than the Marrow, Medium or Pea Bean, and in a wet season will keep dry and healthy while other varieties rust and spot, and are thereby greatly reduced in quantity as well as quality. I have before me a letter from one of the largest concerns handling Beans in New York State; they write that "Burlingame Mediums are, in their opinion, unquestionably the coming Bean for field culture. The ripened seed is pearly white and much handsomer than the old sorts, consequently they can frequently be sold at an extra price." Every reader of this catalogue who has ever grown or thinks of growing Beans for market, should not hesitate to give Burlingame Mediums a trial. Packet, 10 cents; pint, 25 cents; quart, 45 cents.

9

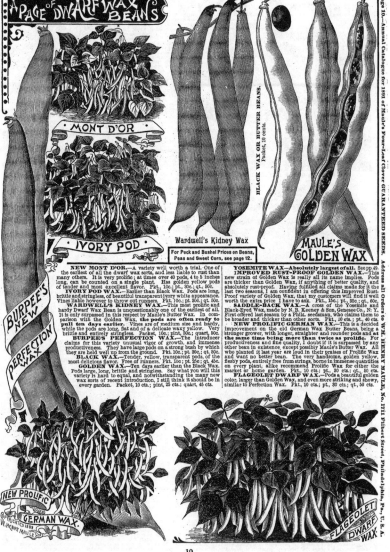

## A PAGE OF DWARF WAX BEANS

MONT D'OR

IVORY POD

BLACK WAX OR BUTTER BEANS.
Packet, 10 cents.

Wardwell's Kidney Wax

For Peck and Bushel Prices on Beans, Peas and Sweet Corn, see page 12.

MAULE'S GOLDEN WAX

BURPEE'S NEW PERFECTION WAX

NEW PROLIFIC GERMAN WAX.
COPYRIGHTED 1889 WM. HENRY MAULE.

FLAGEOLET DWARF WAX

**NEW MONT D'OR.**—A variety well worth a trial. One of the earliest of all the dwarf wax sorts, and less liable to rust than many others. It is very prolific; at times over 40 pods, 4 to 5 inches long, can be counted on a single plant. Has golden yellow pods of tender and most excellent flavor. Pkt., 10c.; pt., 30c.; qt., 50c.

**IVORY POD WAX.**—Earlier than Black Wax. Pods are long, brittle and stringless, of beautiful transparent ivory white appearance. Vines liable however to throw out runners. Pkt. 10c.; pt. 30c.; qt. 50c.

**WARDWELL'S KIDNEY WAX.**—This most prolific and hardy Dwarf Wax Bean is unquestionably one of the earliest of all. It is only surpassed in this respect by Maule's Butter Wax. In comparison with the Golden Wax, **the pods are often ready to pull ten days earlier.** Vines are of medium size and hardy, while the pods are long, flat and of a delicate waxy yellow. Very brittle and entirely stringless. Packet, 10c.; pint, 30c.; quart, 50c.

**BURPEE'S PERFECTION WAX.**—The introducer claims for this variety unusual vigor of growth, and immense productiveness. They have large pods on a strong bush by which they are held well up from the ground. Pkt. 10c.; pt. 30c.; qt. 50c.

**BLACK WAX.**—Tender, yellow, transparent pods, of the most delicious flavor. Free of runners. Pkt. 10c.; pt. 25c.; qt. 45c.

**GOLDEN WAX.**—Ten days earlier than the Black Wax. Pods large, long, brittle and stringless. Say what you will this variety is hard to equal, and notwithstanding the many new wax sorts of recent introduction, I still think it should be in every garden. Packet, 10 cts.; pint, 25 cts.; quart, 45 cts.

**YOSEMITE WAX.**—Absolutely largest of all. See pp. 49.

**IMPROVED RUST-PROOF GOLDEN WAX.**—This new strain of Golden Wax is really all its name implies. Pods are thicker than Golden Wax, if anything of better quality, and absolutely rust-proof. Having fulfilled all claims made for it the last two seasons, I am confident in offering this Improved Rust-Proof variety of Golden Wax, that my customers will find it well worth the extra price I have to ask. Pkt., 15c.; pt., 35c.; qt., 60c.

**SADDLE-BACK WAX.**—A cross of the Yosemite and Black-Eyed Wax, made by N. B. Keeney & Son, Genesee Co., N. Y. First offered last season by a Phila. seedsman, who claims them to be broader and thicker than other sorts. Pkt., 10 cts.; pt., 40 cts.

**NEW PROLIFIC GERMAN WAX.**—This is a decided improvement on the old German Wax Butter Beans, being a stronger grower, with longer, straighter and rounder pods and at **the same time being more than twice as prolific.** For productiveness and fine quality, I doubt if it is surpassed by any other bean in existence except possibly Maule's Butter Wax. All who planted it last year are loud in their praises of Prolific Wax and want no better bean. The very handsome, golden yellow, fleshy pods, entirely free from strings, borne in immense quantities on every plant, alike recommend Prolific Wax for either the market or home garden. Pkt., 10 cts.; pt., 30 cts.; qt., 50 cts.

**FLAGEOLET DWARF WAX.**—Pods a beautiful golden color, larger than Golden Wax, and even more striking and showy, similar to Perfection Wax. Pkt., 10 cts.; pt., 30 cts.; qt., 50 cts.

# POLE BEANS

**WHITE CREASEBACK.**—This very choice pole bean, known through many sections of the South as the Popular Fat Horse Bean, should have been catalogued long ago by Northern seedsmen. One difficulty, however, has been that the seed has always been scarce. I have had, however, a crop grown for me the last four years, and take great pleasure in being able to offer it to my customers. For string beans the Creaseback is especially desirable, being of a beautiful light green color, stringless, about six inches long, perfectly round with a crease in the back, and of most excellent quality. They ripen very early; **in fact, it is the earliest of any green pod pole bean I know,** and pods are thick from one end of the pole to the other. Creaseback for early, Lazy Wives for late, makes an excellent combination. Pkt., 10c.; pt., 30c.; qt., 50c.

**NEW GOLDEN WAX POLE.**—I have given my customers a very fine pole bean above, but have still another that, to say the least, is a perfect beauty. White Creaseback is a green-podded bean. Golden Wax has the finest, rich round, fleshy, stringless, beautiful **golden-yellow** pods, seven to nine inches long, I have ever seen. In flavor it equals any in cultivation, while the vines begin bearing as early as any other pole bean grown, and almost as early as any Dwarf Wax variety. It has only one fault, and that is that the vines do not take the pole quite as readily as the Lazy Wives or Creaseback, but then it is earlier than either, and when its other superior qualities are taken into consideration, not an order for 1891 should omit it. Pkt., 10 cts.; pt., 30 cts.; qt., 50 cts.

**MAULE'S IMPROVED DUTCH RUNNER.**—This new bean is without a doubt **FAR THE MOST PRODUCTIVE POLE BEAN IN CULTIVATION.** The illustration gives but a faint idea of the immense yield. I have never seen anything that could begin to equal them, and all planting Dutch Runner this season I am sure will agree with me. They are also wonderfully early. Pods are very large and handsome, almost equal to the Large Lima. In favor they are superior, and cooked green in Summer **you will find they equal any succotash you** ever made. They continue in bearing from July right up to frost. Packet, 10 cents; pint, 35 cents; quart, 60 cents.

**IT is well to remember that all prices on Beans, Peas, and Sweet Corn, by the pint and quart, include delivery at your post or express office, wherever it may be, free of all charges.**

**NEW GOLDEN CLUSTER.**—This new variety is an improvement on all the good qualities of the Giant and Dwarf Wax, and is distinct in seed, in color and habit of growth. The pods retain their tenderness and plumpness long after the beans have attained a large size, so that only a few days elapse after they cease to be fit for string beans before they are fit to shell. The pods are a beautiful golden yellow, and are from six to eight inches long, borne profusely in clusters of four to six. Commencing to bear ten days after the Golden Wax, it continues to produce an abundance of pods until frost sets in. Pkt., 10 cts.; pt., 35 cts.; qt., 60 cts.

# LIMA BEANS

**SALEM IMPROVED LIMA.**—This is a selected strain of the Large Lima, but it is so far superior to the Lima Beans that I know most of my customers see and grow, that I must give it a prominent notice in my catalogue. In the first place I think you will find it the most productive, and, therefore, best table Lima you have ever grown. Pods are produced in large clusters, five to six large beans often in a pod, and ripens only a very short time after the Extra Early Lima. The vines continue in bearing right up to frost. The King of the Garden is a first-class Lima in every way, but I think the Salem Improved fully equals, if it does not surpass it. It certainly beats it in strong, regular growth on my trial grounds. Packet, 10 cents; pint, 35 cents; quart, 60 cents.

**DREER'S IMPROVED LIMA.**—Very productive, and pods are always full of extra plump beans of the most delicious and superior quality. When green they are nearly as large as the Large Lima, thicker, sweeter and more tender, remaining green in the pod for a long time after maturing. Packet, 10 cents; pint, 20 cents; quart, 50 cents

R. G. Berrett, North Ogden, Utah: "I am pleased to let you know that Maule's Danvers Carrot seed I bought of you last year done extremely well. I raised on 90 rods of ground 24 tons and 1,500 pounds, which would be over 46 tons to the acre. I cannot speak too highly of this carrot. I kept about a tons of the roots for my own use to feed horses and cows; the remainder I sold in Ogden for $8.00 per ton. The Half Long Parsnip also done well, raising 3,000 pounds from ¼ pound of seed."

**FRENCH ASPARAGUS.**—Having had several calls for this bean, I have procured a limited quantity of seed from France. A Philadelphia gardener says of it: "I have grown all varieties of beans, and I consider the Asparagus Bean the most delicious production and best I have ever had." Pods grow **from two to four feet long,** and are produced in great abundance. In color they are a beautiful green, tender and delicious, so that they will not only prove a great curiosity wherever grown, but also a desirable variety as well. E. M. Pace, Virgil City, Mo., raised the prize Asparagus Bean in 1889 It was 36½ inches long. Packet, 15 cents.

Jacob Shisler, Williamsville, N. Y.: "Having used Maule's seeds for two years, have never seen their equal; everything I have tried has proven a representation, and as long as I am in the market gardening business, and Maule's reliable seeds are to be had, they are the seeds for me."

French Asparagus Bean.

SALEM IMPROVED LIMA

$2500 in Cash. see page 68

**11**

A SINGLE PICKING FROM ONE VINE.

COPYRIGHT 1888
W.H. MAULE

LAZY WIVES POLE

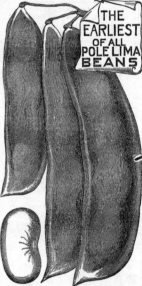

THE EARLIEST OF ALL POLE LIMA BEANS

EXTRA EARLY LIMA

**LAZY WIVES POLE BEAN.**—This variety originated in Bucks County, Pennsylvania, where for a number of years, it has been the most popular Pole Bean grown. Pods are wonderfully broad, thick, fleshy, and, above all, *entirely* stringless. In these respects they surpass any other I know of. Then, again, the pods retain their rich, stringless and tender qualities until they are almost ripe; so much so, in fact, that I am perfectly safe in saying they are the best of all Snap Shorts. They also surpass every other variety in the way vines cling to the pole, and every bean grower will at once acknowledge this is a most important qualification. Its name, I think, implies productiveness, for, the vines being covered all Summer with masses of beautiful pods, it is just the sort to suit lazy wives, as a mess can be soon picked for dinner. Pods are rather flattish, oval shape, and, when fully grown, from 4 to 6 inches long, exceedingly rich, buttery, and fine flavored when cooked. They are hardy, easily grown, and enormously productive. I could furnish hundreds of testimonials from persons who have grown and used the Lazy Wives Bean, all claiming it to be the best Bean they have ever tried, and many have discarded all other kinds, using this for an early and late snap-short, and also as dry, shell or Winter bean ; and such is the peculiar taste and pleasant flavor of this Bean that we have known many persons who could not be induced to eat string beans of any other kind after tasting Lazy Wives. Packet, 15 cents ; pint, 35 cents ; quart, 60 cents.

## ✳ A FEW COMPLAINTS ✳

Borden Lawton, Newport, R. I.: I wish to give every one his due. My vegetable garden has to be replanted in consequence of not using Maule's seeds. The fertilizers were also unsatisfactory, and I've learned a useful lesson.

T. P. Rockey, New Providence, Ind.: I have not sent to you for seeds for the last two years, as I thought I could get as good seed at the store; but I missed it. We have had no garden worth looking at since we stopped getting seeds of you. You have the best seed I ever tried.

Patrick Murphy, Coles Valley, Oregon : I did not send to you last year for seeds, as I was persuaded to patronize seed gardeners at home, and the consequence was that we had no garden the past season. Your seeds prove to be just as they are recommended, and you will get my patronage in the future.

Walter Mincey, Woodbine, Iowa : The seeds I got of you two years ago were very fine indeed ; I never had seed to do as well. Last year I had so much farming to do I neglected to send to you for seeds, and those I purchased from our home dealers were almost good for nothing. From henceforth I am a Maule's man, and don't you ever doubt it.

C. M. Hayhurst, Amarillo, Texas : Because I made an ass of myself in not buying Maule's seeds this last Spring it does not go to show that I do not think Maule's seeds still in the lead, and I want somebody to kick me all over this section of land if ever I commit another such blunder. I did buy some onion seed of you— one ounce of Prizetaker. I planted with my hand, dropping the seed two inches apart; I had to thin out. We have just ended a six weeks drouth, and my Prizetakers have suffered, but still they are from 1 to 2 inches in diameter.

Hattie Rogers, Bloomfield, Ark.: I planted your seeds in 1888 and had better success than I ever had from any seed. In 1889 I failed to get your seeds, and the consequence was a poor garden, on account of seed coming up badly.

**EXTRA EARLY LIMA.**—Also known as Early Jersey. This is 10 days to two weeks earlier than any other pole Lima, and until the introduction of **THE NEW BUSH LIMA** two years ago, was the earliest in cultivation. Notwithstanding the earliness it still equals the ordinary large Lima in quality and productiveness, while the beans are equally as large. Many in the North who have never been able to raise Lima Beans until they planted this variety have had great success with Extra Early Lima. Pkt., 10 cts.; pt., 40 cts.; qt., 75 cts.

J. M. Jones, Smithfield, Tex.: "I will say in behalf of your seeds, I planted them year before last, and had the nicest garden I ever raised. I shall use them in the future, as they have given better results than any I ever tried. My garden was almost a failure last year for I did not use Maule's seeds."

## BULK SEED PRICE-LIST

Peas, Beans & Sweet Corn

All other prices in this catalogue on beans, sweet corn and peas include delivery, all charges paid, at your nearest post or express office. This price-list is for the benefit of those desiring to purchase these three varieties of seeds in quantity.

| BEANS—Dwarf or Bush. | Peck. | Bus. | SWEET CORN.—Continued. | Peck. | Bus. |
|---|---|---|---|---|---|
| Ex. Early Round Pod Valentine | $1 25 | $4 00 | Shoe Peg | $1 50 | $5 00 |
| Early Mohawk | 1 00 | 3 75 | Triumph | 1 00 | 3 50 |
| Imp'd Early Yellow Six Weeks | 1 00 | 3 75 | Stabler's Early | 1 00 | 3 50 |
| Best of All | 1 25 | 4 50 | Amber Cream | 1 25 | 4 00 |
| Nonpariel Green Pod | 1 50 | 5 00 | Perry's Hybrid | 1 25 | 4 00 |
| Round Pod Refugee | 1 25 | 4 00 | Excelsior Sugar | 1 00 | 3 50 |
| White Kidney | 1 00 | 3 75 | Egyptian | 1 00 | 3 50 |
| Large White Marrowfat | 1 00 | 3 75 | Maule's Mammoth | 1 25 | 4 00 |
| Prolific Tree | 1 00 | 3 50 | Stowell's Evergreen | 1 25 | 4 00 |
| Burlingame Medium | 1 00 | 3 50 | PEAS—Maule's Earliest of All | 1 75 | 6 00 |
| Maule's Butter Wax | 2 50 | 8 50 | Maule's Improved Extra Early | 1 25 | 4 00 |
| Wardwell's Kidney Wax | 1 50 | 5 50 | Maule's Family Garden | 1 25 | 4 00 |
| Perfection Wax | 1 50 | 5 50 | Early Prize | 2 00 | 7 00 |
| New Mont D'or | 2 00 | 7 00 | American Wonder | 1 75 | 6 00 |
| Black Wax | 1 50 | 5 00 | Bliss' Everbearing | 1 50 | 5 00 |
| Rust Proof Golden Wax | 2 00 | 7 00 | Bliss' Abundance | 1 50 | 5 00 |
| Ivory Pod Wax | 1 75 | 6 00 | Laxton's Alpha | 1 25 | 4 25 |
| Golden Wax | 1 50 | 5 25 | Improved Dan O'Rourke | 1 25 | 4 0 |
| Prolific German Wax | 1 75 | 6 00 | Tom Thumb | 1 50 | 5 00 |
| New Flageolet Wax | 1 50 | 5 50 | Advancer | 1 50 | 4 50 |
| BEANS—Pole or Running. | | | McLean's Little Gem | 1 50 | 5 00 |
| White Creaseback | 2 00 | 7 00 | Premium Gem | 1 50 | 5 00 |
| Improved Dutch Runner | 2 00 | 7 00 | Laxton's Marvel | 2 00 | 7 00 |
| New Golden Wax | 2 00 | 7 00 | McLean's Blue Peter | 1 50 | 5 00 |
| Golden Cluster | 2 00 | 7 00 | Champion of England | 1 25 | 4 50 |
| Lazy Wives | 3 00 | 10 00 | Dwarf Blue Imperial | 1 00 | 3 50 |
| Salem Improved Lima | 2 50 | 8 00 | McLean's Wonderful | 1 75 | 6 00 |
| Extra Early Lima | 2 50 | 8 00 | Yorkshire Hero | 1 50 | 5 00 |
| King of the Garden Lima | 2 50 | 8 50 | Telephone | 2 00 | 7 50 |
| Dreer's Improved Lima | 2 50 | 8 00 | Pride of the Market | 2 00 | 7 00 |
| SWEET CORN. | | | Stratagem | 2 25 | 8 00 |
| Everbearing | 1 50 | 5 00 | Evolution | 2 00 | 8 00 |
| New Cory | 1 50 | 4 50 | Perpetual | 3 00 | 10 00 |
| Early Marblehead | 1 00 | 3 50 | Horsford's Market Garden | 1 50 | 6 00 |
| Early Minnesota | 1 00 | 3 00 | Large White Marrowfat | 1 00 | 2 50 |
| Adam's Extra Early | 1 00 | 3 00 | Black Eye Marrowfat | 1 00 | 2 50 |
| Crosby's Extra Early | 1 50 | 5 00 | Southern Whippoorwill (field) | 50 | 1 75 |
| Gold Coin | 1 50 | 5 00 | Canada Field | 50 | 1 75 |

AT THE ABOVE FIGURES I DELIVER THESE GOODS ON BOARD CARS IN THIS CITY AND MAKE NO CHARGE FOR BAGS, BUT THE PURCHASER HAS TO PAY THE FREIGHT

12

**MARKET GARDENERS.**—For description of this, the best of all half-long varieties, see colored plate, page 8. Pkt. 10 cents; ounce, 25 cents; ¼ pound, 60 cents.

**MAULE'S DARK RED EGYPTIAN.**—The earliest; the most popular among market gardeners for forcing purposes. Roots when young are hard, crisp and tender, and in color very dark red. I can particularly recommend my seed to those desiring to sow **the best strain of Egyptian Beet on the market.** Pkt., 5 cts.; oz., 10 cts.; ¼ lb., 20 cts.; lb., 60 cts.; 5 lbs., $2.50.

**ECLIPSE.**—Eclipse is as early I find as the Egyptian, and besides is considered by many growers to be of better quality and color. Has a remarkably small top. Is very smooth, fine-grained and tender; bright red in color. Many gardeners have largely discarded Egyptian for Eclipse, and this year the latter will be more largely sown than ever. Pkt, 5c; oz, 10c; ¼ lb, 20 c.; lb. 60 c.; 5 lbs. $2.50.

**BASTIAN'S EARLY RED.**—Very early, quick large growth, fine form and bright red color. Profitable for either market or home garden. Packet, 5 cents; ounce, 10 cents; ¼ lb., 20 cents; pound, 60 cents; 5 lbs., $2.50.

**PHILADELPHIA EARLY TURNIP.**—This is a very early beet, maturing about the same time or a little later than the Egyptian. It is very rich and sugary and highly thought of by all who have ever sown it. Flesh is in alternate rings of light and dark pink, but boils red. It is very smooth and is a decidedly profitable market variety. Pkt., 5 c.; oz., 10 c.; ¼ lb., 20 cts.; lb., 60 cts.; 5 lbs., $2.50.

**MAULE'S BLOOD TURNIP.**—The blood turnip-beet is known the world over as a most desirable variety, and there are any number of strains, good, bad and indifferent. Having grown what I consider **the most desirable and carefully selected** of all these various stocks, I have for several years been supplying it to thousands of my customers to their entire satisfaction. It is nearly as early as the Egyptian, but surpasses the latter variety in flavor. Color a rich dark red; roots fine grained, globular shape with small top. Free from side of fibrous roots, always remarkably smooth. Excellent for forcing, and a very superior keeper, thus making it also desirable for winter use. Cooks sweet, tender and crisp, and **in every way may be considered the standard sort for the market and home gardener.** Has made good crop 7 weeks from sowing. Pkt. 10 cts.; oz. 18 cts.; ¼ lb. 30 c.; lb. 90 c.; 5 lbs. $3.75.

COPYRIGHTED 1890
WM. HENRY MAULE

A. BLANC

13

## TABLE BEETS.—(Continued.)

**EDMAND'S TURNIP.**—This is a very thoroughbred Turnip Beet; very early, good shape, small top. Has given excellent satisfaction on the Boston Market, where it is considered a very popular variety. Pkt., 5 cts.; oz., 10 cts.; ¼ lb., 20 cts.; lb., 60 cts.; 5 lbs., $2.50.

**EARLY BASSANO.**—Grows to a good size; an excellent sort to sow for greens. Pkt., 5 cts.; oz., 10 cts.; ¼ lb., 20 cts.; lb., 55 cents.

**HALF LONG BLOOD.**—An excellent second early. Good also for winter use. Pkt., 5 cts.; oz., 10 cts.; ¼ lb., 20 cts.; lb., 55 cents.

**MAULE'S IMPROVED LONG RED.**—The best strain of long dark red beet in the market, and especially desirable for winter or fall use. Excellent as a feed for cattle, as 12 tons have been grown per acre. Shape shown in cut. Sweet, tender, rich carmine. No garden should be without at least a few beets of this variety. Once sown you will always want them. Pkt. 10c.; oz. 15c.; ¼ lb. 30c.; lb., 90c.; 5 lbs, $3.50.

W. A. Peck, Demorestville, Ont., Can.: "I send you by express to-day, a Blood Turnip Beet, weighing 13 pounds; it was a wonder in this district. Your Parisian Pickling Cucumbers are all you claimed for them and more.

## ✛ SUGAR BEET. ✛

**IMPERIAL SUGAR.**—One of the best beets ever raised for feeding cows and young stock. Can be raised at a cost of 5 cents per bushel, as it has yielded 30 tons and over per acre. Very free of side roots. The $25.00 prize offered in 1888 for the heaviest Imperial Sugar Beet raised from Maule's seeds was secured by J. V. N. Young, Arroyo Grande, Cal., with a specimen weighing 33½ pounds. Packet 5 cts.; oz., 10 cts.; ¼ lb., 20 cts.; lb., 40 cts.; 5 lbs., $1.75.

Frank Scope, South Bend, Ind.: "I send you one of your Improved Blood Turnip Beets. They grow remarkably quick, are of small top, of fine shape, good color and are unsurpassed in quality. In short it is the best Beet I ever raised. They were admired by all who saw them. Their earliness makes them exceedingly desirable for market gardeners to sell them in bunches, and their good size to sell them by the bushel if so desired. They sell best in this market when of medium size."

Remember a $10 bill buys seeds in packets to the value of $15.

## MANGEL WURTZELS

**MAMMOTH PRIZE LONG RED. The best for deep soil.** This splendid variety has created a great sensation wherever grown, on account of its **extraordinary size, wonderful productiveness, and superior quality.** At Smithfield cattleshow specimens have been exhibited weighing **50 lbs.** In 1887 one of my customers raised a Prize Long Red weighing 61 pounds. Pkt., 5c.; oz., 10c.; ¼ lb., 20c.; lb., 40c.; 5 lbs., $1.75.

**MAULE'S CHAMPION YELLOW GLOBE.**—This is the best Yellow Globe in cultivation. It is a splendid keeper, and cows fed on it give an unusual supply of rich milk. I can highly recommend this strain of Yellow Globe Mangel to all. Pkt., 5 cts.; oz., 10 cts.; ¼ lb., 15 cts.; lb., 35 cts.; 5 lbs. $1.50.

**YELLOW TANKARD.**—Best for dairy farming. Considered **indispensable** among English Dairy farmers; it is stated by them they are able to obtain a higher price for milk when feeding cows on Golden Tankard. Sheep thrive on it. Other Mangels cut white, circled with yellow, but Golden Tankard is of a rich, deep yellow throughout. Early, hardy, and a heavy cropper, for on account of its shape roots can be left standing close in rows. **Do not omit this variety when ordering.** Pkt. 5 cents; ounce, 10 cents; ¼ lb., 20 cents; pound, 40 cents; 5 lbs., $1.75.

COPYRIGHTED 1890 BY WM. HENRY MAULE.

14

# 3 HEAVY WEIGHTS

**THE JUMBO.**—Has produced over 50 tons to the acre, and is the very best strain of long red in cultivation. Has been grown to weigh over 50 pounds, yet it is not coarse, but most excellent for stock feeding. A Jumbo Mangel weighing 91 pounds, raised by Forrest Roberts, Arroyo Grande, Cal., secured him the $50.00 premium in 1888. **If you want the heaviest cropper of all Mangels, sow the Jumbo this year.** Packet, 5 cents; ounce, 10 cents; ¼ pound, 20 cents; pound, 50 cents; 5 pounds, $2.00.

**MAULE'S GATEPOST.**—One of the very finest Mangels ever introduced, giving **unbounded satisfaction** wherever grown. The crop is very uniform and the roots heavy, handsome and clean, with single tap root. In 1889 a Gatepost weighing 39 pounds, raised by Mrs. Irene D. Hall, Orange, Cal., secured the $50.00 premium. In flavor they are wonderfully rich and nutritious. With good cultivation will crop at the rate of 2,500 bushels per acre. Particularly recommended to graziers. Pkt. 5c., oz., 10c.; ¼ lb., 20c.; lb., 50c.; 5 lbs. $2.

**NEW GIANT YELLOW INTERMEDIATE.**—This new and entirely distinct strain is sure to make a mark for itself among all growers of Mangel Wurzels. It has a magnificent root, which is easily lifted from the ground, produces enormous crops, and has proven itself to be a most excellent keeper. **It is certainly a novelty of sterling merit,** as can be seen from the illustration. It grows more than half above ground, is remarkable even in shape, rather elongated in form, and of most vigorous habit of growth. Has a fine neck, large leaves with green stems, and a very fine smooth skin. Flesh is firm and sweet, and much liked by cattle. No farmer who has ever grown beet roots for stock should neglect giving this new giant mangel a thorough trial this season; if they do I am confident it will come up to if not, indeed, surpass their highest expectations. Pkt., 5c.; oz., 10c.; ¼lb., 20c.; lb., 50c.; 5 lbs., $2.00.

**DO NOT MAKE A MISTAKE.** It will pay you to read the announcement I make on the back of the order sheet enclosed in this Catalogue; if you have not already done so, you should do so at once.

MAULE'S SELECTED CABBAGE SEEDS

THIS MAN DID NOT SOW MAULE'S SEEDS. RESULT—NOT A CABBAGE.

EVERY PLANT A HEAD FROM MAULE'S SEEDS.

### EARLIEST ETAMPES
Pkt., 10 cts.

90 DAYS AFTER SOWING

**MAULE'S DWARF YORK.—** Very early; firm, of fine flavor. Pkt. 5 cts.; oz. 15 cts.; ¼ lb. 40 cts.; lb. $1.35.

**EARLY TOURAVILLE.—** Coming in early remains a long time without bursting. Produces solid, conical heads, yellow tinge within. Fine flavor; handsome appearance. Pkt. 5c.; oz. 15c.; ¼ lb. 40c.; lb. $1.50.

MAULE'S WINNINGSTADT

**EARLIEST ETAMPES.—**Although a comparatively new cabbage, Earliest Etampes has fairly sprung into public favor, and is unanimously endorsed as the earliest of all, by everyone who has tried it. Full ten days to two weeks earlier than any other variety, excepting New Express, it forms **fine, hard and solid pointed heads of extra quality,** much larger and finer than the Early York. It has a short stem growing close to the ground, and by reason of its few outer leaves can be planted much closer together than any other. **It is in every way one of the most desirable extra early Cabbages ever introduced. Sown in March it is frequently ready for use by 1st of June.** Pkt., 10 cts.; oz., 25 cts.; ¼ lb., 75 cts.; lb., $2.25.

John Brierley, Boulder, Colo.: "The Cabbage seeds purchased of you last winter were the best I have had for several years; the Winningstadt was very true to name, and also the Prize Wakefield. The New Dwarf Champion Tomato is the best I ever had. I tried it two years ago from other firms, but it did not amount to anything; it is the best out of six varieties."

**MAULE'S WINNINGSTADT.—**Is very early, forming large cone-shaped heads of excellent quality, and is very certain to head, as it will grow a solid head in seasons when other sorts fail to produce anything. On account of its very hard heads it keeps well both Winter and Summer. It seems to suffer less from Cabbage worms than any other sort. **Market-gardeners and others desiring a choice strain of this popular Cabbage ought to sow Maule's Seeds.** Pkt., 10c.; oz., 25c.; ¼ lb., 60c.; lb., $2.00.

Jacob K. Smith, Big Run, Pa.: "I must say your seeds have no equal; they are just as you recommend them. We had a very dry season this year but your seeds did remarkably well, and had I sown any others I know I would have been left. Thought I would have no cabbage, but it surpassed all my expectations when fall came and I had a nice crop of Cabbage, and all my neighbors around me were left in the shade in the cabbage line. I had all the cabbage I wanted to use and sold about $100 worth. The Parsnips and Radishes I raised were astonishing. This is the first year I have had parsnips and radishes to amount to anything since I have been making a garden. Maule's Seeds are worth their weight in gold."

MAULE'S WAKEFIELD

IMPROVED BRUNSWICK

**MAULE'S PRIZE WAKEFIELD.—**There is no question that the Wakefield is the best early Cabbage in America to-day, consequently it is not to be wondered at that I should take particular pains in furnishing my customers with an extra choice strain of seed of this variety. I feel perfectly safe in saying that I consider I have to-day the finest and truest stock of Jersey Wakefield in America. Neither pains, trouble nor expense have been spared in producing or selecting my seed of this variety, which I have grown for me right at the fountain-head of the Wakefield Cabbage—on Long Island. The strain I offer is just the sort for market-gardeners and all others who look for quality first and then cost of seed afterwards. Forms an unusually large head; almost as early as Earliest Etampes, while for compactness and regularity of growth it cannot be surpassed. It has remarkably few outer leaves and is always sure to mature fine marketable heads, frequently in 100 days from planting. Market or private gardeners cannot make a mistake by sowing Maule's strain of this justly celebrated, popular and profitable market variety. Pkt., 10c.; oz., 35c.; ¼ lb., $1; lb., $3.50.

**IMPROVED BRUNSWICK, Short-Stemmed.—**Many people who only grow one variety of Cabbage prefer the Brunswick to any other, as if is most excellent planted early or late. Always a reliable header and with ordinary cultivation will readily weigh 20 to 30 lbs. In quality it is most desirable, while there is no question it is the earliest of all the large hard-heading Drumhead varieties of Cabbage. I have long taken pride in furnishing my customers with an extra strain of Short-Stemmed Brunswick Cabbage seed, and for this reason my prices area little higher than for the ordinary strains of Brunswick generally offered, **but the seed is well worth the difference.** Pkt. 10c.; oz. 25c.; ¼ lb. 75c.; lb. $2.50.

J. C. Hill, Bryantsburg, Ind.: "I am highly pleased with the seeds bought of you last spring, and my friends who sent with me are also pleased. I planted Earliest Etampes Cabbage and had Cabbage before any of my neighbors. Turner Hybrid Tomatoes are dandies. It would require too much space to express my opinion on all the different varieties I bought, so will just say they are all good and cannot be excelled. But I must mention your Invincible Zinnia, they were considered by every one the finest they ever saw."

## 3 OF MY CABBAGE SPECIALTIES

### New Early Express

The earliest of all. *First introduced in my 1887 Catalogue and pronounced by one and all the greatest addition in years to the Cabbage family.* Produces fair-sized, marketable heads 70 DAYS FROM SOWING OF THE SEED. I did not think I would be able to offer an earlier cabbage than Etampes, but EXPRESS IS A FEW DAYS EARLIER THAN EVEN THIS NOW FAMOUS EXTRA EARLY. It does not form quite so large a head as the Etampes, but when it is considered that the Express forms a head fit for use in 70 to 80 days from the sowing of the seed, I think I have the pleasure of recommending to my customers the MOST IMPORTANT ADDITION MADE IN YEARS TO THE CABBAGE FAMILY. In quality it is A No. 1; has comparatively few loose leaves, and almost every plant forms a fine head every time. Like the Etampes, it holds its head admirably, and as it can be planted so close together, yields a very large crop. There are many cabbages called "earliest" listed by other seedsmen, but I venture to say that EXPRESS WILL DISCOUNT THEM ALL. Packet, 10 cents; ounce, 30 cents; ¼ pound, $1.00; pound, $3.00.

### Maule's Midsummer

This variety is nearly as early as Early Summer, and at same time produces MUCH LARGER HEADS, which for solidity and compactness are unsurpassed. Its short, compact growth permits its being planted close in rows, so, although the heads are much larger than Early Summer, as many plants can be set to the acre. It is a remarkably sure header, and for a market crop is one of the most profitable varieties in existence. Maule's Midsummer is very similar, in many respects, to the All Seasons lately introduced by Mr. Gregory, and comes from very near the same source on Long Island. Plant Express for early, Midsummer for Summer, and Surehead or Prize Drumhead for winter, and you will have a succession of fine Cabbage all the year round, and the finest heads, both as to solidity and quality, that it has ever been your fortune to raise. Packet, 10 cents; ounce, 40 cents; ¼ pound, $1.35; pound, $4.00.

1 PACKET EACH OF THESE 3 CHOICE CABBAGES FOR 25 CTS

### MAMMOTH RED ROCK

### Mammoth Red Rock

This is the largest and hardiest heading red cabbage in cultivation. Successful Long Island market gardeners will raise no other kind of red cabbage, for they consider this the best of all. The heads frequently average 12 pounds each, and is a very sure cropper. If you want as fine red cabbage as you ever saw, you must sow Red Rock, for it absolutely leads every other red sort, and I know you will be pleased with it. True seed scarce, consequently Red Rock is still very high in price. Pkt. 10c.; oz. 60c.

17

## EARLY BLEICHFIELD — 3 Good Summer Cabbages — EARLY SUMMER
### EARLY FLAT DUTCH

**EARLY BLEICHFIELD GIANT.**—Large, solid heading, short-stemmed, second early sort. Dark-green. Solid. It is sure to please. Pkt. 10c.; oz., 25c.; ¼ lb., 75c.; lb., $2.50.

**MAULE'S EARLY FLAT DUTCH.**—an old variety, but one that is still wonderfully popular wherever grown, unquestionably a good second early, of excellent quality, with large, sound and solid heads. Heads are of a very uniform shape and are flattened on top. Recommended for the South, as it resists heat better than many other varieties. Pkt., 10c.; oz., 25c.; ¼ lb., 75c.; lb., $2.25.

**EARLY SUMMER.**—This variety matures ten days to two weeks after Wakefield but as the heads are almost double the size, it may be ranked as one of the best large earlies. One point in favor of this Cabbage is that on account of its short outer leaves, it can be planted as close as the Wakefield, about 12,000 plants to the acre. Heads are solid, round and rather flat. I offer strictly first-choice Long Island grown seed. Pkt., 10c.; oz., 25c.; ¼ lb., 75c.; lb., $2.50.

**DEEP HEAD.**—This new strain of Brunswick Cabbage well deserves the name, being equal to Fottler's in earliness and other good qualities, but making a larger and thicker head, thus proving a better Winter keeper. All desiring a fine, large, hard-heading early cabbage will find Deep Head just what they want. Pkt., 10 cts.; oz., 30 cts.; ¼ lb., $1.00; lb., $3.00.

**DANISH BALL HEAD.**—One of my customers in Denmark has solicited me to list this Cabbage for several years past. There it is grown in large quantities and considered the best Winter Cabbage, especially for shipment to foreign countries. Heads are very hard, round, of good size and quality. Fine-grained; good keeper. Pkt., 10c.; oz., 30c.

**BLOOD RED ERFURT.**—Good sown early or late. Solid and very red in color, making it very desirable for pickling. Pkt., 5 cts.; oz., 20 cts.; ¼ lb., 60 cts.; lb., $2.00.

THE 50 POUND CABBAGE

**MARBLEHEAD MAMMOTH CABBAGE.** Packet, 10 cents.

M. I. Saunders, Everett's, Va.: "I received my package of seeds over a week ago; have sowed some, and I really think they are coming up two for one that I sowed."

L. L. Guess, Wright's, Cala.: "Was well pleased with seeds last year. Any wayfarer could run and see where Maule's seeds were planted. What do you put on them that makes them grow so rank?"

Aaron L. Stevens, Little Falls, Washington: "I received the first order or seeds just 14 days after ordering. Considering the distance (three thousand miles), I think this breaks the record for promptness and dispatch."

Jos. Bowman, Roswell, New Mexico: "We sold more vegetables than any other gardener in the county last year, from seed bought of you."

John Young, Wallsburg, Utah: "In regard to your seeds, would say all that is required is for the people to give them a trial, and they will find them at the top of the list."

B. J. Rond, Marion, Ind.: "I cheerfully say that the germinating qualities of your seeds, and your generous way of filling orders leave nothing to be desired.

**MARBLEHEAD MAMMOTH.**—This enormous cabbage excels in size all other varieties of its family. If you want to surprise your friends with the largest cabbage ever raised in your neighborhood this is the variety you want. Under high culture it has reached an average weight of thirty pounds per head, and in size equals a two-bushel basket, heads sometimes weighing as high as 50 to 60 lbs. each. The quality, however, is not coarse, but, on the contrary, delicate, and the flavor fine. It is well adapted to the South, and is considered one of the most desirable varieties of late cabbages for the warmer latitudes. Packet, 10 cents; ounce, 30 cents; ¼ pound, $1.00; pound, $3.00.

**RED DUTCH.**—Heads are round, very hard, and in color a dark red. The best for pickling. Packet, 5 cents; ounce, 20 cents; ¼ pound, 60 cents; pound, $2.00.

## 3 GOOD WINTER SORTS OF

**IMPROVED DRUM-HEAD SAVOY.**—Few are aware how excellent are the Savoy Cabbages. They are of a most superior flavor and more resemble the Cauliflower than any other. My strain is unusually choice, heads being large, finely curled and very compact. They are excellent Winter keepers. Pkt., 10 cts.; oz., 20 cts.; ¼ lb., 60 cts.; lb., $2.00.

**STONEMASON.**—This is a very popular variety among New England growers, being a very sure

header, heads at same time being large and solid. IT IS CERTAINLY A VARIETY THAT GIVES GENERAL SATISFACTION. Pkt., 10 cts.; oz., 25 cts.; ¼ lb., 65 cts.; lb., $2.25.

**NEW FELDER KRAUT.**—This new variety from Germany combines so many good qualities that it should be sown by all cabbage growers. It is best of all for kraut. Heads large, very hard, solid, and sure to head. It is very hardy, and thrives well anywhere. Good early or late. Pkt., 10 cts.; oz., 30 cts.; ¼ lb., 60 cts.; lb., $2.00.

MAULE'S SELECTED CABBAGE SEED

21

## A PAGE of CARROTS

**OXHEART**

**E. SCARLET HORN**

**EARLY ½ LONG SCARLET**

**MAULE'S DANVERS 30 TONS PER ACRE**

**Large White Vosges**

**GOLDEN BALL.**— The earliest, consequently is largely grown for forcing purposes. Roots are of small size, round, of good color and excellent flavor. Pkt., 10 cents; oz., 15 cents; ¼ lb., 40 cts.; lb., $1.25.

**OXHEART.**—This new Carrot well deserves general cultivation. In addition to being early, it equals if indeed it does not surpass, every other variety in shape, being an intermediate in length between the Early Horn and the Half Long varieties, while it runs fully 3 to 4 inches in diameter, and specimens have been raised measuring over 7 inches across. In quality it is extra good and will prove profitable in both the home and market garden. Where other sorts require digging, **Oxheart can be easily pulled.** If you want an early, handsome, ready-selling Carrot, Oxheart will suit you. Pkt.10c.; oz. 15c.; ¼ lb., 40c.; lb., $1.25.

**EARLY SCARLET HORN.**—Known favorably by all growers. Considered by many the best early table variety. Flesh fine grained. In color deep orange, has small tops. Grows well in shallow soil. Matures 8 to 10 days sooner than Long Orange. Packet. 5 cts.; ounce, 10 cts.; ¼ pound, 30 cts.; pound, $1.00.

**EARLY HALF LONG SCARLET.**—**Coreless and stump-rooted.** Flesh bright orange. Early, with smooth skin; most excellent for table use. Will mature in shallow soil. Packet, 5c.; ounce, 10c.; ¼ pound, 30c.; pound, $1.00.

**MAULE'S DANVERS.**—Most excellent for all soils, and **will yield greater bulk, with smallest length of roots, of any now grown.** It is of a rich, dark orange color and all the roots are wonderfully smooth and handsome. Forty tons and over per acre have been raised with good cultivation, and has often given 25 to 30 tons per acre. Last year it was the most popular Carrot in my entire list. Pkt. 10c.; oz., 15c.; ¼ lb., 35c.; lb., $1.10.

**MAULE'S IMPROVED LONG ORANGE.**—I consider this **the best strain** of the well-known Long Orange Carrot on the market. Roots of large size, smooth, fine-grained and superior. Always well formed, and of a deep orange color. John T. King, Kent, O., secured the $25.00 offered for the best Long Orange Carrot raised from Maule's seeds in 1888, with a beautiful specimen 16½ inches long. They always grow remarkably uniform, and with a little care and attention **enormous** crops can be grown of this variety, particularly on light deep soil. Pkt., 10 cts.; oz. 15 cts.; ¼ lb. 35 cts.; lb., $1.10.

**NEW CHANTENAY.**—**Very productive,** has an extra large shoulder, is easily dug, and is in every way desirable. It is very smooth, fine in texture, and of a beautiful rich orange color. Well worthy of a thorough trial. Pkt., 10 cts.; oz., 15 cts.; ¼ lb., 40 cts.; lb. $1.25.

**RED ST. VALERY.**—Originated in France, where it is one of the most popular varieties. Of rich, deep orange color. Large and handsome. Very straight roots, broad at the top, often measuring 2¾ to 3 inches across, while they grow 10 to 12 inches long. They have very little foliage for size of root. Of superior quality for table use, also very desirable for stock. Very heavy crops can be grown in light, rich soil. Pkt., 5c.; oz., 10c.; ¼ lb. 25c.; lb. 75c.

**LARGE WHITE VOSGES.**—This new field Carrot is especially suitable for shallow soil. In shape they very much resemble the Oxheart, excepting the roots grow more to a point. When other varieties require digging, Vosges can be pulled. Flesh and skin are white, and it is considered by those who have grown it, **much better in quality than any other white variety.** Pkt., 5 cents; oz., 10 cents; ¼ lb., 25 cents; lb., 75 cents.

**LARGE WHITE BELGIAN.**—Large size, very productive; but coarser than other varieties. It is entirely for stock feeding. Pkt., 5 cts.; oz., 10 cts.; ¼ lb., 20 cts.; lb., 60 cts.

**LARGE YELLOW BELGIAN.**—Similar to white, except in color. Price the same.

**MAULE'S LONG ORANGE**

**28 TONS TO THE ACRE**

**THE PRIZE CARROT**

**16½ INCHES LONG**

COPYRIGHTED 1888 W. HENRY MAULE

**The CHANTENAY**

**RED ST. VALERY**

**WHITE & YELLOW BELGIAN CARROTS**

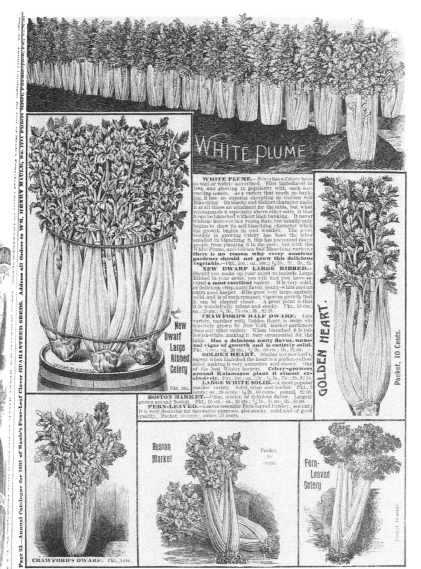

**WHITE PLUME.**

**WHITE PLUME.**—Never has a Celery been so well or widely advertised. First introduced in 1884, and growing in popularity with each succeeding season. As a variety that needs no banking, it has no superior excepting in Golden Self Blanching. Its beauty and distinct character make it at all times an ornament for the table, but what recommends it especially above other sorts is that it can be blanched without high banking. It never whitens however in a young state, but usually only begins to show its self-blanching character when the growth begins in cool weather. The great trouble in growing Celery has been the labor entailed in blanching it, this has prevented many people from planting it in the past; but with the White Plume, and Golden Self Blanching varieties **there is no reason why every amateur gardener should not grow this delicious vegetable.**—Pkt., 10c.; oz., 30c.; ¼ lb., $1; lb., $3.

**NEW DWARF LARGE RIBBED.**—Should you make up your mind to include Large Ribbed in your order, you will find you have secured **a most excellent** variety. It is very solid, of delicious, crisp, nutty flavor, pearly-white and an extra good keeper. Ribs grow very large, entirely solid, and is of such compact, vigorous growth that it can be planted closer. A great point is that it is wonderfully robust and stocky. Pkt, 10 cts.; oz., 25 cts.; ¼ lb., 75 cts; lb., $2.25.

**CRAWFORD'S HALF DWARF.** This variety, together with Golden Heart, is more extensively grown by New York market-gardeners than any other variety. When blanched it is yellowish-white, making it very ornamental for the table. **Has a delicious nutty flavor, unusual vigor of growth and is entirely solid.** Pkt., 5 cts.; oz., 20 cts.; ¼ lb., 60 cts.; lb., $2.00.

**GOLDEN HEART.** Similar to Crawford's, except when blanched the heart is a golden-yellow color, making it very attractive and showy. One of the best Winter keepers. **Celery-growers around Kalamazoo plant it almost exclusively.** Pkt., 10c.; oz., 25c.; ¼ lb., 75c.; lb., $2.50.

**LARGE WHITE SOLID.**—A most popular market variety. Solid, crisp and tender. Pkt., 10 cents; oz., 30 cents; ¼ lb., 60 cents; pound, $2.00.

**BOSTON MARKET.**—Crisp, tender, of delicious flavor. Largely grown around Boston. Pkt., 10 cts.; oz., 30 cts.; ¼ lb., $1.00; lb., $3.00.

**FERN-LEAVED.**—Leaves resemble Fern-leaved Parsley, (see cut.) It is very desirable for decorative purposes, also stocky, solid and of good quality. Packet, 10 cents; ounce, 25 cents.

**New Dwarf Large Ribbed Celery**
Pkt. 10c.

**GOLDEN HEART.** Packet, 10 Cents.

**Boston Market** Packet, 10 cents.

**Fern-Leaved Celery**

**CRAWFORD'S DWARF.** Pkt., 5 cts.

# 3 CHOICE CELERIES AND 2 GOOD NEW SWEET CORNS

### GOLDEN SELF-BLANCHING

The demand the last six years for this magnificent Celery has been something remarkable. Last year was as bad as the year before. Almost every order seemed to want Golden Self-Blanching until I had sold almost every grain of seed on hand. Golden Self-Blanching, besides being remarkably stocky and a wonderfully strong grower, is very heavy, perfectly solid, of a delicious, sweet flavor, and **with all these points is a wonderful keeper**. One would think that these would be a sufficient number of good qualities, but to all these is added **THE WONDERFUL QUALITY OF SELF-BLANCHING** to a very remarkable extent. **Without banking-up, or any covering to speak of, even the outer ribs become of a yellowish white color**, the heart being large, solid, and of a beautiful golden-yellow. Every celery grower should test Golden Self-Blanching this season without fail. As a variety that needs no banking, it is recommended to all. Pkt., 10c.; oz., 40c.; ¼ lb., $1.25; lb., $4.; 2 lbs., $7.

### NEW ROSE CELERY

The Rose or Red Celeries are increasing rapidly in popularity. In quality they are particularly fine, while they are better keepers than either the yellow or white sorts. This variety surpasses all other Red Celeries in handsome appearance and superior flavor; at the same time it makes a beautiful ornament for the dinner-table, the heart and stems being beautifully shaded to a fine rose color. Packet, 10 cents; ounce, 25 cents.

**GIANT PASCAL.**—(See colored plate and description on page 8). No lover of fine celery should neglect including a packet or two in their order. **Certain to more than please every one who sows it.** Pkt., 15c.; two, 25c.

### NEW GIANT PASCAL
THE LARGEST RIBBED CELERY IN CULTIVATION

### Shoe Peg Sweet Corn

This very distinct variety originated in Bordentown, New Jersey, where it is esteemed the sweetest and choicest sort grown, always commanding higher prices than any other variety. It is certainly especially desirable for family use, bearing frequently three to four ears on a stalk, which are always deliciously sweet and luscious, while for drying or canning purposes **it is incomparably better than any variety we know of.** Some of the largest packers of sweet corn in the New England States using it, and preferring it to all other sorts. Accompanying illustration is an exact representation of an ear from nature; from it, it will be noticed, it has an unusually deep grain, and very small cob, two most desirable qualities. The kernel is small, very long, white and exceedingly tender. It matures medium late. Shoe Peg is certain to make a place for itself wherever productiveness and exquisite flavor are desired, **and you need it.** Pkt., 10 cents; pint, 30 cents; quart, 50 cents; postpaid.

SHOE PEG SUGAR CORN

COPYRIGHTED 1890 BY W. HENRY MAULE.

### GOLD COIN SWEET CORN.

**GOLD COIN SWEET CORN.**—For the past four years the New Gold Coin has been compared in all points with Stowell's Evergreen, and in sweetness and delicacy of flavor, it surpasses that old favorite. So far, has proved *ten days earlier*, and in size *one-third larger*. The cob is *snowy white*, compactly covered with large, deep grains. Packet, 10 cents; pint, 30 cents; quart, 50 cents; postpaid.

24

# EVERBEARING

**2/3 SIZE**

COPYRIGHTED 1888 BY WM. HENRY MAULE

## XX SUGAR CORN.

### SPECIAL NOTE

It will pay you to send in your order for MAULE'S SEEDS NOW; by now, I mean the day you are reading this.

**EVERBEARING SWEET CORN.**—In 1888 I first called the attention of my customers to this magnificent variety; but my supply was so very limited I could only furnish it in the smallest quantities. All planting it, however, found it a most profitable investment, so much so, that I certainly expect a very large demand indeed for it this season. The ears are of good size, and are covered with kernels clear to the end of the cob. In growth and appearance it is very distinct, the husk and stalks being of a red color, and in this respect it is different from every other variety. But we now come to a most astonishing quality, which has given this variety its name. Ripening a few days after the Stabler's Early, each stalk will produce one to two well-developed ears; now if these are picked when mature, one to two and even four more ears will set and develop on the same stalks during the next two to four weeks; **single stalks producing during the season frequently as many as six large, well-developed ears.** That this is a most remarkable and desirable qualification all will admit, and Everbearing may at once be classed as the greatest addition in years to our list of Sweet Corns, except, possibly, Maule's XX mentioned below. **3 or 4 dozen hills from one planting will supply a good-sized family with a succession of the most delicious Sweet Corn for weeks.** Packet, 15 cts.; pint, 25 cts.; quart, 40 cts.

**MAULE'S XX SUGAR.**—I took pleasure in offering my customers in 1888, for the first time, a most excellent and desirable variety of Sugar Corn, which well deserves the title XX. This corn comes from one of the most successful market gardeners in the United States, who has grown this variety to the exclusion of all other sorts for the last 30 years; although he has tried every other known variety he has never succeeded in securing anything that **would begin to come up to this sweet corn, either in productiveness, quality, or above all in quick market sales.** It is fit for the table in 9 to 10 weeks from planting, and is of the most delicious, sweet and sugary flavor, while I venture to say that **it remains longer in an edible condition than any other variety, not excepting any.** It is of comparatively dwarf habit, stalks seldom growing more than 4 to 5 feet high. While it matures in a comparatively short period of time for such a large-eared variety, it produces 12 to 16-rowed ears as large as Stowell's Evergreen, which are set low on the stalks. Three well-developed ears are often matured on a single stalk. **Planted as late as the middle of July it has frequently matured a most excellent paying market crop.** To sum up, Maule's XX Sugar, while a medium early variety, produces ears as large as any other, excepting Maule's Mammoth. In flavor it has no equal, if, indeed, it does not surpass every other variety. Its productiveness is simply remarkable. Packet, 15 cents; pint, 30 cents.

**NEW CORY SWEET CORN.**—There is no question but that the Cory is the earliest of all sweet Corns by from 3 to 10 days. Originated by Mr. Cory, of Rhode Island, he has been able to supply for many years the first sweet corn to Providence, Newport and Fall River markets. It is not only much earlier than the Marblehead, but produces much finer, larger and sweeter ears than this well-known extra early. It is very dwarf in growth, producing almost invariably two ears to the stalk. Ears have been fit for boiling 52 days from planting. **Two crops can readily be grown on the same ground in a single season.** A large grower of vegetables near Newport R. I., from about six acres, marketed July 7th, 7,000 dozen ears at 36 cents, and by July 16th 15,000 ears at 30 cents, while Marblehead, not ready until 7 or 8 days later, brought only 30 cents per dozen. Demand has been so great the last four seasons as to soon exhaust my supply, and all pronounced their Cory Corn purchase one of the most profitable they ever made. Pkt., 10 cts.; pt., 20 cts.; qt., 35 cts.

# THE CORY

# A PAGE OF SWEET CORN

**EARLY MARBLEHEAD.**—Undoubtedly the earliest of Sweet Corns after New Corn. Planted with me the middle of May, fair-sized ears were ready for market July 7th. Pkt., 10 cts.; pt., 20 cts.; qt., 35 cts.

**EARLY MINNESOTA.**—Packet, 10 cts.; pint, 20 cts.; quart, 35 cts.

**ADAM'S EXTRA EARLY.**—Not a Sweet Corn, but desirable on account of its extreme earliness. Pkt., 10 cts.; pint, 20 cts.; quart, 33 cts.

**CROSBY'S EXTRA EARLY.**—The old standard early, still very popular. Excellent for private gardens. Pkt., 10c.; pt., 20c.; qt., 35c.

**TRIUMPH.**—It is, after Amber Cream, the very best large-eared early; of most delicious and delicate flavor. Pkt., 10c.; pt., 20c.; qt., 35c.

**STABLER'S EARLY.**—A new variety, of larger size than usual for the early kinds. Remarkable for sweetness and earliness; ripens nearly as early as Marblehead. A desirable gardener's and canning variety. Very popular with Philadelphia truckers. Pkt., 10 cts.; pt., 20 cts.; qt., 35 cts.

**AMBER CREAM.**—I always had a very high opinion of Amber Cream, and I must say this opinion has been both confirmed and strengthened by those who have grown it. Stalks are strong and vigorous; ears from 12 to 16 rows; color, when fit for table, white and handsome, and of very superior, tender and sugary flavor. It is a second early, and grains, when ripe, are of an amber color. Pkt., 10c.; pt., 20c.; qt., 35c.

**PERRY'S.**—**One of the very best.** Earlier than Crosby's, with much larger ear. Packet, 10 cents; pint, 20 cents; quart, 35 cents.

**EXCELSIOR SUGAR.**—Fine, large ears, filled from end to end with extra large grains, cannot be surpassed in delicious flavor. Ripens early and its superior quality and productiveness make it very popular. Pkt. 10c.; pt. 20c.; qt. 35c.

**EGYPTIAN.**—Has proved wonderfully successful wherever grown. It is very sweet, tender and delicious in flavor. Ears large, and remains longer in a green state than any other. Pkt., 10c.; pt., 20c.; qt., 35c.

C. Davis, Gratis, Ohio: "I must say your seeds are the best I ever had. I have been gardening for 15 years and never had such peppers and cabbage as I have this year. I take the lead around here in Mangoes, Cabbage and Tomatoes."

**MAULE'S MAMMOTH SUGAR.**—Not only the largest eared, but also one of the very sweetest corns known. Ripens a little after the Evergreen, and for canning purposes is particularly profitable. Ears frequently weigh three pounds and over. Your garden will be incomplete without it. Pkt., 10 cents; pt., 20 cents; qt., 35 cents.

**STOWELL'S EVERGREEN.**—One of the most popular and desirable. Packet, 10 cents; pint, 20 cents; quart, 35 cents.

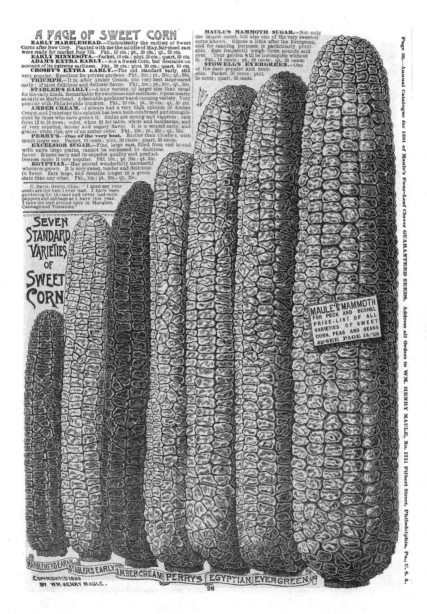

SEVEN STANDARD VARIETIES OF SWEET CORN

MAULE'S MAMMOTH FOR PECK AND BUSHEL PRICE-LIST OF ALL VARIETIES OF SWEET CORN, PEAS AND BEANS SEE PAGE 12.

MARBLEHEAD EARLY · STABLER'S EARLY · AMBER CREAM · PERRY'S · EGYPTIAN · EVERGREEN

COPYRIGHTED 1888 BY WM. HENRY MAULE.

Page 26.—Annual Catalogue for 1891 of Maule's Four-Leaf Clover GUARANTEED SEEDS. Address all Orders to WM. HENRY MAULE, No. 1711 Filbert Street, Philadelphia, Pa., U. S. A.

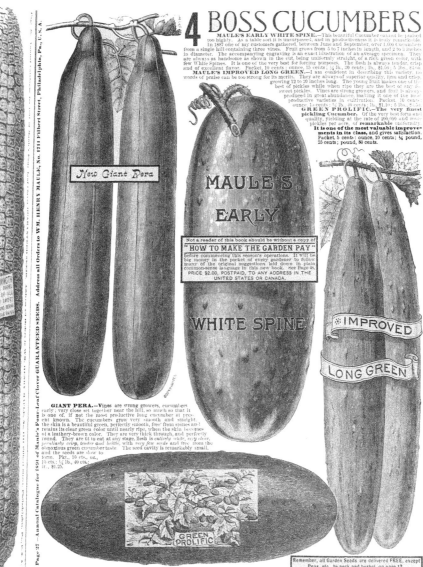

# 4 BOSS CUCUMBERS

**MAULE'S EARLY WHITE SPINE.**—This beautiful Cucumber cannot be praised too highly. As a table sort it is unsurpassed, and in productiveness it is truly remarkable. In 1887 one of my customers gathered, between June and September, over 1,000 Cucumbers from a single hill containing three vines. Fruit grows from 5 to 7 inches in length, and 2 to 3 inches in diameter. The accompanying engraving is an exact illustration of an average specimen. They are always as handsome as shown in the cut, being uniformly straight, of a rich green color, with few White Spines. It is one of the very best for forcing purposes. The flesh is always tender, crisp and of excellent flavor. Packet, 10 cents ; ounce, 15 cents ; ¼ lb., 30 cents ; lb., $1.00 ; 5 lbs., $4.50.

**MAULE'S IMPROVED LONG GREEN.**—I am confident in describing this variety, no words of praise can be too strong for its merits. They are always of superior quality, firm and crisp, growing 12 to 20 inches long. The young fruit makes one of the best of pickles while when ripe they are the best of any for sweet pickles. Vines are strong growers, and fruit is always produced in great abundance, making it one of the most productive varieties in cultivation. Packet, 10 cents ; ounce, 15 cents ; ¼ lb., 40 cents ; lb., $1.10 ; 5 lbs., $5.25.

**GREEN PROLIFIC.**—The very finest pickling Cucumber. Of the very best form and quality, yielding at the rate of 200,000 and more pickles per acre, of remarkable uniformity. **It is one of the most valuable improvements in its class,** and gives satisfaction. Packet, 5 cents ; ounce, 10 cents ; ¼ pound, 25 cents ; pound, 80 cents.

*New Giant Pera*

*MAULE'S EARLY*

Not a reader of this book should be without a copy of
**"HOW TO MAKE THE GARDEN PAY"**
before commencing this season's operations. It will be big money in the pocket of every gardener to follow many of the original suggestions laid down in plain common-sense language in this new book. See Page 48. PRICE $2.00, POSTPAID, TO ANY ADDRESS IN THE UNITED STATES OR CANADA.

*WHITE SPINE*   *IMPROVED*   *LONG GREEN*

**GIANT PERA.**—Vines are strong growers, cucumbers curly ; very close set together near the hill, so much so that it is one of, if not the most productive long cucumber at present known. The cucumbers grow very smooth and straight, the skin is a beautiful green, perfectly smooth, free from spines and retains its clear green color until nearly ripe, when the skin becomes of a leathery-brown color. They are very thick through, and perfectly round. They are fit to eat at any stage, flesh is *entirely white, very clear, peculiarly crisp, tender and brittle,* with *very few seeds* and free from the obnoxious green cucumber taste. The seed cavity is remarkably small, and the seeds are slow to form. Pkt., 10 cts., oz., 15 cts.; ¼ lb., 40 cts.; ½ lb., $1.25.

*GREEN PROLIFIC*

Remember, all Garden Seeds are delivered FREE, except Peas, etc., by peck and bushel, on page 12.

Page 27—Annual Catalogue for 1891 of Maule's Four-Leaf Clover GUARANTEED SEEDS. Address all Orders to WM. HENRY MAULE, No. 1711 Filbert Street, Philadelphia, Pa., U.S.A.

# Cucumbers--2 New Ones

PARISIAN PICKLING

NEW PARISIAN PICKLING.—This entirely new Cucumber comes to me from France. The illustration is an excellent representation of this fine variety, as it represents the natural size of fruit as picked for pickling by Paris gardeners, so it can readily be seen that they make beautiful miniature pickles. Of course, they need not be picked so young if large pickles are desired, but if allowed to grow they will look much smoother. They are of a deep green color, very prickly, and flesh is always firm and remarkably brittle. It is of really startling productiveness, as the vines are completely covered with the little fruit from one end to the other. It is absolutely and positively distinct from every other variety of cucumber. It is sure to become a favorite with all lovers of small pickles, and I can highly recommend it to the attention of my customers. Packet, 10 cents; ounce, 50 cents.

THORBURN'S NEW EVERBEARING.—I desire to call especial attention to this unique variety. It is of small size, very early, enormously productive, and valuable as a green pickler. The peculiar merit of this novelty is that the vines continue to flower and produce fruit until killed by frost, whether the ripe cucumbers are picked off or not, differing in this respect from all other sorts in cultivation. The one vine exhibits at the same time cucumbers in every stage of growth, the small ones being perfect in shape, of a fine green color, and just the size for pickling. In my travels last summer all the market gardeners I visited, who had planted Everbearing were delighted with it, and my friends will make no mistake in giving it a trial. Pkt 10c.; oz, 50c.

EARLY RUSSIAN.—The earliest. It is only about three inches long when fit for use. Packet, 5 cents; ounce, 10 cents; ¼ pound, 25 cents; pound, 70 cents.

EARLY GREEN CLUSTER.—Produces a great abundance of fruit. Packet, 5 cents; ounce, 10 cents; ¼ pound, 25 cents; pound, 60 cents.

EARLY FRAME.—Popular table sort and good for pickles; of medium size, straight and handsome. Packet, 5 cts.; ounce, 10 cts.; ¼ po nd, 25 cts.; pound, 60 cts.

WHITE JAPAN.—Very desirable for table or pickles; productive and of superior quality. Packet, 5 cents; ounce, 10 cents; ¼ pound, 30 cents; pound, 90 cents.

MAULE'S PEERLESS.—This is one of the best strains of pickling cucumbers I consider in the market. All market gardeners desiring an extra choice cucumber for their trade will find it fills the bill. It is very prolific, early, good size, straight, well formed, full at both ends, color a deep green, which it retains until mature. Packet, 10 cents; ounce, 15 cents; ¼ pound, 30 cents; pound, $1.00.

EVERGREEN.—It differs from the Early White Spine, in retaining a deep green color in all stages of growth. It grows very long, is very productive, and matures very early. Its handsome appearance and desirable color will make it a great favorite with all growers, either for pickling or market and table use. Packet, 10 cents; ounce, 15 cents; ¼ pound, 35 cents; pound, $1.10.

TAILBY'S HYBRID.—A hybrid of the White Spine with a large English variety, retaining the proficness of the former, united with large size, hardiness and good market qualities. Packet, 5 cts.; ounce, 10 cts.; ¼ pound, 25 cts.; pound, 80 cts.

JERSEY PICKLE.—Largely grown in New Jersey for a commercial pickle. 150,000 bushels are annually picked in Burlington county alone. Packet, 5 cents; ounce, 10 cents; ¼ pound, 30 cents; pound, 90 cents.

WESTERFIELD'S CHICAGO PICKLE.—For a number of years Chicago has been the centre of a very large pickling industry. This variety is preferred for pickling by almost every large pickling factory in that city, and for commercial pickles it is one of the best. Packet, 5 cents; ounce, 10 cents; ¼ pound, 30 cents; pound 90 cents.

SHORT GREEN.—Makes a beautiful pickle. Pkt, 5c.; oz., 10c.; ¼ lb., 30c.; lb., 90c.

NICHOLS' MEDIUM GREEN.—It is a very handsome variety, in shape between the Early White Spine and the Long Green, always very thick though full at both ends, and of uniform size and shape. "Is worthy of the first place in the list of pickle sorts, second to none as a slicer, and very good for early forcing purposes. In color it is a dark green, flesh crisp and tender, very prolific, medium in size, always straight and smooth, and a real handsome good variety.". Pkt., 5c.; oz., 10c.; ¼ lb., 25c.; lb., 60c.

EVERBEARING

EXTRA LONG WHITE SPINE.—This variety comes to me from the very best and largest grower of cucumbers in the country, and I am very sure my customers will be pleased with it. They grow very straight, to a length of 12 inches or more, and when about 5 inches long, make hard, brittle pickles; dark green and handsome. For table use most excellent. Pkt. 5c.; oz., 10c.; ¼ lb., 30c., lb., 90c.

SMALL GHERKIN.—Exclusively for pickles. Pkt. 10c: oz. 20c; ¼ lb. 50c.

SNAKE.—I have seen this cucumber as long as 6 ft., coiled up like a snake. Singular and remarkable looking curiosity. Pkt 10c

FOR 1891 CASH PRIZES SEE PAGE 68

SHORT GREEN

EARLY CLUSTER

PEERLESS

EVERGREEN

CHICAGO PICKLING

NICHOLS MEDIUM GREEN

EXTRA LONG WHITE SPINE

GHERKIN

SNAKE

COPYRIGHTED BY W. HENRY MAULE 1890

28

Page 35.—Annual Catalogue for 1891 of Maule's Four-Leaf Clover GUARANTEED SEEDS. Address all Orders to WM. HENRY MAULE, No. 1711 Filbert Street, Philadelphia, Pa., U.S.A.

**MAPLEDALE**

**MAPLEDALE.**—Without doubt the most productive Pop Corn in cultivation, some of the reports are fabulous, but are so well substantiated by affidavits that there is no question of their truthfulness. The illustration herewith given is an excellent idea of its prolificness, as well as the size of ears, which are often 8 or 10 inches long, and filled out with bright, handsome white grains. It is of remarkably vigorous habit of growth, the stalks frequently growing 6 ft. high. Its popping qualities are A1 as the grains always pop pure white, and are at all times of delicious flavor. Packet, 10 cents.

**GOLDEN TOM THUMB POP CORN.**—This is certainly a great curiosity. The stalks seldom grow more than 18 inches high. In addition, its dark green foliage certainly makes it an ornament to any flower garden; while stalks only grow 1¼ feet tall, each stalk will produce from two to three perfect little ears, which are only 2 to 2½ inches long. Ears are compactly filled with bright, golden yellow grains, which, when popped, expand to large size. As will be seen from the cut, the ears are set very low down, at times starting only 6 inches from the ground. Stalks do not stool. I venture to say that it will be an attraction to every flower or vegetable garden in which it is planted this season. For the sake of comparison, it would not be a bad idea to plant a hill or two of one of the larger varieties of field corn in the patch with Tom Thumb, as it would be interesting to show the visitor to your garden this summer, this pigmy among giants. Pkt., 10c.

## Pop Corn

**SILVER LACE.**

**SILVER LACE.**—Well deserves its name, for its superior tenderness and beautiful transparency when popped recommend it to all. Grows five to six feet high, very productive, producing three to four perfect ears on a stalk. The ears are very handsome, five to six inches long and always filled out to the end with smooth, round, metallic, white grains. Pkt., 10 cts.; pint, 25 cts.; quart, 45 cents.

**MONARCH WHITE RICE.**

**MONARCH WHITE RICE.**—Every grower of Pop Corn is acquainted with White Rice. This is an improvement on the old variety, ears being much larger and produced in greater abundance. Six ears on a stalk being a frequent occurrence. Grains are sharply pointed and most excellent for popping. Packet, 10 cents; pint, 25 cents; quart, 45 cents.

**QUEEN'S GOLDEN.**

**QUEEN'S GOLDEN.**—This is the handsomest of all Pop Corns, and every one of my customers should plant at least a few hills of it. It surpasses all others in yield, size and color. It pops perfectly white and a single kernel will expand to nearly one inch. Often produces from three to four ears to the stalk. In former years demand has exceeded my supply; but I have grown for this season's trade a very large stock, so that I think I can promise to fill all orders. Pkt., 10c.; pt., 25c.; qt., 45c.; postpaid.

**NEST-EGG GOURD**

## ❈ GOURDS ❈

**NEST-EGG GOURD.**—A capital nest-egg. Produces fine, white fruit, exact size and shape of an egg, and so similar as to often deceive growers. Do not crack and will last for years. A rapid grower, very ornamental, useful for covering screens, etc. Boys can make lots of money by sowing this gourd, and selling them to their neighbors for nest-eggs. Pkt., 10 cts.; oz., 45 cts.

**SUGAR TROUGH.**—This variety grows to a very large size, holding from 4 to 10 gallons each, having hard, thick shells, very strong, but light and durable, lasting for many years. They are used for a great variety of purposes, such as buckets, baskets, soap and salt dishes, nest-boxes, etc., and have been used for packing lard. They are as easily grown as pumpkins. Plant in hills 8 feet apart each way, when the ground is warm and settled. Pkt., 10 cents; oz., 25 cents.

**DISH-CLOTH GOURD.**—The peculiar lining of this fruit, which is sponge-like, porous, tough, elastic and durable, makes a natural dish-cloth. The fruit grows about two feet in length, and the vine is very ornamental, producing clusters of large yellow blossoms, in pleasing contrast with a silvery-shaded dark green foliage. Many ladies prefer this dish-cloth to anything that can be made. For the bath and for all uses of the toilet in general the Dish Rag Gourd is taking the place of the sponge. It is, in fact, a sponge, a soft brush and a bath-glove combined and are almost indestructible, for the fibre wears away imperceptibly and as long as any part is left they are as good as new. Even with daily use they will last for years, and taking into consideration that a packet of seed contains sufficient to raise at least 30 to 50 gourds and the different uses it can be applied to around the house, it is something everyone should grow. In the North the seed should be started in a hot-bed. The dried interiors of these gourds have already become an article of commerce. They are sold by druggists in New York, Philadelphia and Boston, while in England their sale and use are quite general. Every housewife should procure a packet of this seed. Packet, 10 cents.

Henry Wurtenburg, Wysox, Pa.—I have planted your seeds for the past eight years, and they are always good and just as represented.

**DISH-CLOTH GOURD.**

**JAPANESE CLIMBING GOURD.**—This beautiful Japanese climbing annual, with its handsome cut leaved foliage, is one of the most remarkable and novel climbers the East has ever produced. Of rapid growth and easy culture, bears most profusely odd and attractive fruits, about the size of a cherry, of light green color striped with white. Worthy a place on every suburban home. Packet, 10 cents.

**DIPPER GOURD.**

**DIPPER GOURD.**—When grown on the ground the stems will be curved, as shown in the engraving, while if raised as a climbing vine on the trellis, the weight of the blossom end will cause the stem to grow straight. They are very easily prepared for use as dippers, will last for years, and are particularly valuable for dipping hot liquids—the handles do not readily become hot. Dippers of various sizes, of a capacity from a pint to a quart and a half, can be had from a few vines. Packet, 10 cents; ounce, 25 cents.

**JAPANESE CLIMBING GOURD.**

# The Practical Farmer

## ESTABLISHED 1855—WEEKLY—$1.00 PER YEAR.

The Practical Farmer enters the season of 1891 thoroughly prepared to work for the best interests of its patrons. For 36 years it has labored unceasingly in its chosen field, and has performed its part in elevating American Agriculture. But in all the 36 years of its publication, it has never been so well equipped to do battle for the farmer as now; its corps of writers never so strong; its ability and disposition to enlist the best talent in the country in the service of the farmer never better than now. To prove it, here is

## The Bill of Fare for '91.

**FIRST.** A general editorial policy that will be a vigorous and aggressive championship of the farmers' interests. The present agricultural depression, its causes and cure, will receive the careful attention of the best writers. The important questions of taxation, railroad discrimination, proper representation of the farmer in Congress and the State Legislatures, and other kindred subjects will receive their due share of attention, and be treated from an independent standpoint. While the farmer by his individual efforts on his farm must do the largest share of the task of bettering his condition, much also can be achieved by co-operation and organization. These twin topics will be intelligently treated.

**SECOND.** The following able writers will contribute weekly something from their busy brains to lighten the labor of every tiller of the soil in this great and glorious country, in which it is our good fortune to live:

T. GREINER, of New York, that celebrated common-sense writer on all topics pertaining to general agriculture.

T. B. TERRY, of Ohio, whose success both as a writer and farmer gives peculiar point to what he says.

JOSEPH MEEHAN, of Pennsylvania, one of the leading horticulturists of the country.

JOHN M. STAHL, of Illinois, who combines in a high degree clearness of style and knowledge of his subject.

PROF. HENRY STEWART, of North Carolina, one of the most advanced thinkers and workers in the agricultural field.

WALDO F. BROWN, of Ohio, who for years has stood in the front rank of agricultural writers. He talks straight from the shoulder.

JOHN E. READ, of New York, a well-known writer on agriculture, stock and garden topics.

C. L. ALLEN, of New York, an acknowledged authority on all horticultural subjects.

BENJ. F. JOHNSON, of Illinois, a close observer of agricultural matters and whose thoughts are expressed in language attractive to the reader.

GALEN WILSON, of New York. In the front rank of the progressive thinkers of to-day; he is doing yeoman service for the farmer everywhere.

DR. C. E. BRIDGE, of Pennsylvania, who brings to our Veterinary Department a trained intellect in his profession, second to none.

JOHN GOULD, of Ohio, who stands at the head of writers on Dairy topics.

J. McLAIN SMITH, of Ohio, than whom there is no better authority on all matters relating to Live-Stock.

G. H. TURNER, of Mississippi, well known as a practical writer on every subject relating to Southern agriculture.

C. E. CALDWELL, of Louisiana, who writes understandingly and eloquently on the advantages and possibilities of the New South.

J. M. SMITH, of Wisconsin, one of the most celebrated gardeners in the country, whose views are always concisely expressed.

In addition special papers will be contributed from a score or more of correspondents of national reputation in all sections of the country.

**THIRD.** Our Postal Card Correspondence, which has proven such a success in the past, will be continued, and each week we will award the two prizes of $3.00 and $2.00 for the two best cards sent us by subscribers. While we do this for fifty issues during the year, in two issues we will increase the prizes from $5.00 to $25.00, thus making $300 paid during the year for postals written by our subscribers.

**FOURTH.** In addition to the above-mentioned $300 offered our subscribers, we will also offer $700 in cash prizes during 1891, in part, for the best articles written by subscribers to the PRACTICAL FARMER on various subjects pertaining to farm work, hereafter to be announced, and partly to those securing the largest clubs for us during the next subscription season. It is a point worth noticing that this $1000 in cash is to be divided among actual subscribers to the PRACTICAL FARMER and no one else

**FIFTH.** The Home Circle will continue to be a strong feature, as no one realizes better than the management of this paper that if the women folks are not looked after they had better quit publishing the PRACTICAL FARMER. Mrs. Melville promises to take good care that her department will not be surpassed by any other, and we promise that we will do our best for every farmer's wife who reads our paper.

**SIXTH.** The Markets. No more important duty attaches to the farmer than to know when and where best to sell his products. Our market reports are carefully compiled from the leading trade centres of the country, and from their study, from week to week, can be obtained this indispensable information for the proper disposal of every product of the farm.

**SEVENTH.** The Week's Happenings can be depended on to contain each week everything of importance occurring at home or abroad. We thoroughly realize that while the PRACTICAL FARMER is what is called a class publication, yet our ambition is also to make it a newspaper in every sense of the word. We will not be satisfied until its opinion will be as highly thought of, and its circulation will compare with that of any of the largest metropolitan weeklies published in America.

**EIGHTH.** Our Three Inquiry Departments—General, Veterinary and Legal—are under the supervision of the best authorities. All inquiries sent by subscribers under any of these heads are answered fully and satisfactorily. They have been the source of much valuable information and will be kept up to the high standard already established.

**NINTH.** Our Occasional Foreign Letters; the Weekly Letters from New York and Chicago, and the Car Window Impressions made on our staff correspondents in their journeys through the country, are magazines of facts and opinions. Our correspondents are in position to intelligently and thoroughly chronicle and discuss the different topics which arise from week to week.

**FINALLY.**—If push and pluck will make a paper, whose weekly visits will be eagerly looked for by every reader, we propose to get there. We shall spare no expense to try to make the PRACTICAL FARMER a power for good in every household into which it comes; but without the help of you who are now reading this, we realize that our efforts will not be as successful as we could wish.

We want you to give The Practical Farmer a trial, either for three months or a year. It will cost you only 30 cents for three months, or a dollar bill for a year. "Once a subscriber, always a subscriber." That is our motto. Send for a sample copy. We shall be glad to send you one or more.

## THE FARMER CO. Publishers of The Practical Farmer,

P. O. Box 1317

## PHILADELPHIA, PA.

mer

Address all Orders to WM. HENRY MAULE, No. 1711 Filbert Street, Philadelphia, Pa., U. S. A.

Page 31.—Annual Catalogue for 1891 of Maule's Four-Leaf Clover QUARANTEED SEEDS.

# Egg Plants

**Earliest Dwarf.** Packet, 10 cents.
**EARLIEST DWARF PURPLE.**—It resembles the N. Y. Imp. Purple exactly in shape, but in size is considerably smaller; on the other hand, is a **month earlier.** Pkt., 10c.; oz., 30c.

**New York Purple.** Pkt. 10 cts.

**New York Improved Purple.**—Large, fine, free of thorns skin a rich purple, flesh white and of excellent quality. I can especially recommend my select carefully grown seeds of this profitable variety to market-gardeners. Pkt., 10 cts.; oz., 50 cts.; ¼ lb., $1.50.

**EARLY LONG PURPLE.**—Early; prolific. Pkt., 5 cts.; oz., 25 cts.; ¼ lb., 60 cts.

**BLACK PEKIN'**—Weight, 4 to 8 lbs. It is **very productive,** with handsome, nearly round, solid fruit, which matures early. Pkt., 10 cts., oz., 50 cts.; ¼ lb., $1.50.

**Long Purple.** Pkt., 5c.

## KALE GREEN CURLED.
—Very desirable for greens, being remarkably tender and delicate in flavor. It is very hardy and is improved by frost. Leaves, rich green and very curly. Pkt., 5c.; oz., 10c.; ¼ lb., 30c.; lb., 90c.

**Black Pekin.** Packet, 10 cents.

**GREEN CURLED SCOTCH KALE.**—Grows about 2 feet high with an abundance of dark green leaves, which are very curly and wrinkled. Will stand the winters in the Middle States without protection. Pkt., 5 cts.; oz., 10 cts.; ¼ lb., 30 cts.; lb., 90c.

**BROAD FLAG.**—Large, with broad leaves, growing on two sides like flag. Packet, 5 cents; ounce, 10 cents; ¼ pound, 40 cents; pound, $1.25.

**NEW GIANT ITALIAN.**—This new variety has given great satisfaction everywhere; it grows to an enormous size, of which the illustration fails to scarcely convey an idea. It is very hardy, easily grown and of monstrous size. Packet, 10 cents; ounce, 20 cents; ¼ pound, 50 cents; pound, $1.75.

**Giant Italian Leek.** Packet 10 cents.

## COLLARDS TRUE Georgia
—Collards are extensively grown in the South, as they are an easy, sure crop, and afford an abundance of food for both man and beast. It forms a mass of leaves on a tall stem, which are the better for freezing.

**True Ga. Collards.** Pkt., 5 cts.

**MARTYNIA PROBOSCIDEA.**—When young and tender the seed-pods make excellent pickles, and as they are produced in great abundance, a few plants will suffice for an ordinary garden. Packet, 10 cents; ounce, 30 cents; ¼ pound, $1.00; pound, $3.00.

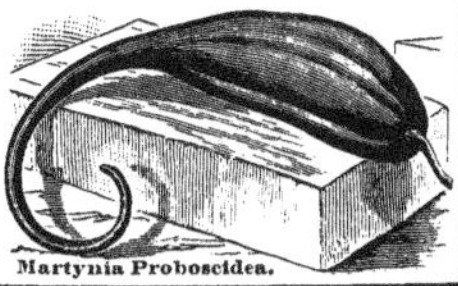

**Martynia Proboscidea.**

**MUSHROOM SPAWN.**—Mushrooms can be grown in a dry cellar, or in sheds where the temperature can be kept from 50 to 60 degrees through the winter. Boxes ,containing two lbs., $1.00 per box by mail, or 75 cents per box by express at expense of purchaser.

**224,160 PACKETS OF MAULE'S SEEDS WERE PRESENTED TO CUSTOMERS FREE, FOR TRIAL, IN 1890.**

**NEW WHITE EGG PLANT.**—One of my customers received two plants of White Egg Plant from a friend who brought the seed from Sweden. They were set out at the same time with some of the Purple varieties, and proved hardier and more prolific, and very much superior in every way, having no green color under the skin whatever, and being very much firmer in flesh. The shape is excellently shown in illustration given herewith. The originator writes as follows: "They are a true egg shape, very smooth, and nearer the color and smoothness of polished ivory than anything I can compare them to. If they have a fault, it is in their propensity to over-produce. A plant no thicker than a lead-pencil and less than 12 inches high, will blossom and if not taken off the fruit will lay on the ground and grow ill-shaped. I had the best success where I took off all blossoms until the plant had attained a growth of 18 inches. As regards earliness, will say that with me the white variety were fully two-thirds grown before plants of the New York Purple began to blossom, yet both were set at same time, though I have had too little experience to be certain there would always be that much difference. As a curiosity they attract more attention than any other plant." The supply of White Egg Plant is limited this year to a few ounces, so I can offer it by packet only. Pkt., 20c.; 3 pkts, 50c.

**White Egg Plant.**

**UPLAND CRESS.**—Water Cress requires running water to perfect it; but the new Upland Cress, which is similar in its characteristics, can be raised without any care. It is indestructible by frost to such a degree as to remain green nearly the whole year round; it comes to use at a time when green vegetables are scarcest, when the appetite for anything like this is the strongest, and when wished for the most; it is the first from the open ground, weeks ahead of lettuce, asparagus or spinach. In quality it is the very best, having the identical, very agreeable and highly-prized flavor of the Water Cress; it grows with surprising and unequaled rapidity, so that in a few days after the opening of Spring, it is ready to use. The young and tender leaves can be eaten raw or as a salad. It is excellent prepared the same as lettuce, or when the leaves become large and plentiful, boiled as greens, being far superior to spinach. It is of easy culture, thriving on any soil, wet or dry, and when once established remains, appearing regularly every Spring, requiring no further care. Upland Cress endures more cold, more freezing without injury than any other plant; from 15 to 20 degrees of frost will not change the color of the leaves, and if wanted to use during the whole Winter, a covering of two inches of straw will fully protect the foliage from spoiling, when the thermometer runs below zero. Packet, 10 cents.

**UPLAND CRESS.**

## ENDIVE GREEN CURLED.
—Popular for greens. When leaves are properly blanched it will make excellent salad. The hardiest variety. Pkt., 10c.; oz., 20c.; ¼ lb., 60c.; lb., $2.00.

**EVER WHITE CURLED.**—(Self-blanching.) An improvement on old White Curled. Large growth, tender, crisp. Pkt., 10c.; oz., 30c.; ¼ lb., $1.0 ; lb., $3.50.

**Ever White Curled Endive.** Packet, 10 cents.

**Mushroom Spawn.**

# HERBS AND OTHER ODDS AND ENDS.

## ※ HERBS. ※

Anise.—Pkt, 5 cts.; oz., 15 cts.
Balm.—Pkt, 5 cts.; oz., 25 cts.
Basil, Sweet.—Pkt, 5c.; oz., 20c.
Caraway.—Pkt, 5c.; oz., 10c.
Coriander.—Pkt, 5c.; oz., 10c.
Dill.—Pkt, 5 cents; oz., 10 cents.
Fennel, Sweet.—Pkt, 5c.; oz., 10c.
Horehound.—Pkt, 5c.; oz., 30c.
Lavender.—Pkt, 5c.; oz., 25c.
Marjoram, Sw't.—Pkt.5c.; oz. 20c.
Rue.—Pkt, 5 cents; oz., 25 cents.
Rosemary.—Pkt, 10c.; oz., 40c.
Sage.—Pkt, 5 cents; oz., 15 cents.
Summer Savory.—Pkt. 5c; oz.20.
Thyme.—Pkt, 10 cts.; oz., 30 cts.
Winter Savory.—Pkt.5c; oz.,20c.

**BRUSSEL SPROUTS.**
Imp.—Should be more largely grown. The sprouts grow as shown in cut, and are used as greens. They become very tender and of rich flavor when touched by frost. Pkt, 5 cts.; oz., 20 cts.; ¼ lb., 45 cts.; lb., $1.35.

**CELERIAC.**—(Turnip Rooted Celery. Used as a salad as well as for seasoning and flavoring Soups. Pkt, 5c.; oz., 30c.

**CHICORY.**—Used when dried as a substitute for Coffee. Pkt.5c.; oz., 10c.; ¼ lb., 30c.; lb., 80c.

**CORN SALAD.—New Large Round-Leaved.** Matures in 4 to 5 weeks. One of the hardiest of all salads. Pkt, 5 cts.; oz., 10 cts.; ¼ lb., 25 cts., lb., 75 cts.

**CRESS. Extra-Curled, or Pepper Grass.** Pkt, 5 cts.; oz., 10c.; Water.—Pkt, 10c.; oz., 40c.

**DANDELION IMPROVED. Large-Leaved.** Cultivated for spring greens. The leaves of this variety are fully double the size of the common sort. Pkt, 10 cents; oz. 50 cents.

**HORSE-RADISH.—Sets.** 40 cts. per doz. By mail postpaid.

**MUSTARD—White.—Pkt,** 5 cts.; oz., 10 cts. **Black.—Pkt.,** 5 cts.; oz., 10 cts. **New Chinese.** —Grows twice the size of the ordinary mustard. Pkt.5c.; oz.10c

**NASTURTIUM. Tall.** Pkt., 5 cts.; oz., 15 cts. **Dwarf.**—Pkt. 5 cts.; oz., 15 cts.

**OKRA.—Dwarf Green.—** Pkt., 5 cts.; oz., 10 cts. **Long Green.**—Pkt., 5 cts.; oz., 10 cts.

**RHUBARB, Victoria.—** Pkt., 5 cts.; oz., 10 cts. **Roots.** 35 cts. each, $3.50 per dozen.

**IMPROVED IMPERIAL.**—The best for table use. Has small greens, but extra large roots thus producing a very heavy crop per acre. It will not only out-yield all others, but is a better keeper. When matured, most excellent, and even better than Mangels or SwedeTurnips for feeding stock, and especially fine for feeding cows, as ½ imparts no unpleasant taste to the milk. It is well to remember that in places where Turnips fail, Kohl Rabi or Turnip-Rooted Cabbage, will produce good crops. Unquestionably the most profitable variety ever offered. Pkt, 5 cents; ounce, 20 cents; ¼ lb, 50 cents.

**LARGE-WHITE.**—Excellent for the table. Packet, 5 cents; ounce, 20 cents; ¼ lb., $2.00.

**PERSIAN INSECT POWDER PLANT.**—A hardy perennial of easy culture, yielding a large quantity of flowers which somewhat resemble Ox Eyed Daisy, except in color, this being rose color. The flowers are gathered when in full bloom, and dried, and when finely powdered they make the Genuine Persian Insect Powder, which is sold from 60 to 75 cents per pound, and often much adulterated. Any one, by growing their own, can, at a trifling expense, keep their houses free from Flies, Ants, Roaches, Fleas and Bedbugs. Dogs, Cats, Horses, Cattle and Poultry can quickly be relieved of Fleas and Lice. It will also destroy the worms that infest the currant and gooseberry. In fact, all insect life is destroyed when brought in contact with the fine powder, at the same time it is not poisonous to animals or the human family. A solution, made by steeping the flowers in water, will be found useful to persons camping out, or hunting, in fact, in any situation exposed to Mosquitos or Vermin of any kind; by applying the wash to parts exposed, their attacks will be prevented; and a strong solution will be found to be a good way to apply it to animals to destroy Fleas and Lice, and will in a measure prevent flies tormenting horses. A beautiful, showy flower, as well as a valuable insecticide. Pkt, 15c.; 2 Pkts., 25c.

## IMPROVED GROUND CHERRY.

**Imp. Ground Cherry,** Packet, 10 cts.

Unequaled for canning, preserving and pies. Dried in sugar as Raisins or Figs, they are unexcelled. They are a handsome purple color, and will keep till mid-winter. They have a strawberry flavor, produce fruit in great abundance, from one to two inches in diameter. In sections devoid of fruit, many esteem them highly; a great curiosity, and sell well in market.

A correspondent to the Chicago Inter-Ocean writes as follows: "One thing which with me is one of the most important of all the fruits in my cookery. I do not recollect of ever seeing the Ground Cherry (not the wild one.) They grow well on almost any dry soil, are easier raised than the tomato, and are prolific bearers, and oh! such luscious fruit. For sauce they are excellent, and for pies I know of nothing that can equal them in flavor or taste. They are just as well dried in sugar, and they will keep, if put in a cool, dry place in the shuck, nearly all winter. I have never seen them named in any seed catalogue, and from what I learn from friends in different parts of the country they seem to be very little known. No one after raising them once will ever make a garden again without devoting a small portion to the Ground Cherry. Pkt, 10 cts.; oz., 30 cts.

## UPRIGHT OR TREE TOMATO.

There have been many varieties of so-called Tree Tomatoes offered in recent years, but I think this more nearly fills the bill than any other. Standing up like a tree, without support of any kind, as shown in illustration, even herewith. It bears abundantly, fruit being of medium size, smooth in shape, bright red in color and fine flavor; a valuable and curious acquisition; very ornamental as well as useful. Sure to excite remark in any garden. Packet, 15 cents; 2 Packets, 25 cents.

**Upright or Tree Tomato.**

**Imp. "Ground Pea" or Peanut.**—Pkt, 10 cts.

**IMPROVED "GROUND PEA" OR PEANUT.**—A variety that combines the following good qualities, viz: earliness, size and prolificness, yielding fewer imperfect pods, and makes less "popps" than any other kind, yielding on medium land one hundred bushels per acre; the vines average three and a half to four feet across, which makes valuable forage for stock; color of nut red, two to three in a pod, large and rich flavor. An excellent paying crop in the South, as the demand has often exceeded the supply, and growers of the "Peanut" have always found ready sale at remunerative prices for their product. It does not require a rich soil. Pkt., 10 cts.; pt., 25 cts.; qt., 40 cts

## THE MELON PEACH.

—This is considered by the introducer the most valuable and unique novelty offered to the public in many years. Those who have tried them, consider they are interesting vegetables of value. They grow on vines same as melons, are a beautiful golden yellow, almost resembling oranges in color, shape and size. The flesh is snow-white, and makes excellent and handsome preserves. They are delicious fried as eggplant, and for mangoes are considered superior to peppers. They are hardy, very productive, and keep a long time after being picked. Pkt., 10 cts.; oz., 35 cts.

WITH EVERY ORDER FOR EITHER GROUND CHERRY OR MELON PEACH I WILL SEND A NUMBER OF RECIPES FOR COOKING AND PRESERVING THESE NOVELTIES, WRITTEN BY A PRACTICAL HOUSEWIFE.

# Brussels Sprouts

**NEW HALF DWARF PARIS MARKET.**—This delightful vegetable is at present only cultivated to a limited extent in this country; but the demand for the seed is becoming greater and greater, particularly as market-gardeners are finding out that the demand for this vegetable is greater, and rapidly increasing every year, as its merits become better known to the American people. The largest French seed house, last season, for the first time, put this new strain on the market, recommending it as the best variety of Brussels Sprouts that has ever been offered on account of its regularity of growth (18 to 20 inches,) its hardiness and sureness of setting. The sprouts are of medium size, very hard and thickly set on the stem, etc. It can not be compared with the large, coarse-looking, new English varieties. Flavor excellent, with no strong taste. Packet, 10 cents; ounce, 50 cents.

**NEW HALF DWARF PARIS MARKET.**

**BIG HAVANA TOBACCO.**—A hybrid of Cuban seedleaf. Heavy cropper, fine texture, delightful flavor and earliest cigar variety, to mature and ripen. Pkt. 10c.; oz. 75c.

**TOBACCO, Connecticut Seed Leaf.**—Packet, 10 cents; ounce, 25 cents. **Havana.**—Packet, 10 cents; ounce, 40 cents. **Sweet Oronoco.**—Pkt., 10c.; oz., 25cts.

**STACHYS AFFINIS.**—A new and valuable ground fruit. The bulbs are the size and shape as seen in the cut, and taste exactly like the tuber of artichoke, and are cooked in a variety of ways—fried, roasted, baked, etc., but are particularly valuable for stock, owing to their enormous productiveness. They are a most valuable feed to raise for swine. Planted in ordinary soil they yield a bushel of tubers to every 10 ft. of row. The bulbs are very sweet, tender and nutritious. Dozen, 20 cents; 75 cents. per 100.

STACHYS AFFINIS.

**NEW PRIMUS TOBACCO.**—This entirely new and extra early Tobacco, which I offered for the first time in '88, matures and ripens the earliest of any variety grown. Succeeds in Canada, where few kinds will ripen. Leaves large. Others fine and texture silky. Yields big crops of extra fine quality. Pkt. 10c.; oz. 80c.

**NEW PRIMUS**

**WHITE VELVET OKRA**

This new Okra produces pods larger than any other. They are never prickly to the touch, and always round and smooth, while in other varieties they are either ridged or square-edged. At the same time it is very productive and will out-yield every other sort. It is certainly worthy of a trial by all my customers. Pkt., 5 cts.; oz., 10 cts.; ¼ lb., 30 cts.

**CHUFAS or EARTH ALMOND.**—A species of "grass nut," much used to fatten hogs. It is not to be confounded with Cocoa or Nut Grass, for though it belongs to the same class, the Chufa is eradicated with ease and is never a pest. The nuts or tubers are larger and more elongated, very sweet and nutritious. The nuts grow under ground, very near the surface, easily reached by pigs or poultry, and destroyed by them if they have free access. Easily and cheaply grown, abundant in yield, greedily eaten by hogs, which take on firm fat rapidly from them. They fill a decided want wherever there are a number to be fattened. Plant in April, 10 to 12 in. apart, in 2½ to 3 ft. rows. Cover lightly. If seed is very dry, soak well before planting, to secure a good stand. Mature about Sept. 1st.. and lie in the soil till wanted. Pkt. 10c.; pt., 35c.; qt., 60c.; by express, peck, $2.00.

CHUFAS.

**ASPARAGUS CHICORY.**—This remarkable vegetable is quite new. It is a wonderful curative for all disorders of the stomach. It produces a large quantity of compact short stems, which, when cut, are reproduced time after time. The benefit derived from the consumption of these stems for only a short time, by those having weak digestion, is said to be remarkable. The leaves when boiled make a very wholesome and delicious salad. Can be blanched and rendered very tender by simply covering. When fully known, this vegetable will prove to be a valuable acquisition to our gardens and vegetable markets, and no gardener should be without it. Pkt., 10c.

H. C. Rogers, Hillsborough, N. H. "I wish to say I consider your seeds superior to others. I cannot get along without them, so send along the order for 1890."

**ASPARAGUS CHICORY.**

The GARDEN LEMON

**NEW GARDEN LEMON.**—I was pleased to introduce this to my customers last year as a novelty of merit well worthy their attention. It resembles the Melon Peach in manner of growth and shape of fruit, but is distinct in that the unripe fruit is striped with very dark green, nearly black, while the Melon Peach is plain green, and when ripe is not russeted like the Vine Peach. Fruit is somewhat smaller than Vine Peach, has thinner flesh and is decidedly more acid, thus dispensing with the sliced lemons, which are so important in putting up the Melon Peach. Cultivate like Musk-melon in hills three feet apart each way. Full directions for cooking in various manners accompany each packet. Don't fail to try it. Packet, 10 cents.

**CHINESE YAM.—Cinnamon Vine.**—One of the most valuable esculents in cultivation, though but little known; stem 12 to 20 ft. in length, rapid growth, creeping or climbing habit, forming an excellent covering for a screen; flowers small, white, in clusters; leaves heart-shaped. A correspondent writes the *Rural New Yorker.* "The Chinese Yam possesses merits that should commend it to the Agricultural classes of the U. S. They have no insect enemy, and drouth affects them but very little, as they root so deeply. There is no necessity for their being dug, except when wanted. You can plant enough at one planting to last for years, each year bringing larger Yams. I consider them safer to depend on than the Irish Potato, which has its enemies, and is so sensitive to a little freeze." Small bulbiets which form roots about a foot in length in 1 year, 30 cts. per doz.; 1-year-old roots, $1.25 per doz.; $6.00 per 100.

CINNAMON VINE.

## MAULE'S IMPROVED HANSON LETTUCE.

**MAULE'S IMPROVED HANSON LETTUCE.—I have no hesitancy in saying that its superior does not exist.** These may appear to be strong words to use, but I think every customer this season planting this strain of Hanson Lettuce will willingly acknowledge the above to be correct. The branching leaves are of a beautiful green color, slightly curled, while the inner leaves, which form the head present a white appearance, **and are as tender as if blanched.** It forms a **very large head**, at times attaining a weight of 5 lbs. each and over. The $50 premium in 1888 was awarded to Alfred Fuller, East Ashford, N. Y., for raising a head weighing 12½ pounds, which was the heaviest head of any variety I have ever known. When eaten, it has a rich, **nutty flavor, and is almost absolutely free from any strong or bitter taste. It resists wonderfully well Summer heat and drought,** and is in every way the sort for the market or family gardener. **NO PRAISE IS TOO HIGH FOR ITS MERITS.** Pkt., 10 cents; oz., 35 cents; ¼ lb., 75 cents; lb., $2.50.

H. J. Horton, Hendersonville, N. C. "The seeds I bought of you last spring were good. Each kind coming squarely up to representation as per catalogue. The prize Jumbo Watermelon can not be beat. I got a Justice of the Peace to weigh two of them; one weighed 45, the other 48 pounds. I cut one after we weighed them, and the Justice declared it was too sweet, he could not eat it. Extra Early Hackensack Musk-melon is a No. 1. for size and sweetness; it is a delicious melon; when good and ripe it will melt in the mouth like sugar."

J. T. Paine, Gillentine, Tenn. : "I am well pleased with my seeds. I sold from one vine three Jumbo Melons for $1.00 and had nine left on the vine. I have been raising melons for 14 years but never had so many from the same amount of hills."
U. G. Daniels, Lowrianesville, Ky.: "I take pleasure in writing you a letter to-day that I had no idea I should write last spring when I received my seeds; but I am proud to say, and not only to say, but to prove to you, that the seeds have done more than anything you recommended them to do. I raised two Jumbo Watermelons that beat anything in the melon line that was ever raised in this county. Every one who sees them say they are the largest melons by half that they ever saw. One weighs 97 lbs. and 13 ounces, the other 78¾ lbs.; they were grown in 3 months and 14 days."

John W. Harmon, Poseyville, Ind.: "I was well pleased with the seeds purchased from you last Spring. I raised one Jumbo Melon that weighed 87 pounds. The Stubborn Seeder Lettuce, and Matchless Tomato are excellent."
A. D. Hawes, Blissfield, Mich.: "I have some very fine Jumbo Melons, they are ahead of any thing that was every raised here."

## FOUR SUPERIOR CABBAGE LETTUCES FOR 1891

**LARGE PASSION.**—While in California in 1887 I was particularly struck with this fine Lettuce. Its large handsome heads are of a delicate, crisp flavor. Leaves resemble the Cal. Butter, except that the outer ones contain no brown spots. **Stands the Summer heat wonderfully well.** As it grows slowly, and forms a very hard head, it remains fit for use a **long time.** Pkt., 10c.; oz., 15c.; ¼ lb., 40c.; lb., $1.50.

**CALIFORNIA BUTTER.**—Very similar to the Large Passion. Forms a fine head, which is very compact and solid. The outside leaves are of a medium green color, slightly marked with brown spots, while within the leaves are of a rich creamy yellow color. Packet, 10 cts.; ounce, 15 cts.; ¼ pound, 40 cents; pound, $1.50.

**BUTTERCUP.**—This new variety comes very highly recommended. For beauty of foliage, extreme tenderness and delicacy of flavor, it is hard to beat. Always forms good solid heads. It is a medium early and is equally suitable for either Summer or Winter growth. It is undoubtedly **one of the best** of all the new varieties. Packet, 10 cts.; ounce, 15 cts., ¼ pound, 40 cts.; pound, $1.50.

**MARBLEHEAD MAMMOTH.**—Frequently grows as large as a good Drumhead Cabbage. It is a second early, leaves being of a lightish green color. In quality it is tender, crisp and free from bitterness. It is a splendid Lettuce, a very hard header, and slow to run to seed. **If you want the largest Lettuce you have ever sown,** you should sow Marblehead. It is the largest heading variety of the lettuce family in cultivation. Pkt., 10c.; oz., 15c.; ¼ lb., 40c.; lb., $1.50.

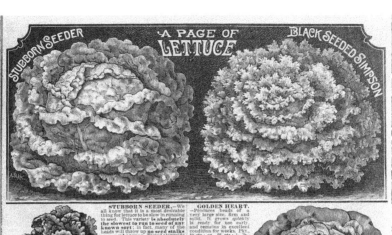

**STUBBORN SEEDER**     A PAGE OF **LETTUCE**     **BLACK SEEDED SIMPSON**

**STUBBORN SEEDER.**—We all know that it is a most desirable thing for lettuce to be slow in running to seed. This variety **is absolutely the slowest to run to seed of any known sort**; in fact, many of the heads will throw up **no seed stalks whatever.** Tested alongside of almost 100 other sorts, it surpassed all by long odds in this important qualification, while it **formed magnificent large solid heads of the most superb quality.** It stands drouth better than any other variety, and is equally desirable for market or home use. Pkt., 10 cts.; oz., 25 cts.; ¼ lb., 75 cts.; lb., $2.50.

**GOLDEN HEART.** Packet, 10 cents. Of the very best introduced in years. Stands Summer heat splendidly, and remains a long time fit for use. **No customer sowing it this season will regret it.** Packet, 10 cents; ounce, 25 cents; ¼ pound, 60 cents; pound, $2.00.

**TENNISBALL.**—One of the earliest of heading sorts, and most excellent for forcing under glass. Pkt., 5 cts.; oz., 15 cts.; ¼ lb., 40 cts.; lb., $1.50.

For a $1.00 remittance you can always select seeds, in packets, to the value of $1.30. $2 buys $2.75. This reduces the cost of each packet considerably.

**GOLDEN HEART.**—Produces heads of very large size, firm and solid. It grows quickly is ready for use early, and remains in excellent condition for weeks. Pkt., 10 cts.; oz., 25 cts.; ¼ lb., 60 cts.; lb., $2.00.

**SALAMANDER.**—Large, compact heads. New York market-gardeners consider it the best for Summer use on account of its heat-resisting qualities. Pkt., 5c.; oz., 15c.; ¼ lb., 40c.; lb., $1.50.

**ALL THE YEAR ROUND.**—Crisp and compact. Valuable for forcing. Pkt., 5c.; oz., 15c.; ¼ lb., 40c.; lb., $1.50.

**BOSTON CURLED.**—Excellent superior quality. Pkt., 5c.; oz., 15c.; ¼ lb., 40c.; lb., $1.50.

**GREEN FRINGED.**—A most distinct and beautiful sort. Pkt., 5c.; oz., 15c.; ¼ lb., 40c.

**OHIO CABBAGE.** Packet, 10 cents.—Early Ohio is good either for Spring or Summer use; forms a large, solid head, of a beautiful light green color. Is early and very pleasing to the sight. Very tender and of delicious flavor. Packet, 10 cents; ounce, 20 cents; ¼ pound, 50 cents.

**MIXED LETTUCE.**—12 to 15 varieties in a single packet, early, medium and late. Packet, 10 cents; ounce, 15 cents; ¼ pound, 40 cents; pound, $1.50.

**COS LETTUCE.**—Cos Lettuce are all of fine and tender quality. Pkt., 5c.; oz., 15c.

**SALAMANDER.** Packet, 5 cents.

**BOSTON CURLED.** Packet, 5 cts.

**ALL THE YEAR ROUND.** Pkt., 5 cts.

**GREEN FRINGED.** Pkt., 5 cts.

**MAULE'S PHILADELPHIA BUTTER.**—Produces fine heads of large size white, tender crisp and of fine flavor. Sure to head, and to please in every way. Packet, 10 cents; ounce, 25 cents; ¼ pound, 75 cents; pound, $2.25.

**EARLY PRIZE HEAD.**—Forms a large, tender and crisp mass of leaves of superior flavor, and very hardy. Slow to run to seed and does not become bitter as early as many other sorts. Pkt., 5 c.; oz., 15 c.; ¼ lb., 40c.; lb. $1.25.

35

# MAULE'S NEW SUPERIOR MUSK MELON.

**(See illustration on last page of cover.)**

No one is better aware than I that during the last few years any number of new Muskmelons have been offered the American public; consequently I have been unusually careful in growing and examining into the merits of this new variety before offering it to my customers. **I now do so, however, with the full confidence that Maule's Superior Muskmelon will prove the most profitable market variety in cultivation, for the Superior unquestionably leads all other Muskmelons in quality, productiveness and quick market sales.** Ripening about the same time as the Jenny Lind, they are wonderfully strong and vigorous growers, producing frequently 5, 6 and 7 melons to the vine that in quality will equal, if not surpass, every known variety, and that for transportation purposes cannot be excelled. They have never been known to crack or rot at the blossom end, and they are so attractive in appearance that they will always command from 10 to 25 cents per basket more than any other variety. I do not think a better name could have been chosen than Superior for this excellent Muskmelon, and my customers can rest assured that if they want **the most profitable variety for market** they should select this one, and if they desire **the most desirable Muskmelon for the home garden** they cannot do better than plant Superior the coming season. Packet, 10 cts.; ounce, 20 cts.; ¼ pound, 60 cts.; pound, $2.00.

**Netted Gem.** Pkt., 5c.

**NETTED GEM.**—A small melon, weighing from 1¼ to 1½ pounds each. They are thick-meated, the flesh is light green in color, and uniformly of fine, luscious flavor; skin green, regularly ribbed and thickly netted. They are almost as solid as a cannon ball, and will keep well five to seven days after picking. They are a very heavy cropper, and are extra early in ripening. I offer seed grown from stock obtained direct from introducer, and can recommend it to all. Packet, 5 cents; ounce, 10 cents; ¼ pound, 30 cents; pound, 90 cents.

**MAULE'S PRIZE JENNY LIND.**—It is astonishing that this, **the most delicious small melon,** is so little known outside of the State of New Jersey. There it is more largely grown than any other variety, and thousands upon thousands of baskets are annually shipped to New York and Philadelphia markets, where they always meet with ready sale. My strain of this popular variety has been carefully selected for years. It is **the earliest** of all the green-fleshed sorts. Pkt., 5 cts.; oz., 10 cts.; ¼ lb., 25c.; lb., 70 cts.

**Maule's Prize Jenny Lind.**

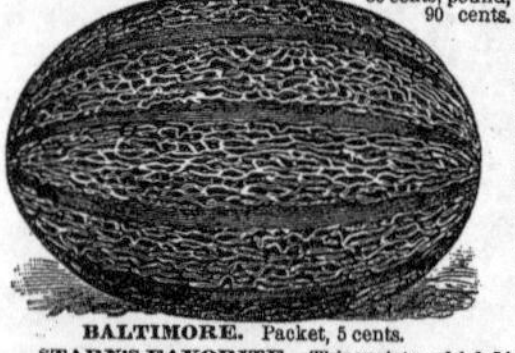

**BALTIMORE.** Packet, 5 cents.

**STARN'S FAVORITE.** Packet, 10 cents.

**MAULE'S BAY VIEW.** Packet, 5 cents.

**STARN'S FAVORITE.**—This variety, which I introduced in 1887, was also catalogued the same year under the name of "Champion Market." It originated with one of my customers, Mr. E. N. Starn, of New Jersey, about ten years ago. Mr. Starn has grown it to the exclusion of all other varieties ever since, annually planting from 10 to 20 acres, the products of which have always sold at good prices the entire season, and **many times at two to three times the price of other sorts.** They are nearly round, just a little oblong, thickly netted, with thick, green flesh. Rich and spicy and one of the very best flavored in cultivation. They are shy seeders; the cavity for seed in many of them is so small that if they were all seed inside the flesh they could not contain many. They are very attractive in appearance and a good shipper. Mr Starn has never had a grower to see or taste them but wanted some of the seed. In addition to their attractive appearance and most excellent shipping qualities, they are also an enormous cropper and will be pronounced by all who plant them **as most certainly a favorite and most profitable market variety.** Pkt., 5 cts.; ounce, 10 cents; ¼ pound, 30 cents; 1 pound, $1.00.

**EARLY IMPROVED CHRISTIANA.**—This is a most popular early in New York State, being 10 days earlier than than the Nutmeg. Many market growers, having once planted it, always continue to do so, pronouncing it just the sort for early market on account of its extreme earliness. Try it. Pkt., 5 cents; ounce, 10 cents; ¼ pound, 25 cents; pound 70 cents.

**CASABA.**—It has thick green flesh, of delicate and delicious flavor. Weight from 10 to 12 lbs. Pkt., 5 cents; ounce, 10 cents; ¼ lb., 25 cts.; lb., 70 cts.

**HACKENSACK.**—Large size, well known in N. Y. market. Round shape, flattened ends; deeply netted, very productive, excellent quality. Liked by market gardeners. Pkt. 5c.; oz. 10c. ¼ lb. 25 c.; lb. 70c.

**MONTREAL.**—Often weighing from 20 to 25 lbs. In 1883, three melons were raised, weighing respectively 39½, 38½, and 38¼ lbs. each. In addition to their large size, the flesh is remarkably thick, of delicious melting flavor, regular shape, nearly round flattened ends, skin green, densely netted, and very productive. At considerable expense, I procured a few lbs. of Montreal direct from original source in Canada. Pkt. 10c. oz., 15 c.; ¼ lb., 35 c.; lb., $1.10.

MONTREAL

**BALTIMORE.**—Quite early and very large and showy. A fine netted, green fleshed variety, for either market or private gardeners. Pkt., 5c.; oz., 10c.; ¼ lb., 25c.; lb., 70c.

**MAULE'S BAY VIEW.**—Under ordinary cultivation will reach 12 to 15 lbs. **Very productive,** and most excellent in many other ways; they are firm when ripe; excellent for shipping. Packet, 5 cents; ounce, 10 cents; ¼ pound, 25 cents; pound, 70 cents.

**NUTMEG.**—Skin deep green, finely netted; flesh of rich and delicious flavor. Pkt., 5 cts.; ounce, 10 cts.; ¼ pound, 25 cents; pound, 70 cents.

**NUTMEG.** Packet, 5 cents.

**HARDY RIDGE.**—This is a great favorite in France. Flesh is wonderfully thick, 4 to 5 in. through; juicy and sugary, with few seeds. Pkt., 10c.; oz., 30c.

**BANANA.**—At first Banana Melon was cultivated more as a curiosity than anything else, but the last few seasons have seen them bring such high prices, 50 cents to $1.00 a piece in Philadelphia, New York and Boston markets, that they prove **a most profitable market crop.** They must not be confounded with the old Log of Wood, as they are entirely distinct and resemble no other melon. They attain a length of from eighteen inches to two feet six inches, and are from two to four inches thick. Flesh, very thick, of a salmon color; in flavor remarkably delicious, and equal to almost any melon you have ever eaten. It looks almost like an overgrown banana, and, **moreover, smells like one.** It is not only a curiosity, but in flavor is unquestionably fine. Packet, 5 cents; ounce, 10 cents; ¼ pound, 30 cents; pound, 90 cents.

BANANA

EMERALD GEM.—They are about the size of Netted Gem, but unlike that variety, the skin while ribbed is smooth and of a very deep emerald green color. Its salmon flesh is thicker than any other of its size, and ripens thoroughly to the thin green rind. The vines are hardy and thrifty in growth, very prolific; the melons mature early and are uniformly of the most superb quality. Pkt. 5 cts.; oz., 10 cts.; ¼ lb., 30c.; lb., 90c.

EXTRA EARLY HACKENSACK.—This is a selection of the popular Hackensack, but is a decided improvement, from the fact that they will produce melons almost equal the size at least ten days earlier. In shape and color it is similar to the old Hackensack, the only difference being in its greater earliness, but this alone is sufficient **to highly recommend it to all.** Pkt., 5 cents; oz., 10 cents; ¼ lb., 30 cents; lb. 90 cts.

OSAGE.—The Osage has brought higher prices in Chicago, as well as many other Western markets, **than any other Musk-melon, and is considered by many the most profitable market variety in cultivation.** It is a medium size, nearly round, salmon colored flesh, finely netted, of rich, luscious flavor; gains friends with both growers and consumers, wherever tried. Packet, 10 cents; ounce, 20 cents; ¾ pound, 50 cents; lb., $1.50.

PERFECTION MUSKMELON.—No words of praise can be written that would recommend this most excellent of the muskmelon too highly. It is simply the perfection of the muskmelon family, equally desirable and profitable to the planter of a dozen hills or the planter of tens of thousands, and it has no superior among muskmelons, except Maule's New Superior, offered on the next page of this catalogue. In the last seven years it has been planted by thousands of melon growers in all sections of the country and it has given one and all entire satisfaction. I really believe that I can show at my office three times the number of testimonials in regard to the good qualities of Perfection than have been written concerning any other variety of muskmelon ever introduced.

Originated ten years ago in Chenango Co., N. Y, by one of my best customers, I secured a small sample of seed from him in 1883. In sending it to me I could not help but think he praised it too highly, stating as he did, that he had tested almost all known varieties and found Perfection **superior to them all.** After a careful test on my trial grounds, I discovered it was fully up to his recommendation, and a **wonderful acquisition.**

It is nearly round, as may be seen by the cut, of good size, frequently weighing 8 to 10 lbs. each. Of a dark green color outside, heavily netted, while inside they are of a rich orange color, and I venture to say with thicker flesh than any other variety in cultivation, there being scarcely room for the seeds. As to flavor, they take the lead of all and are far ahead of everything else at present cultivated. **It can be recommended alike for either home or market use,** and has fully demonstrated that it well deserves the name of **PERFECTION. It surpasses all others with the single exception of Superior in delicious flavor and unusual productiveness, beauty of form and desirable shipping qualities.**

Nothing is so delicious as a really good muskmelon; consequently I look the coming season for a large demand for this, the **sweetest and most delicious of all.** Packet, 10 cents; ounce, 20 cents; ¼ pound, 50 cts.; pound, $1.50.

A. C. Niswander, Broadway, Va.; "New Superior is the finest muskmelon I ever tasted, and sells the best. I have Montreal Nutmegs weighing 15 pounds and over. Colorado preserving melons are a wonder to all who see them grow. I have one vine now over 40 feet long, with 16 melons on it."

FOR the Best Market Muskmelon and the Largest of all Watermelons, see last cover page.

37

KOLB'S GEM

DARK ICING

IRON CLAD

PRIZE JUMBO

CUBAN QUEEN

AN EXACT ILLUSTRATION DRAWN FROM NATURE OF A JUMBO WEIGHING 80 lbs. RAISED BY GARVER BROS. ATTICA, KANSAS.

COPYRIGHT 1892 BY W. HENRY MAULE

**KOLB'S GEM.**—This variety, on account of its earliness and excellent shipping qualities, is largely grown for shipping purposes. They grow nearly round; dark green, with narrow stripes of lighter shade. Flesh, bright red and of good flavor. Melons raised vary in weight from 30 to 50 lbs. each. It is not only one of the best shipping, and most profitable sorts for the South, but it is hardy and productive at the North. Pkt., 5c.; oz., 10c.; ¼ lb., 20c.; lb., 60c.

**TRUE DARK ICING.**—Taking everything into consideration, I think there are but few better melons than the True Dark Icing. In flavor it is simply delicious, and cannot be excelled. It is very solid, rind very thin, and an excellent shipper. It is round in form, and white seeded. Having sold it by the hundreds of pounds for years, I have yet to hear from a customer who does not praise it. By purchasing the True Dark Icing from me, you will discover you have secured a melon very hard to beat in all the points that go to make a perfect melon. Packet, 5 cts.; ounce, 10 cts.; ¼ pound, 20 cts.; pound, 60 cts.

**MAMMOTH IRON-CLAD.**—Iron-clad grows uniformly to a larger size, will yield a far greater bulk and more A1 marketable melons than any other, with the single exception of Prize Jumbo. They have frequently been dropped three feet, and even from the shoulders of a man without bursting or showing any bruise. The heart is very large; the flesh next to rind is fully equal to the heart in luscious taste. The flesh is never mealy, but always solid. They ripen with the Cuban Queen. They can be allowed to remain on the vines one month after they are ripe. Melons taken in the first of October keep in good condition till Christmas. Packet, 10 cents; ounce, 20 cents; ¼ pound, 40 cents; pound, $1.25.

**CUBAN QUEEN.**—This variety has become justly celebrated alike with both producer and consumer. Its large size, great productiveness, bright scarlet, solid flesh, crisp, luscious and spicy flavor, thin rind and superior shipping qualities, recommend it to all growers. In flavor it is the equal of the Icing. Pkt., 10 cts.; oz., 20 cts.; ¼ lb., 40 cts.; lb., $1.35.

**FRAME'S PRIZE, THE JUMBO OF ALL WATERMELONS.**—This new watermelon is a cross between those two grand melons, Cuban Queen and Iron-clad, perfected by Mr. Paynter Frame, originator of Iron-Clad, new Delaware and Fordhook Early. Mr. F. writes me concerning it as follows: "The Prize Melon is a cross between Iron-clad and Cuban Queen. It resembles Cuban Queen somewhat, but is of finer quality than either that variety or Iron-clad. They ripen medium early, flesh solid, very sweet and juicy. They will grow the largest of any melon now known, and if you want to put the largest watermelon in the world on the market, now is your time to strike." I followed Mr. F.'s advice and found that it fully equals all he claims for it. I take pleasure in offering seed of this new variety, confident that you will find it the largest as well as finest melon you have ever planted. Coming from such a source and with such a recommendation, it certainly must be A GOOD ONE to surpass both its parents in size as well as quality. At same time it is fully equal to Iron-clad for shipping purposes; rind, while unusually thin for so large a melon, is so tough that it will bear transportation in first-class condition for long distances. Shape, which is well shown in illustration, also on last page of cover, all will acknowledge a most desirable one. Color, dark green, striped light; flesh, rich cardinal; stringless; seeds drab with dark centers. From what I know of Mr. F.'s previous introductions, I am satisfied Jumbo will prove the most satisfactory as well as largest melon ever introduced. Pkt., 10 cts.; ¼ lb., $1.00; lb., $2.50; 5 lbs., $4.00.

**EARLY RIPE.**—I regret to say that unfortunately my grower has allowed my strain of this variety to become mixed, consequently, I do not offer it this season; but trust to straighten out the damage done in a year or two, when I will be able to offer this excellent sort again to my customers.

**VICK'S EARLY.**—One of the earliest. Small, long, solid and sweet; flesh bright pink. Pkt., 5 cts; oz., 10 cts.; ¼ lb. 20 cts.; lb., 60 cts.

**PHINNEY'S EARLY.**—Deep red flesh; excellent flavor; prolific and very early. Pkt., 5 cts.; oz., 10 cts.; ¼ lb., 20 cts.; lb., 60 cts.

**MOUNTAIN SWEET.**—Flesh, bright scarlet; old but good. Pkt., 5 cts.; oz., 10 cts.; ¼ lb., 20 cts.; lb., 50 cts.

**MOUNTAIN SPROUT.**—A large, long variety; skin, dark green, marbled with lighter shades. Pkt., 5c.; oz., 10c.; ¼ lb., 20c.; lb., 50c.

**BOSS.**—An excellent shipper, very productive and of delicious flavor. Color, very dark; flesh of an unusually deep scarlet, rich in sugar. It well deserves the name of Boss, and you should not neglect to plant it. Packet, 5 cents; ounce, 10 cents; ¼ pound, 30 cents; pound, 90 cents.

**CHRISTMAS.**—It is claimed they can readily be kept in good condition till Christmas. Packet, 5 cents; ounce, 10 cents; ¼ pound, 20 cents; pound 60 cents.

**VOLGA.**—Originally from Russia. Of small size, round in shape. Much esteemed by many for home use. Packet, 5 cents. ounce, 10 cents; ¼ pound, 20 cents; pound, 60 cents.

**FORDHOOK EARLY.**—This new Watermelon, first offered in 1890, is the largest of all the early varieties. At the same time, flesh is of a deliciously sweet flavor, bright red in color. Rind is tough, thus making it a valuable shipper. Seed we offer was grown especially for us by Mr. Frame, of Delaware, the originator. Packet, 10 cts.; ounce, 20 cts.; ¼ pound, 60 cts.

**PEERLESS.**—An excellent sort for garden cultivation. Size, medium; color, mottled green; flesh, rich scarlet; thin rind, sweet and productive. Pkt., 5c.; oz., 10c.; ¼ lb., 20c.; lb., 60c.

**SEMINOLE.**—This new Watermelon comes from Florida, where it originated with Mr. Girardeau, the originator of the Florida Favorite. Mr. Girardeau is one of the largest melon growers in the United States, having tested all known varieties, and he claims that while his Florida Favorite is a most excellent

**SEMINOLE.** Packet, 10 cents.

and desirable variety, that his new Seminole lays on the shelf every watermelon at present known. Flesh, a brilliant carmine, very solid, of a rich melting flavor; rind thin, but so tough as to make it a most superior shipping and market melon. I am sure my customers will find the Seminole will come up to Mr. G.'s recommendation, and I have no doubt that every one who grows this variety this season will find it will even surpass every claim made for it. Pkt., 10c.; oz., 20c., ¼ lb., 40c.; lb., $1.10.

## SEE PAGE 68 — FOR THE 1891 CASH PRIZES OFFERED FOR PREMIUM VEGETABLES RAISED FROM — MAULE'S SEEDS

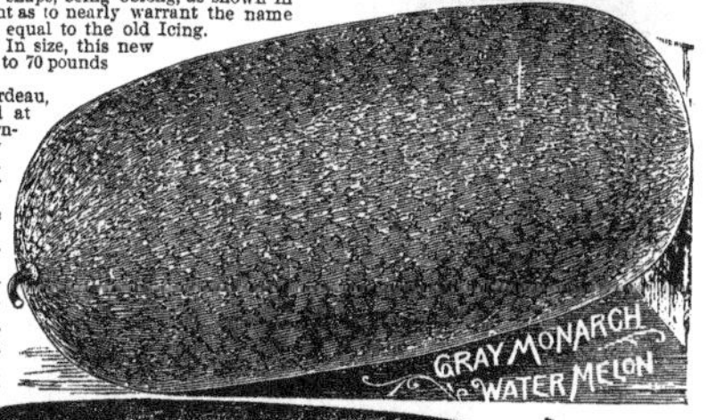

**GRAY MONARCH OR LONG WHITE ICING.**—For several years past a few melon growers of New Jersey have had a type of the favorite Icing Watermelon, entirely distinct in shape, being oblong, as shown in illustration. The skin is of an attractive, mottled, very light green color, so light as to nearly warrant the name white or gray. The flesh is deep red in color, and of very fine quality, fully equal to the old Icing which has long been recognized as one of the finest-flavored melons grown. In size, this new variety is much larger than the old, specimens having been raised to weigh 60 to 70 pounds each. Packet, 10 cents; ounce, 20 cents; ¼ pound, 40 cents; pound, $1.10.

**FLORIDA FAVORITE.**—This new melon, also originated by Mr. Girardeau, has ripened 10 days earlier than Kolb Gem, Iron-Clad or Rattlesnake, planted at the same time. Its superior oblong shape, brilliant color, rind being alternately striped with dark and light green, bright crimson, crisp and deliciously sweet flesh, are sure to make it a favorite indeed with every melon grower. Thousands of my customers planted Florida Favorite last season to their entire satisfaction. Pkt., 10 cts.; oz., 20 cts.; ¼ lb., 40 cts.; lb., $1.10.

**COLORADO PRESERVING MELON.**—This new melon, immensely productive, one vine produced twenty-five melons weighing from ten to forty lbs. each. Preserving qualities are the very finest. It makes beautiful, clear, nearly transparent preserves of surpassing flavor. Pkt., 5c.; oz., 10c.; ¼ lb., 30c.; lb., 90c.

**PRIDE OF GEORGIA.**—Another Southern melon that is of particularly crisp, delicious flavor, and very firm. An excellent shipper. Packet, 5 cents.; ounce, 10 cents; ¼ pound, 30 cents; pound, 90 cent.

**GEORGIA RATTLESNAKE.**—An improved Gipsy; excellent for shipping and very popular. Flavor, first class; rind very thin; flesh, bright red. Pkt., 5 cts.; oz., 10 cts.; ¼ lb., 20 cts.; lb., 60 cts.

**BLACK SPANISH.**—Large size; round; dark green skin; flesh red and of fine flavor. Packet, 5c.; ounce, 10c.; ¼ pound, 30c.; pound, 60c.

**HUNGARIAN HONEY.**—This small sweet-flavored watermelon came originally from Hungary. They weigh from 10 to 15 pounds each, and are almost round, as shown in illustration. Color of the skin is a medium dark green, while the flesh is of a brilliant red color, and absolutely stringless. They ripen early, vines are very productive and strong growers. Packet, 5 cents; ounce, 10 cents; ¼ pound, 30 cents, pound, 90 cents.

**GREEN AND GOLD.**—Rich green color outside, flesh is of a golden orange color. They grow to a good average size, 25 pounds and over in weight; in productiveness they equal any red flesh variety; thin rind. They make a desirable ornament for the table, if arranged in contrast with the red flesh of other varieties. Pkt., 5c.; oz., 10c.; ¼ lb., 30c.; lb., 90c.

Mrs. Marion Elwood, Walton, N. Y.: "We tried your seeds last year and they are the best we ever used. You were very liberal with your extras."

N. White, Lorton Valley, Va.: "I received the seeds all right and much more than I ordered or expected. Such liberality is something unusual in my experience. I thank you most sincerely and shall not forget you when in need of anything more."

VICK'S EARLY. Packet, 5 cents.

PHINNEY'S EARLY. Packet, 5 cents.

PEERLESS

GRAY MONARCH WATER MELON

Florida Favorite

BOSS WATERMELON

# MAULE'S RELIABLE ONION SEED FOR 1891

AN 1888 CROP OF MAULE'S WETHERSFIELD FROM A PHOTOGRAPH

A SPECIMEN BULB OF MAULE'S WETHERSFIELD FROM NATURE

ENG. BY A BLANC
COPYRIGHTED 1888 BY
N. HENRY MAULE

## 3 Better Varieties

Than Maule's Wethersfield, Danvers, and Prizetaker cannot be found THE WORLD OVER.

NEW CUSTOMERS

Should remember that Maule's Reliable Onion Seed is only grown from **carefully hand-sorted** and **selected bulbs,** is always of high germinating quality and of unusual vigor of growth by reason of **its superlative vitality.** My onion seed now has a reputation in almost every prominent onion growing district in America unsurpassed by any other house in the trade.

**MAULE'S WETHERSFIELD.**—There are many strains of this justly-celebrated Onion offered, but none that can surpass Maule's famous stock of this popular variety. Growing to a large size, one to two-pound onions from seed the first year are of frequent occurrence. The $50 prize offered in 1887 for the heaviest was secured by one of my customers for a specimen weighing 2¾ pounds. It grows with unusual regularity, scallions being almost unknown. 600 to 800 bushels have frequently been raised on a single acre; and in 1888, in competition for the $250 prize, several of my customers produced even a larger quantity. The premium being finally secured by Randolph Byers, of Arroyo Grande, San Luis, Obispo Co., Cal., he having raised the enormous quantity of 66,905 pounds of marketable onions on one acre of ground. The shape is well shown in illustration above. In color the skin is deep purplish red, and the flesh white. Moderately grained and of a good strong flavor, it is a magnificent keeper. Maule's Red Wethersfield is unquestionably the king of all red onions as Prizetaker is king of all yellow, and Silver King the king of all white.

50,000 of my customers unanimously endorse it as the best they have ever sown. I trust no onion grower receiving this catalogue will fail to try at least a small quantity of Maule's Red Wethersfield, for all ought to know just how superior it is. Pkt., 10c.; oz., 15c.; ¼ lb., 40c.; lb., $1.35 ; 5 lbs., $6.25 post-paid ; 10 lbs., $11.50, by express or freight, purchaser paying transportation charges.

## $4.50--3 ONION PREMIUMS

Last year I offered three onion prizes of $150 each. One for the largest amount of Prizetaker raised from 1 pound of seed. Another for the largest amount of Red Wethersfield raised from 5 pounds of seed, and the other for the largest amount of Danvers raised from 5 pounds of seed. On account of the large edition of my catalogues, I have to start to print them about the 1st of Oct. of each year, and as I always desire to publish a list of the prize winners of the preceding season in each year's catalogue, I have required all reports to be sent me by Oct. 1st for prize crops and vegetables. Now Oct. 1st was too early, I find, for my customers to send in their reports of yields of onions; consequently, last Sept. **only one came to hand,** which, on investigation, proved to be unreliable. For this reason I again offer the same prizes for 1891 as I offered for 1890, namely : **$150** for the largest yield of Prizetaker raised from one pound of seed purchased of me in '91- **$150** for the largest yield of Maule's Red Wethersfield raised from 5 pounds of seed purchased of me in '91. **$150** for the largest yield of Maule's Yellow Danvers raised from 5 pounds of seed, purchased of me in '91 ; **and I will allow my customers until Nov. 1st, 1891, to send in their reports.** It must however, be borne in mind that the other prize Vegetables must reach me by Oct. 1st., the same as heretofore. I trust that by reason of my extending the time, it may also increase the competition for these prizes, and **I certainly should now hear from more than one of my customers.** Reports of these Onion yields must be signed by two thoroughly reliable and well-known witnesses and sworn to before a Justice of the Peace. By well-known witnesses, I mean country storekeepers or others in good standing in the community. Said reports must reach me on or before Nov. 1st, 1891, and in all cases must fully bear witness as to the facts of the amount of seed sown, amount of ground occupied by same, and weight of the crop, in pounds, when ready for market. Competition is open to all my customers excepting those to whom I have paid $100 in prizes within the last three years.

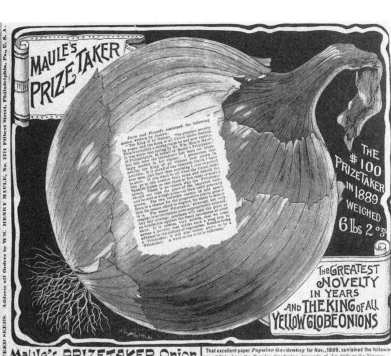
## Maule's PRIZETAKER Onion

First offered in 1888, and it proves to be the greatest acquisition in years, **THE LARGEST, HANDSOMEST, FINEST FLAVORED, BEST SHAPED, FINEST KEEPING, MOST SUPERIOR, YELLOW GLOBE ONION EVER INTRODUCED.** This simply magnificent onion **is certainly a wonder.** There has never been an onion in these United States that could equal it, and I believe **it will supplant all other Yellow Globe Onions now in cultivation, as soon as its sterling qualities are known,** for it is certainly perfection. Of a clean, bright straw color, it always grows to a uniform shape, which is a perfect globe. It has a very small neck and always ripens up hard and fine, without any stiff-necks. In market it attracts marked attention, and although only offered to a limited extent, has always been picked out and selected at three times the price of any other sort on sale, either red, white or yellow. Readily produces 700 and more bus. per acre, its keeping qualities are simply wonderful, late in the Spring the Bulbs being apparently as firm and solid as when put away in the Fall. I regret very much indeed that my supply of seed of Prizetaker is again short this year, hence have still to ask a very high price for it. Pkt., 15cts.; oz., 60 cts.; ¼ lb., $2.00; lb., $6.00.

# DON'T BE HUMBUGGED

Into purchasing seed said to be MAULE'S PRIZETAKER offered at low prices. The genuine article can not be sold at a profit at lower figures than those given above.

That popular publication, the *Orchard and Garden* for November, 1888, contained the following: "The finest Onion we have ever raised is Maule's Prizetaker, as beautiful and as large as the Spanish Onion on sale at our fruit stands, and surpassing, by far, the excellent Spanish Onion sent out by —— & ——. The Prizetaker in short is the acme of beauty and perfection, and will undoubtedly become the most popular yellow onion in cultivation. Mark what we say."

That excellent paper *Popular Gardening* for Nov., 1889, contained the following: "*Note from the Popular Gardening Grounds at La Salle-on-the-Niagara.* A PRIZETAKER. We always try every new Onion that we hear of, and the older ones, too. This season again we had a great number of varieties, among them Silver King, Mammoth Pompeii, Spanish King, and various other mammoth sorts. Owing to the new condition of the soil, lateness of the season, and lack of various requisites at the proper time, our success was nothing to brag about although we have a fair crop. Among the score or more of choicest sorts however, none can hold the candle to Prizetaker, a variety introduced last year by Mr. William H. Maule. Our specimens last year were the finest Onions we ever raised equalling in size and beauty the imported Spanish Onions of our fruit stores and groceries, and our experience with them this year only strengthens our good opinion of it. A few rows grown with root care, but otherwise by no means under the most favorable circumstances, gave us bulbs the smallest of which weighed over one-half of a pound each, and which yielded at the rate of over 1000 bushels per acre. With special care we think we could even double this yield, and propose to do this next year. Its name is undoubtedly proper. No other variety can take the prize at any exhibition in competition with a well-grown Prizetaker: at least this is the conclusion of two seasons' trials with it. It has proved itself to be the Onion *par excellence.*"

Wm. Perry, Cool Spring, Del.: "From the ounce of Prizetaker Onion seed sown this spring, I grew some specimens weighing a pound, notwithstanding the unprecedented drought of the early summer."

Willard Robinson, Cisco, Texas: "I have been growing Prizetaker Onions on a small scale for three years, and consider them for a main crop twice as valuable as any other variety. I have sold all my Prizetakers this year when about two-thirds grown at $2.50 to $3.35 per 100 onions. They are worth beaten for size, beauty, &c."

C. J. Koempel, St. Paul, Minn.: "Prizetaker Onions are by all odds the best, finest and most prolific onion in cultivation: they gave me a fine crop in spite of drought. It is magnificent and has such a beautiful color and shape that it commands much higher prices in market than any other sort."

Charles W. Stone, Nuevo, Cal.: "Prizetaker onions are splendid. They certainly are the most superb onion I ever raised."

Milton W. Rose, Deep Vale, N.Y.: "Our Prizetaker Onions go ahead of all other onions in this section. This has been a poor season for onions around here, first wet weather then dry; but the Prizetakers do not seem to mind the weather. Ours are the admiration of all who see them."

Mrs. J. E. Beighton, Shirleyville, Ohio: "The Prizetaker Onions cannot be beaten: I feel safe in saying every seed in the ounce packet grew, as did all other seeds purchased of you. I took $10 worth of premiums at the Portage Co. Fair last week."

Henry N. Rand, Argos, Ind.: "We had a very excellent garden from the seeds purchased of you last spring, notwithstanding the very dry season. We of those your seeds are splendid. From one ounce of Prizetaker we had the enormous yield of 1,725 pounds of onions."

M. D. Dozier, Camden, C. H., N.C.: "I have been growing onions for some years: have experimented with all the leading sorts, and also some new ones, but Prizetakers beat the world. They are the kind for everybody to plant if they want to raise onions."

Fred Clarke, West Jordan, Utah: "I wish I could send you a picture of my Prizetaker Onions: but I cannot describe them better than a friend of mine did last Sunday. He was looking at them, and I asked him what he thought of them: he replied, 'They are a picture.' Your Peas, Beans, Tomatoes and Cabbage are excellent."

# MAMMOTH SILVER KING

Attains a weight of **2½ to 4 lbs** first year from seed

ALTHOUGH I offered Silver King for the first time in 1884, I do not believe any other variety, excepting possibly my Sure-head (cabbage, has in 6 years' time been more unanimously endorsed by one and all in all sections of the country. I received thousands of letters and postals the past six seasons, all containing **words of the highest praise AS TO THE SIZE, EARLY MATURITY AND QUALITY OF THIS NOW FAMOUS ONION,** seed of which I have sold to tens of thousands of my customers. **It grows larger than any other white Onion in cultivation.** Bulbs are of attractive shape, flattened, but thick through, as shown in illustration. Average diameter of Onions, from 5 to 7¼ in.; bulbs often attain weights of 2½ to 4 lbs. each. **No other White Onion attains such mammoth size, nor will any other White variety grow uniformly so large.** Skin, a beautiful silvery white; flesh, of particularly mild and pleasant flavor, so sweet and tender that it can be eaten raw, like an apple. Everyone desiring the **largest and handsomest onions**, of the **finest flavor** will be more than satisfied with **Silver King.** Cannot be too highly recommended either for family use, exhibition at fairs or restaurants, or for sale in market where its size and beauty will prove very striking. **If you have not already sown Silver King, you should not neglect to sow it another year.** In 1887-88-89-90, over 100,000 gardeners found it to EQUAL and SURPASS ALL CLAIMS HEREIN MADE.

Packet, 10 cts.; ounce, 30 cts.; ¼ pound, $1; pound, $3.

4 lbs. 9 ozs.

The Prize Silver King of 1888, raised by J. V. N. Young, Arroyo Grande, Cal.

# WHITE BARLETTA

**WHITE BARLETTA.—**As Silver King is the largest White Onion in cultivation, I think this is a very good place for the New Barletta, **as it is not only the earliest but also the smallest Onion grown.** This new variety, which I now offer for the first time, comes in **3 weeks ahead of New Queen.** In color, is a beautiful waxy-white; bulbs are 1¼ inches in diameter, flattened on top and ¾ inch thick. They make a beautiful pickle and are **in every way the most desirable of all small Onions.** Packet, 10c.; ounce, 30c.

THE SMALLEST ONION GROWN

2 SPECIMENS OF NATURAL SIZE

COPYRIGHTED BY WM. HENRY MAULE PHILADA.

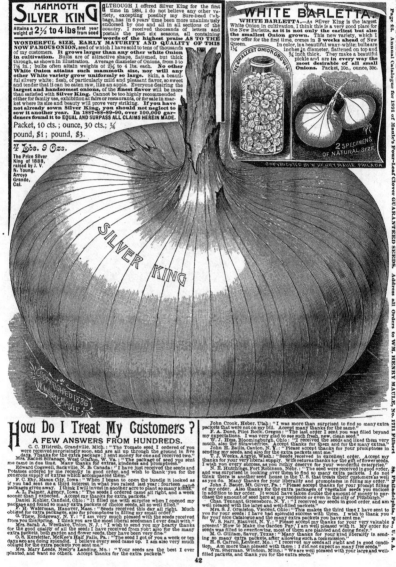

SILVER KING

COPYRIGHTED 1886 WM. HENRY MAULE

# How Do I Treat My Customers?

## A FEW ANSWERS FROM HUNDREDS.

C. C. Hildreth, Grandville, Mich. : "The Tomato seed I ordered of you were received surprisingly soon, and are all up through the ground in five days. Thanks for the extra package; I sent money for one and received two."

Mrs. Rachel Schanage, West Grafton, W. Va. : "The package of seed you sent me came in due time. Many thanks for extras, kindness and promptness."

Edward Cogswell, Sackville, N. B. Canada: "I have just received the seeds and Potatoes ordered by me recently in good order, and wish to thank you for the generous supply of extras which accompanied them."

F. C. Eby, Mason City, Iowa: "When I began to open the bundle it looked as if you had sent me a third interest in what you raised last year; fourteen packages given away. I think I will invest in another acre to plant so many kinds."

A. L. Palmer, Agency, Iowa: "The seeds I ordered came all right, and a week sooner than I expected. Accept my thanks for extra packets."

Daniel Kohler, Canfield, Ohio : "It filled me with surprise when I opened my package and found so many extra packets of choice seeds, all so well-filled."

J. H. Waterman, Hanover, Mass. : "Seeds received this day all right. Much obliged for extra packages, also for promptness in filling my small order."

O. Thew, Ridgeway, N. Y. : "I am very much pleased with the seeds received from you this Spring. I think you are the most liberal seedsman I ever dealt with."

Mrs. Sarah A. Westlake, Union, N. J. : "I wish to send you my hearty thanks for the good quality of all the seeds I have received from you; also for the many extra packets, both garden and flower seeds, they have been very fine."

O. S. Kerstetter, McKee's Half Falls, Pa. : "The seed I got of you a week or ten days are are doing splendidly. I believe every seed came up. I am also very much obliged for the extra packets you sent me."

Mrs. Mary Leeds, Neely's Landing, Mo. : "Your seeds are the best I ever planted, and want no others. Accept thanks for the extra packets."

John Crook, Heber, Utah : "I was more than surprised to find so many extra packets that were not on my bill. Accept many thanks for the same."

F. A. Done, Pilot Rock, Oregon : "The last order I sent you was filled beyond my expectations. I was very glad to see such fresh, new, clean seed."

W. J. Hess, Bloomingburgh, Ohio : "I received the seeds and liked them very much, also the strawberries. Accept thanks for them and for the many extras."

John H. Ballis, Canton, N. Y. : "Please accept thanks for your promptness in sending my seeds, and also for the extra packets sent me."

T. J. Weeks, Argyle, Wash. : "Seeds received in excellent order. Accept my thanks for your very liberal supply. Wife returns thanks for the gift of flower seeds. I wish you every success, as you richly deserve for your wonderful enterprise."

N. E. Hutchings, Fort Robinson, Nebr. : "The seed were received in good order, and was surprised in looking over them to find so many extra packets. I do not think there is another seed house in the U. S. that treats their customers as well as you do. Many thanks for your liberality and promptness in filling my order."

John J. Bauer, Mt. Oliver, Pa. : "Please accept thanks for your prompt filling of my order. Also thanks for the extra packages of vegetable seeds you enclose in addition to my order. It would have taken double the amount of money to purchase the amount of seed here at my residence or even in the city of Pittsburgh."

Chas. Tennant, Greensboro, N. Y. : "I received my seeds in good order and am well pleased with the large and well-filled packets."

Mrs. S. J. Ormiston, Vincent, Ohio: "This makes the third time I have sent to you for your seeds; I have had splendid success with them. I wish to thank you for your nice Catalogue and the many extra packets you have sent me."

W. S. Barr, Blauvelt, N. Y. : "Please accept my thanks for your very valuable present 'How to Make the Garden Pay.' I am well pleased with it. My order for seeds was filled to overflowing, most of them are planted and doing nicely."

M. O. Gilliam, Savoy, Texas : "Many thanks for your kind liberality in sending so many extra packets, after allowing such a commission."

H. S. Carroll, Lentner, Mo. : "I received my seeds all right and in good condition. Am more than pleased with them : I did not expect so many free seeds."

Wm. Sherman, Windom, Minn. : "We are well pleased with your large and well-filled packets, and thank you for the extra seeds."

42

Address all Orders to WM. HENRY MAULE, No. 1711 Filbert Street, Philadelphia, Pa., U.S.A.

Page 43.—Annual Catalogue for 1891 of Maule's Four-Leaf Clover GUARANTEED SEEDS.

MAULE'S DANVERS YELLOW

A CROP of DANVERS YELLOW 800 BUSHELS to the ACRE

GROWING MAULE'S DANVERS for SEED

**MAULE'S DANVERS YELLOW.**—Of good size, globular form, very thick bulb, with small neck. **Very choice**, well flavored, rather mild and very early. In many markets it will find ready sale **at much higher prices** than any other variety. **Frequently produces 600 bushels and more** per acre from seed, the first year. **After Maule's Prizetaker it is best of all Yellow Onions.** Packet, 10 cts.; ounce, 15 cts.; ¼ pound, 40 cts.; pound, $1.25; 5 pounds, $5.50.

Mrs. D. Curry, Norwalk, Cal.: "From seeds purchased of you last spring, we have some fine Jumbo Melons; have one vine that raised 5 large melons, all growing within a yard of each other. The largest one weighed 66 pounds, and the other two 63 pounds. Mr. Curry took the 66 pounder to the Chamber of Commerce, and they sent it to 'California on Wheels.' We have one hill of Early Ripe and All Heart that is very fine; some of them will weigh 30 pounds. Have one vine of Potiron Pumpkin that has six large Pumpkins on it. The largest measures 98 inches in circumference, the smallest measures 64 inches."

### EXTRA EARLY PEARL.

**EXTRA EARLY PEARL.**—This is among the earliest, if not the earliest of white Onions. Keeps well. Of a fine, showy, waxy appearance; the flesh is snow white; flavor mild and pleasant; grows 5 to 6 inches in diameter the first year from seed. Packet, 10 cts.; oz., 25 cts.; ¼ lb., 75 cts.; lb., $2.50.

**NEW QUEEN.**—Remarkable keeper and rapid grower. If sown in March it will produce onions from **1 to ½ inches in diameter in early Summer**. Pkt., 5c.; oz., 20 c.; ¼ lb., 60c.; lb., $2.00.

Harold Fowler, Madeira, Ohio: "I was very much pleased with your seeds last year: I took half a dozen premiums at the County Fair with them. Your Yellow Danvers Onion are the finest I have ever seen, they took the premium. Everbearing Sugar Corn is very fine; three ears to the stalk. All the Surehead Cabbage headed out."

Delbert Williams, Shane's Crossing, Ohio: "The Jumbo Watermelon seed I received from you last, grew with the greatest rapidity. I never saw such melons as I raised in my patch; they were more than half as large again as any melons that were seen in Mercer Co. in 1890, therefore I say that the seeds put up by you are the best in the market."

SOUTHPORT YELLOW GLOBE

**SOUTHPORT YELLOW GLOBE.**—This is similar in shape to the Red and White Globe, but differing in color. A wonderfully heavy cropper; remarkably handsome in appearance and large in size. Pkt. 10c.; oz. 25c.; ¼ lb. 75c.; lb. $2.25.

### NEAPOLITAN MARZAJOLA

**NEAPOLITAN MARZAJOLA.**—One of the earliest. Grows first season to large size, silvery white skin. Good keeper. **Sown in February or March will produce fine crop early in season.** Pkt., 5c.; oz., 20 c.; ¼ lb., 60 c.; lb., $2.00.

Chas. W. Arnor, Farmington, Kan.: "I got four first prizes on vegetables raised from seed bought of you, and got three diplomas on three on which there were no premiums offered: I took two first premiums on Maule's Prizetaker Onions; first premium on Maule's Blood Turnip Beet, and on your Everbearing Sweet Corn: could also have taken first prize on Maule's Surehead Cabbage, but did not look to see how large it was until too late. I never saw seed do as well as they did this summer, an hot and dry as it was here, the thermometer running up to 110 in the shade for over five weeks, and still they grew. My largest Jumbo Mangel weighed 20 pounds. I am well pleased with Mastodon Corn. Kaffir Corn was a wonder to all; I got a diploma on it, also on Jumbo Beets. I came home from the Fair well pleased with Maule's seeds; they beat all competition and got premiums over all."

### NEW GIANT ROCCA OF NAPLES   GIANT POMPEII   MAMMOTH RED TRIPOLI

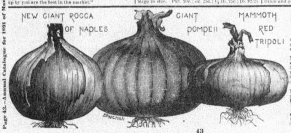

**NEW GIANT POMPEII.**—Notwithstanding the large size attained by this variety, they retain their perfect shape and fine quality. The skin is very thin and delicate in appearance, of a beautiful, handsome, reddish-brown color; the flesh is pure white, very fine grained, and remarkably mild. Pkt., 5 cts.; oz., 20 cts.; ¼ lb., 60 cts.; lb., $2.00.

**NEW GIANT ROCCA OF NAPLES.**—An onion of immense size, single bulbs having weighed 3¼ lbs., of handsome, globular form, mild and tender flesh. Valuable for both Spring and Autumn sowing. Pkt., 5 cts.; oz., 20 cts.; ¼ lb., 60 cts.; lb., $2.00.

**MAMMOTH RED TRIPOLI.**—Flavor excellent, being both mild and pleasant. **Bulbs have weighed as heavy as 2¼ lbs. and over.** Pkt., 5 cts.; oz., 20 c.; ¼ lb., 60 cts.; lb., $2.00.

**GIANT WHITE TRIPOLI.**—Quick growth, mild flavor, similar to the Red. Pkt., 5 cts.; oz., 20 cts.; ¼ lb., 60 cts.; lb., $2.00.

# EXTRA EARLY RED

# SILVER

SKIN.

**EXTRA EARLY RED.—Ten days earlier than the large Red.** My seed has frequently produced fine marketable onions 90 days from sowing. Very hardy and reliable. Desirable for early market; keeps well. Packet, 10 cents; ounce, 15 cents; ¼ pound, 50 cents; pound, $1.50.

**SILVER SKIN.—(White Portugal.)** Also known as **Philadelphia White.** A mild, pleasant onion, handsome shape, and very popular for family use; one of the best for pickling. In this vicinity grown largely for sets. Packet 10 cents; ounce, 20 cents; ¼ pound, 60 cents; pound, $2.15.

# RED WHITE GLOBE

YELLOW DUTCH

**RED GLOBE.—**Very similar to the Large Red, differing principally in form. Packet, 10 cents; ounce, 15 cents; ¼ pound, 50 cents; pound, $1.40.
**WHITE GLOBE.—**Fine symmetrical bulbs; flesh, firm, fine grained and mild flavor. Packet, 10 cents; ounce, 20 cents; ¼ pound, 60 cents; pound, $2.00.

**YELLOW DUTCH.—**Very productive, keeping well and being excellent for shipping. In Philadelphia and many other sections largely grown for sets. Flesh fine grained, mild, and of good flavor. It is certainly a very profitable market variety. Packet, 5 cts.; ounce, 15 cts.; ¼ pound, 40 cts.; pound, $1.25.

## ONION SETS

Philadelphia has long been esteemed in all sections of the country as headquarters for Onion Sets. In my estimation the best way to grow onions is from the black seed, but still, a great many people prefer to plant sets, which I will be pleased to furnish at the following prices:

**WHITE BOTTOM.—**Grown from my best selected seed of the White Silver Skin or Portugal variety, which will produce White Onions very early in the season. Pt., 20 cts.; qt., 35 cts.; 5 qts., $1.50, by mail, postpaid.

**YELLOW BOTTOMS.—**(See illustration of a tumblerful of sets taken from a photograph.) Pt., 20 cts.; qt., 35 cts.; 5 qts., $1.50, by mail, postpaid. Above two varieties are produced from seed. Potato, Egyptian and Multiplier Onions do not produce seed, and can be obtained from bulbs only.

**EGYPTIAN OR PERENNIAL TREE.—**When once set out, without having the slightest Winter protection, will come up year after year, as soon as frost breaks the ground, and grow very rapidly. The bottoms divide, making several irregular shaped onions. The young sets grow on top of the stalks. Pt., 30c.; qt., 55c.; 5 qts., $2.50, by mail, postpaid.

**POTATO ONIONS.—**Small bulbs when planted increase in size, and the parent bulbs produce quantities of small bulbs in clusters. They mature early and are of a mild, pleasant flavor. Pt., 30 cts.; qt., 55 cts.

**NEW WHITE MULTIPLIER ONION.—**Is enormously productive; of pure white silvery color, very hardy and will unquestionably prove a great acquisition to this class of onions, for its handsome appearance will make it one of the most salable varieties that can be grown; it is also very useful for pickling. White onions being usually higher priced than any other color, the advantage of a White Multiplying Onion can be readily understood. Pint, 35 cents; quart, 60 cents

·EGYPTIAN OR PERENNIAL TREE.

BOTTOM SETS.

44

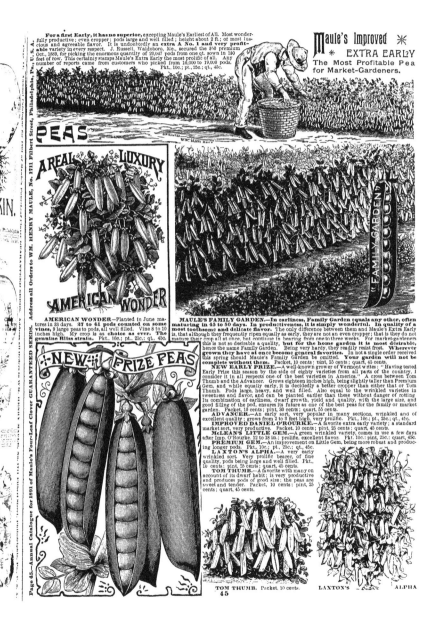

**For a first Early, it has no superior,** excepting Maule's Earliest of All. Most wonderfully productive; even cropper; pods large and well filled; height about 2 ft.; of most luscious and agreeable flavor. It is undoubtedly an **extra A No. 1 and very profitable** variety in every respect. J. Russell, Waldoboro, Me., secured the 880 premium Oct., 1889, for picking the enormous quantity of 20,047 pods from one qt. sown in 150 feet of row. This certainly stamps Maule's Extra Early the most prolific of all. Any number of reports came from customers who picked from 16,000 to 19,000 pods. Pkt., 10c.; pt., 25c.; qt., 45c.

# Maule's Improved ✳
## ✳ EXTRA EARLY
### The Most Profitable Pea for Market-Gardeners.

A REAL LUXURY

AMERICAN WONDER

FAMILY GARDEN

SKIN.

PEAS

**AMERICAN WONDER**—Planted in June matures in 33 days. **27 to 41 pods counted on some vines,** 9 large peas to pods, all well filled. Vine 8 to 10 inches high. My crop is as **choice as ever. The genuine Bliss strain.** Pkt., 10c.; pt., 25c.; qt., 45c.

**MAULE'S FAMILY GARDEN.**—In earliness, **Family Garden equals any other, often maturing in 45 to 50 days. In productiveness, it is simply wonderful. In quality of a most toothsome and delicate flavor.** The only difference between them and Maule's Extra Early is, that although they frequently ripen equally as early, they are not an even cropper; that is they do not mature their crop all at once, but continue in bearing from one to three weeks. For market-gardeners this is not so desirable a quality, **but for the home garden it is most desirable,** hence the name Family Garden. Being very hardy, they readily resist frost. **Wherever grown they have at once become general favorites.** In not a single order received this spring should Maule's Family Garden be omitted. **Your garden will not be complete without them.** Packet, 10 cents; pint, 25 cents; quart, 45 cents.

**NEW EARLY PRIZE.**—A well-known grower of Vermont writes: "Having tested Early Prize this season by the side of eighty varieties from all parts of the country, I consider it in all respects one of the best varieties in America." A cross between Tom Thumb and the Advancer. Grows eighteen inches high, being slightly taller than Premium Gem, and while equally early, it is decidedly a better cropper than either that or Tom Thumb. Pods large, heavy, and well filled. Also equal to the wrinkled varieties in sweetness and flavor, and can be planted earlier than these without danger of rotting. Its combination of earliness, dwarf growth, yield and quality, with the large size, and good filling of the pod, ensures its future as one of the best peas for the family or market garden. Packet, 10 cents; pint, 30 cents; quart, 55 cents.

**ADVANCER.**—An early sort, very popular in many sections, wrinkled and of excellent quality; grows from 2 to 3 feet high, very prolific. Pkt., 10c.; pt., 25c.; qt., 45c.

**IMPROVED DANIEL O'ROURKE.**—A favorite extra early variety; a standard market sort, very productive. Packet, 10 cents; pint, 25 cents; quart, 45 cents.

**McLEAN'S LITTLE GEM.**—A green wrinkled variety, comes in use a few days after Imp. O'Rourke. 12 to 18 in.; prolific, excellent flavor. Pkt., 10c.; pint, 25c.; quart, 45c.

**PREMIUM GEM.**—An improvement on Little Gem, being more robust and producing longer pods. Pkt., 10c.; pt., 25c.; qt., 45c.

**LAXTON'S ALPHA.**—A very early wrinkled sort. Very prolific bearer, of fine quality, pods being large and well filled. Pkt., 10 cents; pint, 25 cents; quart, 45 cents.

**TOM THUMB.**—A favorite with many on account of its dwarf habit; is very productive and produces pods of good size; the peas are sweet and tender. Packet, 10 cents; pint, 25 cents; quart, 45 cents.

NEW PRIZE PEAS

TOM THUMB. Packet, 10 cents.

LAXTON'S

ALPHA

## BLISS'S EVERBEARING PEA.

—The want of a reliable first-class pea for Summer and Autumn use has long and seriously been felt by everyone. In this choice and remarkable variety I am confident I place before the public a pea which, when sufficiently known, will everywhere be recognized as an excellent sort for a Summer and Autumn crop. Season late, to very late. Height of vines 18 inches to 2 feet. Its habit of growth is of a peculiar branching character, forming as many as ten stalks from a single root stalk. One hundred pods have been counted on a single vine. After repeated pickings of quantities of full-sized pods, the vines continue to be covered with blossoms and buds, developing to maturity, making it practically a perpetual bearer. On account of its branching habit, a pint of seed will plant as much ground as a quart of most other kinds. Pkt., 10 cts.; pt., 25 cts.; qt., 45 cts.

**STRATAGEM.**—The Stratagem is a pea for everybody, whether rich or poor; it is a Pea that will always pay, whether for the best table in the land or the people's market. It is of wonderfully vigorous habit, and immensely productive. It is dwarf in habit, growing 18 to 24 inches high, and is no doubt, the best green wrinkled marrow in cultivation; pods long, large, and always well filled. **You should surely put down Stratagem on your order, if only for a single packet.** Packet, 10 cts.; pint, 30 cts.; quart, 55 cts.; 2 quarts, $1.00.

**YORKSHIRE HERO.**—A splendid large marrow pea, growing 2 feet high; has a branching habit, and is an abundant bearer; of fine quality and the pods keep a long time before becoming hard. Pkt., 10c.; pt., 25c.; qt., 45c.

**DWARF BLUE IMPERIAL.**—A favorite sort for either private use or for market-gardeners. Pods are large and well filled, and when young are exceedingly tender. The dry peas are sold in large quantities in our market during the winter season. Pkt., 10c.; pt., 20c.; qt., 35c.

**McLEAN'S BLUE PETER.**—Is a remarkable dwarf variety, with dark green foliage. Splendid bearer and of exquisite flavor. It is sometimes called the Blue Tom Thumb. Pkt., 10c.; pt., 25c.; qt., 45c.

A. M. Stevens, Williamstown, Mass.: "I send you a box of vegetables raised from your seeds to compete for prizes. I received first Premium for Market Garden, also on best collection of garden vegetables, at the Hoosick Valley Fair, at North Adams, and at the Berkshire Agric. Soc. at Pittsfield, Mass."

E. Morrow, Norfolk, Neb.: "Our fair is over, and thought I would let you know what success I had with vegetables raised from seeds bought of you. I took first premium on Long Orange Carrots; Long Parsnips and Tree Beans. Competition was great, there being a magnificent display of vegetables. I should not hesitate to put your seeds against the world."

BLISS'S EVERBEARING.

HORSFORD'S MARKET GARDEN.

BLISS'S "ABUNDANCE PEA"
—COPYRIGHT 1888 by B.K. Bliss & Sons—
SINGLE PLANT, ENGRAVED - FROM A PHOTOGRAPH.

**NEW ABUNDANCE.**—The most striking feature of this variety is its remarkable tendency for branching directly from the roots, forming a veritable bush. Plant, half dwarf, 15 to 18 in. high; pods, 3 to 3½ in. long roundish and well-filled, containing 6 to 8 large wrinkled peas of excellent quality. Packet, 10 cents; pint, 25 cents; quart, 40 cents.

**TELEPHONE.**—These Peas are wrinkled, of a pale green color, and superior sugary flavor. It is second-early, very robust in habit, a great bearer, averaging 18 to 20 unusually long pods to the stalk. **No private garden should be without this grand Pea, as it is one of the very finest yet introduced.** Pkt., 10c.; pt., 30c.; qt., 55c.; 2 qts., $1.00.

**HORSFORD'S MARKET GARDEN.**—This most excellent new second early Pea is from a cross between the Alpha and American Wonder. As a first-class wrinkled variety, it has excited favorable comment wherever grown, particularly on account of its superior flavor and great productiveness, 154 pods have been counted on a single plant. Grows 20 to 30 inches high, and is very stocky. On the grounds of the New York Experimental Station it has proved among the most desirable of almost 160 varieties. Pkt., 10 cts.; pint, 30 cts.; quart, 50 cts.

Edward Reynolds, Bradshaw, Md.: "The seeds sent me have arrived all right, they were packed very nicely indeed. Thank you very much for the extra packets, you are very generous with them."

W. J. Potter, Glens Falls, N. Y.: "Allow me to express my appreciation for the amount and variety of seeds given for the amount of money sent you."

Kate L. Rogers, Boston, Mass.: "Seeds came and in good condition. Am much pleased with the liberal way in which my order was filled and with the extras."

**EVOLUTION.**—Evolution grows 3 to 3½ feet high, is of a very branching habit, and bears continuously an abundant crop of pods, some containing as many as 10 peas. Packet, 10 cents; pint, 30 cents; quart, 55 cents; 2 quarts, $1.00.

**LAXTON'S MARVEL.**—This new Pea, is truly a marvel in flavor and productiveness. Originated by that celebrated grower and introducer of so many desirable varieties, Mr. Laxton, of England, it was awarded a first-class certificate by the English Horticultural Society. It grows about 3 feet high, matures about the same time as the Champion of England, and produces at all times and under all conditions an enormous quantity of fine handsome pods, which are always full of fine large peas, that in quality are very hard to beat. Marvel is certain to please, and you ought to have a row in your garden this year. Packet, 10 cents; pint, 30 cents; quart, 50 cents.

I WISH TO CALL the attention of my customers to the fact that Mr. Jas. E. Way, P. M., Clove, N. Y., sent me an order last Spring amounting to $3.10. From this investment in Maule's Seeds, he succeeded last Oct. in capturing $200 in premiums. See page, 51. Will not every one admit this was a big return? And it is well for my customers to bear in mind that such a thing is just as liable to happen to anyone of them this year.

**WHITE MARROWFAT.**—Extensively cultivated for summer crops by market-gardeners; a strong grower and very productive; height about 5 feet. Pkt., 10 cts.; pint, 20 cents; quart, 35 cents.

**BLACK-EYED MARROWFAT.**—Popular in all parts of the country. Both of the Marrowfats are very extensively grown as a field pea; very hardy and productive; largely used by the canning establishments. Pkt., 10 cts.; pt., 20 cts.; qt., 35 cts.

**DWARF SUGAR, (Edible Pods).**—Height about 3 feet. Can be used either shelled or cooked in the pods, which, when young, are very tender and sweet. Pkt., 10 cts.; pint, 30 cts.; quart, 50 cts.

**CANADA FIELD.**—Extensively used for field culture, also make excellent feed for pigeons. Packet, 10 cents; quart, 40 cents.

**SOUTHERN WHIP-POOR-WILL, (Field)**—Used for soiling. Packet, 10 cents; quart, 40 cents.

**PRIDE OF THE MARKET.**—They require no sticks, and are quite unequaled in productiveness. They have a robust, free-branching habit, 18 to 20 inches high, and are immensely productive. They are, indeed, such heavy croppers, that I know of no peas from which so large a bulk of produce can be obtained from a given space. The pods are large in size and handsome in appearance, and the peas are of so splendid a quality, that it would be difficult to overpraise them. Pkt., 15c.; pt., 30c.; qt., 55c.; 2 qts., $1.00.

**SANDER'S MARROW.**—A tall, very late and immense cropping variety. The pods are produced in pairs, and are well filled with fine, large wrinkled peas, the largest that we have ever seen; the quality is sweet and delicious. It has the desirable peculiarity of retaining its deep green color when dished for the table. It is a great favorite with experts in Great Britain, and should be grown by every one desiring a really first-class Pea. Height, 5 ft. Pkt., 10 cts.; pt., 30 cts.; qt., 50 cts.

**CHAMPION OF ENGLAND.**—This good old standard sort is still as popular as ever. Very productive and of delicious flavor. **I can particularly recommend my stock to market-gardeners.** Pkt., 10 cts.; pt., 25 cts.; qt., 45 cts.

**McLEAN'S WONDERFUL.**—The most prolific of the White Wrinkled Peas in cultivation, bearing its pods near the tips in clusters. Height 2½ feet. Ripens about the same time as Champion of England. Quality excellent, as it is very sweet flavored, and on account of its well-filled pods and unusual prolificness, it is always a very large cropper. Pkt., 10 cts.; pint, 30 cts.; quart, 50 cts.

**NEW PERPETUAL.**—This is the **best** late variety, on account of its continued bearing, maturing just after the Telephone, and continues growing and branching until cut by frost; thus one can have green peas the whole season, from June to October. It has proved superior to the Everbearing. It requires no bushing; a wonderful cropper, strong, and robust; foliage attractive; very desirable for family use and worthy of trial for market. Pkt., 15 cts.; pint, 30 cts.; quart, 50 cts.

47

# My Colored Plate Specialties No. 2.

**MAULE'S EARLIEST SCARLET RADISH.**— Nothing in my whole catalogue is more worthy to be pictured in colors than this **the Earliest of all Turnip Radishes,** and if you are at all anxious to have Radishes four or five days to a week earlier than any of your neighbors, Maule's Earliest is what you should sow. Its crisp, brittle flavor, as well as its remarkably quick growth, alike recommend it. Color of skin a rich scarlet, while the flesh is a pure white; of mild flavor, always remarkably crisp and tender. Has a very small short top, and is equally valuable for forcing or open ground; in favorable weather maturing in from 20 to 25 days from the sowing of the seed. Not one of my customers should fail to sow this Earliest of All Radishes in 1891. Packet, 10 cents; ounce, 15 cents; ¼ pound, 40 cts.; pound, $1.25.

**MAULE'S EXTRA EARLY CUCUMBER.**—This new Cucumber is a cross between Early Russian and Green Prolific. Fully as early as the former, while it combines all the fine pickling qualities of the latter. Always grows uniformly, and wonderfully productive; seldom, if ever, produces a cucumber too large for pickling. That celebrated grower of cucumbers, E. L. Coy, of Washington Co., N. Y., writes: "It not only makes a standard commercial pickle, but in its younger and smaller state it is a perfect gem for bottling. Its extreme earliness, in addition to its many other good qualities, will make it of great value to market-gardeners for bottling or commerce. **IF YOU WANT the Earliest Cucumber you have ever grown you must plant Maule's Extra Early.** Pkt., 10 cts.; oz., 15 cts.; ¼ lb., 50 lbs.; lb., $1.50.

**YOSEMITE WAX BEAN.**—The Yosemite Valley in California is known the country over as one of the wonders of the world. The Yosemite-Mammoth Wax Bean was named after the valley on this account, for it is certainly **one of the wonders of the Bean family.** No other dwarf Bush Bean can anywhere near approach it in size, the pods being more often 8 to 9 inches long than 5 to 6 inches, and as thick as a man's finger. It is really a distinct new type of the dwarf wax sorts, that in the near future may lead to many important improvements in this very popular vegetable. The pods are nearly all solid meat, the seeds being very small when the beans are fit for use. The pods are a rich golden yellow color, and are absolutely stringless, always cooking tender and delicious. It is enormously prolific, and is unquestionably one of the novelties of the year that no one should neglect to include in their order, particularly if you wish to show your neighbors pods of a bush bean twice as long and thick as they ever dreamed of. Packet, 15 cents; pint, 40 cents; quart, 75 cents, postpaid.

**PEACH TOMATO.**—This the greatest novelty in Tomatoes is sure to attract attention and the most favorable comment, whether growing in the garden, served on the table either raw or preserved, or on the exhibition table. If you want to surprise yourself as well as your friends and neighbors, include a packet of Peach Tomato in your order. **It is almost identical with some forms of peaches, both in shape and color.** The fruit is produced in clusters, is very solid, with red interior, with red, pinkish and green blush outside. Vines compact in habit and very productive. For preserving Peach Tomato has no superior. Packet, 10 cents; ounce, 40 cents.

---

Mr. T. Greiner, that justly-celebrated writer and authority on gardening and horticultural topics, in 1889 compiled the results of his notes and experience for many years into a voluminous and exhaustive book on the subject entitled

# ◄ "HOW TO MAKE THE GARDEN PAY" ►

HOW TO MAKE THE GARDEN PAY
PRICE $2.00

I have undertaken the publishing and placing before the American public of this the best and most practical work ever written for the benefit of the American vegetable gardener. I am confident it will prove the stepping-stone to successful gardening for many thousands who are now unacquainted with this, the noblest calling on earth, while I know it will give many profitable common-sense ideas to those who are even now high up in the profession. In giving a brief summary of the work, I cannot do better than quote the following from Mr. Greiner's introductory remarks: "How to Make the Garden Pay?"

"Gardening," is the minds of average people, is a dreadful combination in its requirements of skill and unceasing drudgery. Many, especially farmers, doubt their ability to acquire the one without giving more time and thought than they can afford to devote to the garden, and fear the other; hence, home gardening is often at a discount. To disabuse the minds of the masses of this only too common error, to convince people in rural districts and in the suburbs of cities, that gardening in reality is a very strong combination of pleasure, health and profit, and to point out the ways and means how to relieve the task of all semblance of drudgery—that is one of the aims, and perhaps the chief one of this volume.

"While in the following pages I shall attempt to teach the whole of the art, in the aspects that have been revealed to me during long years of practice, study and experiment, and propose to conform these instructions with the needs of the new beginner, both in kitchen and market gardening, I am quite certain that even the experienced horticulturist can find new truths and valuable suggestions in it, and it will pay all—novice and expert—to look these pages over carefully.

"Any one of the readers who thus far has remained in the old ruts, let him turn over a new leaf and try the newer ways that I point out; for gardening, like life, is what you yourself make of it—a paradise of pleasure or a veritable shed of drudgery. You have the decision in your own hands. You may leisurely accompany your visitors through the well-kept grounds that are teeming with thrifty, sparkling vegetation, as your own countenance is beaming with pleasure and satisfaction, and that is as free from weeds as your face is free from care; or you may crawl through the beds on hands and knees, tiling up masses of weeds, with a face sour and distorted in discontent and in hatred of yourself and the life you are leading. My instructions, if faithfully followed, will insure you the former conditions and save you from the curse of the latter."

"HOW TO MAKE THE GARDEN PAY" Contains almost one hundred thousand words, is finely printed in large readable type, is handsomely bound, copiously illustrated at great expense, with almost 200 practical illustrations, and is, in all respects, both as to the matter it contains and the manner in which it has been printed, bound and published, superior to any work of its kind ever issued.

It is not only a common-sense helper for every gardener, large or small, but will also prove an ornament to any centre table.

## PRICE, $2.00 POSTPAID TO ANY ADDRESS.

CHAPTER I. HOME GARDENING.—Gardening for Pleasure, Health, Profit and Morality.
CHAPTER II. MARKET GARDENING AND TRUCK FARMING.—Gardening for profit only.
CHAPTER III. FARMER'S KITCHEN GARDEN.—Selection of locality and arrangement of beds.
CHAPTER IV. REQUIREMENTS OF SUCCESS IN MARKET GARDENING.—Selection of soil and location.
CHAPTER V. HINTS IN MARKETING.—Secrets of success exposed.
CHAPTER VI. MANURES FOR THE GARDEN.—I. Stable manure and how to manage it.
CHAPTER VII. MANURES FOR THE GARDEN.—II. Commercial Fertilizers, their value and uses.
CHAPTER VIII. MANURES FOR THE GARDEN.—III. Nitrates, wood-ashes, and other specific fertilizers.
CHAPTER IX. GARDEN IMPLEMENTS AND HOW TO USE THEM.
CHAPTER X. COLD FRAMES.—Their construction and use.
CHAPTER XI. MANURE HOT BEDS.—Their construction and use.
CHAPTER XII. FIRE HOT BEDS AND THEIR CONSTRUCTION.
CHAPTER XIII. FORCING HOUSES.—How to build and manage.
CHAPTER XIV. HOT FORCING HOUSES.—Simple, sensible structures, successfully managed; cost, construction, etc.
CHAPTER XV. EARLY PLANTS FOR THE HOME GARDEN.—Various means and devices for everybody.
CHAPTER XVI. DRAINAGE.—Where needed and how done.
CHAPTER XVII. IRRIGATION.—Surface soaking, and Sub-Earth Flooding.
CHAPTER XVIII. INSECTS AND OTHER FOES.—Their ways of sowing mischief, and how to keep them in check.
CHAPTER XIX. FUNGUS DISEASES OF PLANTS.—How to prevent and cure them.
CHAPTER XX. SEEDS AND SEED SOWING.—By machine and by hand.
CHAPTER XXI. NOVELTIES, AND WHY WE TEST THEM.
CHAPTER XXII. SYSTEM AND ROTATION OF CROPPING.
CHAPTER XXIII. WEEDS, AND HOW TO MANAGE THEM.
CHAPTER XXIV. THINNING AND TRANSPLANTING.
CHAPTER XXV. PROTECTION AGAINST DROUTH AND FROST.
CHAPTER XXVI. HIRED HELP.—Employment and treatment of labor.
CHAPTER XXVII. MONTHLY MEMORANDA.—A Chronological Summary of the year's work.
CHAPTER XXVIII. CULTURAL DIRECTIONS. How the various crops of our gardens are grown most easily and profitably.

---

PEACH
TOMATO
Packet 10 cts.

SEMITE MAMMOTH WAX BEAN

Maules Earliest
Scarlet Radish.
Packet 10c.

MAULE'S
EXTRA EARLY
CUCUMBER
PACKET 10 CENTS

# THE PRACTICAL FARMER.

ESTABLISHED 1855.—PUBLISHED WEEKLY BY THE FARMER COMPANY.

Vol. 60.  No. 17.  Philadelphia, April 26, 1890  Price, 5 Cents. [$1 Per Year in advance.]

## CONTENTS OF THIS NUMBER

## THE PRACTICAL FARMER

### TERMS OF SUBSCRIPTION.

One year, in advance, postage paid, ............ $1 00
Foreign subscriptions may be sent to our European Agents, the International News Company, 11 Bouverie Street (Fleet Street), London, England.

### RATES OF ADVERTISING.

A limited number of strictly legitimate and respectable advertisements will be inserted :—
Regular advertisements, per line, ............ 25 cts.
Outside pages, ............ 35 cts.
Special Notices, ............ 50 cts.
Preferred location 25 per cent, extra.
No advertisers on business should be inserted, and all drafts, checks, or orders be made payable to the FARMER COMPANY, P. O. Box 1817, Philadelphia, Pa.

## POSTAL CARD CORRESPONDENCE

This department of our paper is intended to contain short communications received on postal cards from week to week from our subscribers. In order to encourage every subscriber to send us a line once in a while, we offer and award each week a cash prize of $5.00 for the best postal received and a second prize of $3.00 in cash for the next best that comes to hand. Every postal received during the week will be published in so far as we have the space. The first prize postal at the head of the first column, the second prize postal immediately underneath, the others following.

TERMS OF COMPETITION: All communications must be written on a postal card. They must come from a yearly paid in advance subscriber. They must be short, and to the point: those giving prices for produce and statements as regards the weather, progress of farm work and crops being especially desired. We shall try to be perfectly fair in awarding the weekly prizes, but all our postal card correspondents must distinctly understand that after the prize for any week have been awarded the decision is final, and that the subject will in no case be re-opened for any one.

Lat. 41° 50' North, Long. 3° 29' East from Washington; 80 miles North of New York City and 11 miles East of the Hudson. We have had a very warm, wet Winter. Highest temperature 60°, lowest 15° (March 7th) 3°. Farmers have plowed every month this Winter. Nearing here for two years. March 10 and 11 gave us all the snow we have had, and the quality was inferior. The wet weather last Summer was detrimental to all crops, and many farmers did not finish haying until September. Fruit of all kinds was plenty. Farmers in this locality raise but little produce for the New York market and local factories. Heretofore farmers have been subject to the extremely small prices dictated by the New York Milk Exchange, but this Winter they have become aroused and have formed a Milk Producers Union which has fixed its price at 2½c per qt. until further notice. Prices: corn, 55c per bu.; oats, 30c.; rye, 50c.; potatoes, 75c. per bu.

for $2.50 to $3.00 per acre cash, or one-third to two-fifths of crop in crib, and is in good demand. Tame grasses and clover do well. The latter, when sown in field, will run under fence and occupy roadside, driving out the native grass; when sown on prairie soil it "catches" and improves the match. Corn is the staple crop. Now land is check-rowed; old land mostly "listed." Crop averaged last year 35 bushels per acre. Large acreage of oats raised is mostly cultivated in corn ground; was tilled in corn ground; was injured by rust, average 40 bushels; wheat averaged 25 bushels. Acreage small on account of chinch bugs. Apples and small fruit crops good. Apples sell at picking time for $2 per bushel; Ben Davis and Genitors lead. No peaches; trees were badly winter-killed and many Winters ago. Stock healthy and looks well. Very few sheep raised; too many wolves, and takes too much fence. Horse-raising receives much attention; is now running many onions $1 to $2 per bu.; apples, $2 to $4 per bbl.; beans, 15c per bu.; butter, 15 to 20c.; beef, 5c; lard, 7 to 10c; beef, 6c; cows, $20 to $40; horses, $50 to $100; hens, 10c each; eggs, $10 to $16 per 100; corn, $15 to $20 per acre; hay is plenty, of poor quality and not raised here. Hay is plenty, of poor quality and not much changing hands.

he was ambuscaded and killed by the Indians. Farm land in the Muncy Valley, $50 to $100 per acre, according to location and improvements. The Muncy Hills, reaching from the West branch of the Susquehanna to the North branch of the same river, is proverbial for good health and pure water; the land sells from $15 to $40 per acre. Peach culture is becoming quite an industry on those hills, with prospects of a good crop of peaches the coming season. Prices of farm produce: wheat, 95c; corn, 50c; oats, 40c; potatoes 90 to 75c. per bu.; horses, $50 to $300; cows, $15 to $50; sheep, $3 to $4 per head; calf fed cattle, 20 to 3c per hundred lbs.; butter, 25c; honey, 18c. per lb.; chickens, 50c to 60c. each; clover seed, $5 per bu.; farm hay, $12 to $15 per month and board, the year round. J. V.

A mild Winter; just snow enough for good sledding, except in rough places. Principal industries, farming and lumbering; logs are driven down the different streams to large saw-mills, where they are cut up for commerce. Hardwoods mostly worked up in local factories into spools, chairs, sleds, etc. These mills furnish profitable employment for most of our young men. But few farmers can afford to buy as good wages as these mills, so most of the farms are being tilled by old men, or are left to grow up in wood, which seems more profitable. This is a favorite resort for Summer travel, as the scenery is grand, and the air and water the purest; fish and game are quite plentiful. The local demand for nice fruits, berries and garden truck is good. Poultry and eggs sell well. Those who are favorably located and devote their energies to these crops are not complaining of hard times. Apples, pears, plums cherries, and all hardy fruits and berries thrive. Too cold for peaches and but few grapes ripen. Main exports, lumber, grain(e), potatoes, apples, school-marms, Governors and legislators.
Loch's Mills, Oxford Co., Me.    W. H. P.

This place is 44° N. Lat., and 43° W. Long. Crops last year were short, owing to the drouth. Last Winter was hard on stock, which is the principal industry in this county. Below is a few of the prices paid for produce: Hay, average price $12 per ton in stack; oats, 12c. per lb.; barley, 15c. per lb.; wheat, $1 per 100 lbs.; corn, $25 to $100 per head, according to what kind wanted; cattle, $30 per head; beef, 2½c. per lb.; live weight; sheep $3 per head, mutton sheep, $2.50 per head; wool, per lb., 17c; improved land, from $5 to $25 per acre; poultry and garden produce in good demand. M. E. S.
Hardin, Crook Co., Oregon.

We farm here altogether by irrigation; raise alfalfa, corn, barley, potatoes, and all kinds of vegetables. Watermelons, pumpkins and cabbages grow to enormous size; nothing uncommon to see melons weighing 60 lbs., and pumpkins 100; cabbages will average in the one patch over. Alfalfa is the principal crop; we mow it three times, and get a ton each time; sells here for $12.50 per ton in the stack. Corn, 50c. per bu.; potatoes, 75c. per lb.; cabbage, 5c. per lb.; land high; no water, only on the river. This is a mining country. Silver City, Lordsburg and Clifton our markets. Altitude 6,000 feet.    N. S. H.
Carlisle, Grant Co., N. M.

10 miles N. E. of Florida City, Mich. Latitude 43° 3' N. Longitude 3° W. of Washington. Our part Winter has been quite out of the common line for this climate. We have had no sleighing, but a succession of light snow-storms, the snow remaining on the ground but a few days at any time. The feeds here either been very muddy or very rough most of the Winter. The weather is now very pleasant. Fruit buds are swelling, and birds singing. Our fruit is uninjured except peaches, which are nearly killed. We have a good country for plums, apples and pears, and a part of the time for peaches. Prices in 100's are, wheat, 75c.; corn, 60c; oats, 35c.; potatoes, 50c per bu.; hay, $6 per ton; butter, 18c. to 20c. eggs, 10c.    N. S.
Polo, Jones Co., Mich.

Weather here in Southwest Va., very good till the last few weeks, which have been pretty tough. Farmers are beginning to sow oats; wheat looks fine; rye is beginning to look green; grass the apple tree buds are swelling. The peach crop is killed, even many of the trees badly damaged. The Farmers' Alliance is being organized in the county. Wheat is worth 95c; corn, 50c; oats, 40c; rye, 60c; potatoes, 80c. per bu. Cattle don't seem to look very well, owing to the weather plenty of feed though. Fat cattle are worth 3½ to 4c per lb. on foot; pork, $6.50c; sheep, $3 to $4 per head; milk cows, $20 to $30; horses, $60 to $100; mules, $75 to $200. This is a great country for fine horses and cattle, no less than 30 thoroughbred stallions on the stand in this county, and some four or five Ken. Jacks. Butter is worth 20c. eggs, 10c.; fat hens, 30c to 60c.; turkeys, 6c. per lb. on foot; farm hands pay from $10 to $20 per month and board.    W. C.
Thompson Valley, Tazewell Co., Va.

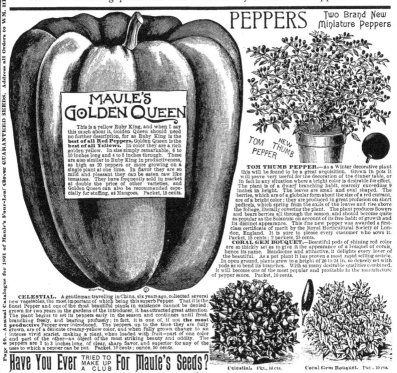

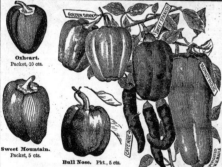

# RUBY KING

**L**argest of All ● ●
    Most Productive of All
      ● Best of All ●

**12 to 18 Peppers 6 to 8 inches long and 4 inches thick on a single plant at one time.**

During the last six years I furnished seed of Ruby King to tens of thousands of gardeners who have all found it ahead of everything they had ever tried. Every one who has ever grown Peppers will want Ruby King, **and you need it. This new Pepper attains a larger size than the Spanish Monstrous and is of different shape.** They are remarkably mild and pleasant in flavor. **Unequaled by any other variety.** They can be sliced and eaten with pepper and vinegar, like tomatoes, and make a very pleasant and appetizing salad. Pkt., 15 cts.; oz., 35 cts.; ¼ lb., $1.00.; lb., $3.00.

**BLACK CHILL.**—This new Pepper, which I offer my customers this year for the first time, is not only beautiful and compact in growth, but as prolific and vigorous as any of the most productive sorts bearing yellow or red fruit. Black Chill produces an abundance of fine dark violet colored peppers, which keep well and are hot to the taste, but when cooked in green state they make a very agreeable vegetable, and striking novelty. The odd color of this pepper will recommend it to all growers of novelties, and it will be sure to make a striking contrast when planted with either the yellow or red sorts, or both. As supply of seed is necessarily limited. I can only offer it by the packet, 10c.

Wm. J. Williams, Brownville Maine: "I have always been well pleased with your seeds, so you will find my order double what it was last year, and if I am alive a year from now it will be doubled again."

THE BEST OF ALL PEPPERS.

● RUBY KING ●

PROCOPP'S GIANT

3 REMARKABLE PEPPERS

Oxheart.
Packet, 10 cts.

Sweet Mountain.
Packet, 5 cts.

Bull Nose. Pkt., 5 cts.

"RED CLUSTER"

**GOLDEN DAWN.**—All reports from those who have tested Golden Dawn have been of **the most favorable character.** In shape it resembles the Bull Nose, except that it is a little more pointed on the end; in color, it is a beautiful golden yellow, which, as all will recognize, is a very distinctive feature. It is very sweet, not the slightest suspicion of a fiery flavor about it, and withal, very productive. Packet, 10 cts.; ounce, 30 cents; ¼ pound, $1.00.

**SWEET SPANISH.**—The earliest; very mild and pleasant. Packet, 5 cts; ounce, 25 cts.

**LARGE BELL, OR BULL NOSE.**—It is early; bright red in color; very mild; thick flesh and of large size, excellent for stuffing. Pkt., 5 cts.; oz., 25 cts.; ¼ pound, 75 cts.; pound, $2.50.

**SWEET MOUNTAIN.**—Larger and of milder flavor than above. Productive and very desirable. Packet, 5 cents; ounce, 25 cents; ¼ pound, 75 cents; pound, $2.50.

**LONG RED CAYENNE.**—True. Pkt., 10 cts.; oz., 30 cts.; ¼ lb., $1.00; lb., $3.00.

**SPANISH MONSTROUS.**—The largest of all except Ruby King and Procopp's. Frequently grows six inches long and two inches thick. Pkt., 5 cts.; oz., 25 cts., ¼ lb. 75 cts.

**OXHEART.**—A hot Pepper all my customers will like. **It is one of the very best for pickles,** of medium size and heart-shaped. Packet, 10 cents; ounce, 40 cents.

**PROCOPP'S GIANT.**—A mammoth indeed, for while not as large around as Ruby King they frequently grow 9 inches long. Their shape being well illustrated in the above cut. Flesh is very thick, flavor mild and pleasant. They are of a brilliant red color. It is very sure to please, and I do not hesitate to highly recommend Procopp's Giant to my customers. Pkt., 15c.

**NEW RED CLUSTER.**—This is one of the most distinct and beautiful varieties I have ever seen—in fact, the plants are so ornamental as to deserve a prominent position in the flower garden. The illustration shows habit of growth. The small thin peppers, of a most conspicuous coral-red color, are curiously crowded together in bunches at the top of each branch. A single plant will bear hundreds of these handsome little peppers, which are very hot and pungent in flavor. Packet, 10 cts.; ounce, 40 cts.

Mrs. Thos. Davison, Freetown, N. Y.: "I send you by express to-day, two Ruby King Peppers raised from seed purchased of you last spring. These Peppers are the largest ever seen in this section and they are a third larger than any I saw at the New York State Fair. A seedsman of Rochester had twelve kinds on exhibition there, but nothing to compare with these in size."

**Maule's Seeds are not sold to dealers, and can only be obtained by ordering them direct from Philadelphia.**

50

# Where the Money Went

## ✳ LAST OCTOBER ✳

**$100 for the Longest Pod of Yosemite Wax Bean.** The competition for this prize was very strong, and hundreds of fine samples were sent me by my customers. On summing up the competition, I found that five customers had sent me pods of the same length, consequently $20.00 was sent to each of the five following persons, who each sent in a pod 8¾ inches long: **Moses H. Kelsey, Salisbury, Vt., Forrest Boodey, Melvin Village, N. H.; John T. Allen, Manchester, Iowa; R. Neiley, Durell, Pa.; S. V. Lynde, Machias, N. Y.**

**$25 for the Longest Pod of Asparagus Bean.** This premium was secured by **D. G. Pulaski, Georgiana, Ala.,** with a pod 34 inches in length.

**$50 for the Finest Blood Turnip Beet.** This premium was secured by **Smith Bros., Villa Nova, Pa.**

**$50 for the Largest Jumbo Mangel.** This premium was secured by **G. B. Huston, Arroyo Grande, Cal.,** with a Jumbo weighing 35½ pounds. The competition for this premium was very limited the past season, and only a few reports came to hand.

**$100 for the Heaviest Head of Surehead Cabbage.** This premium was secured by **Jas. E. Way, P. M., Clove, N. Y.,** with a head weighing 58¼ pounds. Mr. G. B. Schooley, Luzerne, Pa., raised a Surehead weighing 67 pounds, but sent in no sworn statement, while Mr. Spencer N. Lynde, Machias, N. Y., and Mr. J. V. N. Young, Arroyo Grande, Cal., closely followed Mr. Way, each of them reporting having raised a Surehead weighing 52 pounds.

**$25 for the Longest and Best Ear of Pop Corn.** This premium was secured by **T. B. Young, Rock City, Ills.,** with an ear of Queen's Golden measuring 10¾ inches in length.

**$100 for the Heaviest Jumbo Watermelon.** This premium was secured by **John A. McGirk, El Monte, Cal.,** with a melon weighing 131¼ pounds. J. D. Seaford, Selena, N. C. reported having raised a Jumbo weighing 134 pounds, but failed to send in a sworn statement; while Mr. Robert M. Helton, Neodesha, Kan., was not far behind Mr. McGirk with a melon weighing 110 pounds 1 ounce. **This competition certainly puts Jumbo in the lead of all heavy Melons.**

**$50 for the Largest Amount of Prizetaker Onions raised from an ounce of seed.** This premium was secured by **Mr. James Moss, Westminster, Cal.,** with a yield of 8384 pounds. Mr. Moss reports that his onions averaged almost 2 pounds apiece; and while the above statement seems phenomenal, we have every reason, from the evidence submitted, to believe it to be a truthful one.

**$50 for the Largest Ruby King Pepper.** This premium was secured by **J. D. Randolph, Mount Union, Ohio,** with a fine specimen weighing 11½ ounces.

**$100 for the Heaviest Potiron Pumpkin.** This premium was secured by **Jas. E. Way, P. M., Clove, N. Y.,** with a Pumpkin weighing 242 pounds. It will be noticed Mr. Way also secured the $100 premium on Surehead Cabbage. His order last spring amounted to $3.10, and he received in cash last fall $200, consequently his investment in Maule's seeds certainly paid.

**$50 for the Best and Heaviest Hubbard Squash.** This premium was secured by **Vander Moon, Evergreen, Pa.,** with a Hubbard Squash weighing 54 pounds.

**$100 for the Heaviest Turner Hybrid Tomato.** This premium was secured by **T. S. Davis, Daisy, N. C.,** with a tomato weighing 5 pounds, 15½ ounces. Thomas Helton, Neodesha, Kan., was very close after Mr. Davis with a tomato weighing 5 pounds 14 ounces, while Spencer N. Lynde, Machias, N. Y. followed Mr. Helton very closely with a Turner Hybrid weighing 5 pounds 12 ounces.

**$50 for the Heaviest Heavy Cropping Ruta Baga.** This premium was secured by **Henry Shields, Centralia, Wash.,** with a Ruta Baga weighing 33 pounds.

**$25 for the Largest Sunflower.** This premium was secured by **Mrs. Mattie L. Blanchard, Pownal, Vt.,** with a Black Giant 29 inches in diameter.

**$100 for the Six Heaviest People's Potatoes.** This premium was secured by **Thomas Wend, Shoup, Idaho,** who sent me 6 specimens whose aggregate weight amounted to 17 pounds.

The number of years this competition has existed, and the results obtained, unquestionably demonstrate my claim that Maule's Seeds lead all.

**$2500 in Cash.** see page 68

For **1891 CASH PRIZES** see page 68

**$2500 in Cash.** see page 68

DOUBLE CURLED. Pkt., 5 cts.

## Parsley

**FERN-LEAVED.**—Most beautiful, splendid for table decoration. More like a crested fern. Packet, 5c.; oz., 10c.; ¼ lb., 30c.; lb., 90c.

**DOUBLE CURLED.** Packet, 5 cents; ounce, 10 cts.; ¼ lb., 25 cts.; lb., 65 cts.

**PLAIN.**—The hardiest; excellent for flavor or seasoning. Pkt., 5 cts.; oz., 10 cts.; ¼ lb., 20 cts.; lb., 55 cts.

# PARSNIPS

EARLY SHORT ROUND. Packet, 5 cents.

**EARLY SHORT ROUND.**—Earliest; does well in shallow soil. Packet, 5 cents; ounce, 10 cents; ¼ pound, 25 cents; pound, 65 cents.

Harvey Kandall, Kirwin, Kansas. "The seeds I bought of you last year were the best I ever planted. My garden was the wonder of the neighbors. I took $12.50 in premiums at our County Fair. **It takes the political orators three hours to tell the Western farmers how to get the mortgages off their farms; I can tell the same thing in three words—buy Maule's Seeds."**

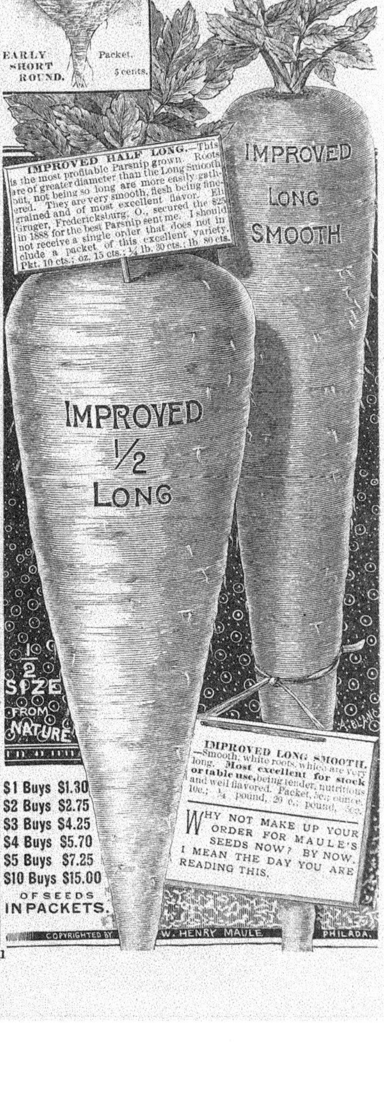
IMPROVED LONG SMOOTH
IMPROVED 1/2 LONG
1/2 SIZE FROM NATURE
A. BLANC
COPYRIGHTED BY W. HENRY MAULE PHILADA.

**IMPROVED HALF LONG.**—This is the most profitable Parsnip grown. Roots are of greater diameter than the Long Smooth, but, not being so long are more easily gathered. They are very smooth, flesh being fine-grained and of most excellent flavor. Eli Gruger, Fredericksburg, O., secured the $25 in 1888 for the best Parsnip sent me. I should not receive a single order that does not include a packet of this excellent variety. Pkt. 10 cts.; oz. 15 cts.; ¼ lb. 30 cts.; lb. 80 cts.

**IMPROVED LONG SMOOTH.**—Smooth, white roots, which are very long. **Most excellent for stock or table use,** being tender, nutritious and well flavored. Packet, 5c.; ounce, 10c.; ¼ pound, 20 c.; pound, 50c.

WHY NOT MAKE UP YOUR ORDER FOR MAULE'S SEEDS NOW? BY NOW, I MEAN THE DAY YOU ARE READING THIS.

$1 Buys $1.30
$2 Buys $2.75
$3 Buys $4.25
$4 Buys $5.70
$5 Buys $7.25
$10 Buys $15.00
OF SEEDS IN PACKETS.

# ✳ PUMPKINS ✳

TENNESSEE SWEET POTATO.

Page 53.—Annual Catalogue for 1891 of Maule's Four-Leaf Clover GUARANTEED SEEDS. Address all Orders to WM. HENRY MAULE, No. 1711 Filbert Street, Philadelphia, Pa., U. S. A.

**TENNESSEE SWEET POTATO.**—Grows to medium size, pear-shaped, a little ribbed, color creamy white, sometimes lightly striped with green. Flesh thick, creamy-white; remarkably fine-grained, dry, and brittle, and of most excellent flavor. Hardy, very productive, and keeps perfectly sound until late in the Spring. It speedily becomes a general favorite wherever it has been introduced. When cooked it has somewhat the appearance of sweet potatoes, but of more delicious taste. Pkt., 10 cts.; oz., 20 cts.; ¼ lb., 50 cts.; lb., $1.50.

**QUAKER PIE.**—This comes from Wash. Co., N. Y. It is both hardy and productive, and can be depended on to make a crop when others fail. Especially valuable for pies, being fine grained and of rich flavor, having none of the stringy nature common to so many varieties. It is early and keeps late, being oval shaped, tapering towards each end; of a cream color, both inside and out.

Packet, 5 cents; ounce, 10 cents; ¼ pound, 30 cents; pound, $1.00.

**POSSUM NOSE.**—Matures early, and is an excellent keeper, hardy and productive. Has a thick, yellow flesh, of very fine quality, better than Hubbard Squash. Excellent, either used as a squash or made into pies. Packet, 10 cents; ounce, 20 cents; ¼ pound, 50 cents; pound, $1.50.

**JAPANESE.**—This new Pumpkin, originally from Japan, is said to surpass every other variety in flavor. Flesh being unusually fine grained, and when cooked almost as dry and mealy as a sweet potato. It is especially desirable for making pies, custards, etc. They grow to a medium size, are very productive, ripen very early, and are excellent keepers. Pkt., 10c.; oz., 25c.; ¼ lb., 60c.; lb., $2.00.

**YELLOW SWEET POTATO.**—This great pie pumpkin is an unusually handsome variety. It is wonderfully prolific, six to eight large pumpkins setting on a single vine. Flesh is remarkably fine grained, very thick, of a beautiful golden yellow. It keeps in magnificent condition until late in the Spring, and for making pies or custards it cannot be surpassed even by that wonderfully good variety, the Tennessee Sweet Potato. Pkt., 10c.; oz., 25 c.; ¼ lb., 60 c.; lb., $2.00.

**MAMMOTH OR LARGE TOURS.**—Grows to enormous size; has weighed as high as 300 pounds, frequently weighs 100 to 150 pounds. Packet, 5 cents; ounce, 10cts.; ¼ pound, 25 cts.

**CASHAW, or CROOK-NECK.**—Flesh yellow, solid and sweet. Popular for table use. Packet, 5 cents; oz., 10 c.; ¼ lb., 25 c.; lb., 70 c.

**LARGE CHEESE.**—Far superior in every way to ordinary field sorts. Desirable for table. Pkt., 5 cts.; oz., 10 cts.; ¼ lb., 20 cts.; lb., 60 cts.

**MAMMOTH ETAMPES.**—Attains immense proportions. Pkt., 5 cts.; oz., 15 cts.; ¼ lb., 30 cts.; lb., $1.00.

**GOLDEN MARROW.**—Flesh of fine flavor; cooks soft and tender. A perfect keeper. Packet 5 cts.; ounce, 10 cts.; ¼ pound, 30 cts.; pound, 90 cts.

**FIELD PUMPKIN.**—Quart, 35 cents, postpaid; by express, at expense of purchaser, bus., $3.50.

YELLOW SWEET POTATO. Pkt., 10 cts.

THE GREAT PIE PUMPKIN

For **1891 CASH PRIZES** see page **68**

Mammoth Etampes. Pkt., 5 cts

**ONE PACKET EACH OF ALL THE VARIETIES ON THIS PAGE 75C.**

QUAKER PIE PUMPKIN

**MAULE'S PRIZE POTIRON.—The largest of all,** as it has grown to simply immense proportions when given rich soil and extra cultivation, 1886 was beaten out of sight in 1886; for, whereas in the former year 190 lbs. was the weight of the premium pumpkin, in 1886 it weighed 248¼ lbs. In 1889 John Robinette, Kidder, Mo. secured the prize with a 280 pounder. It is one of the varieties sure to carry off all the honors wherever exhibited. It has salmon-colored skin; flesh bright yellow, fine grained, and of excellent quality. Put in a few hills of Potiron this year and see just how large you can grow a Pumpkin. You will surprise yourself. Pkt., 15 cts.; oz., 25 cts.; ¼ lb., 75 cts.

**MAMMOTH CHILI SQUASH.**—I think I can justly claim to have the best strain of this squash in the market, certainly there is no better. Outer color is rich orange-yellow; flesh very thick and of rich yellow color; quality good, very nutritious. Most profitable to grow for stock particularly when root crops are not largely grown. Keep well throughout entire winter and spring. Very productive. In 1883 Mr. Hewitt, of Nova Scotia, exhibited one at Dominion Exhibition, weighing 292 lbs. Pkt., 10 cts.; oz., 25 cts.; ¼ lb., 75 cts.; lb., $2.50.

Prize Potiron Pkt, 15 cts.

**$100 OCTOBER 1, 1891.**

I AGAIN OFFER $100 for the largest Potiron Pumpkin or the largest Mammoth Squash raised from Maule's Seeds the coming season. For several years, I have been offering this premium of $100 for the largest Pumpkin or Squash raised from seed purchased from me of these two varieties. So far the Pumpkin has always beaten the Squash in weight. Last year Mr. Jas. E. Way, P. M. Clove, N. Y., secured the premium with a Potiron weighing 242 lbs. I trust in 1891 my customers will enter this competition with renewed vigor, and that I may have the pleasure next Oct. of awarding this $100 for a Pumpkin or Squash larger than ever before raised from Maule's Seeds.

52

Mammoth Chili Squash. Pkt., 10 cts.

# A PAGE of RADISHES.

**MAULE'S EARLIEST SCARLET.**—Earliest of all. See page 48.

**EARLY SCARLET ERFURT.**—This new radish is most desirable as an extra early, and is particularly fine for forcing purposes. Shape is well shown in cut; flesh, white, crisp, solid and very mild. Has a very small top. It will not disappoint a single customer who sows it, and should be included in every order sent me this Spring. Pkt. 10 cents; oz., 15 cents; ¼ lb., 40 cents; lb., $1.25.

**THE 18.14.**—Most excellent all the year round. See next page.

**FRENCH BREAKFAST.**—Of quick growth, crisp and tender. This is still an exceedingly popular variety. Pkt., 5 cts.; oz., 10 cts.; ¼ lb., 25 cts.; lb., 60c.

**EARLY DEEP SCARLET OLIVE.**—This is of the same quick growth and rich carmine red as Round Dark Red, differing only in shape. It is equally desirable either for market or private garden. **Absolutely the very best Olive-shaped Radish.** Pkt., 5 cts.; ounce, 10 cts.; ¼ pound, 30 cts.; pound, 90c.

**EARLY WHITE TURNIP.**—Of quick growth; fine, sharp flavor; has always been held in high esteem. Pkt., 5 cts.; oz., 10 cts.; ¼ lb., 20 cts.; lb., 50 cts.

**EARLY SCARLET TURNIP.**—Similar to the White Turnip, differing only in color. Pkt., 5 cents; ounce, 10 cents; ¼ pound, 25 cents; pound, 50 cts.

**WHITE BOX.**—This new White Turnip Radish is most excellent for forcing purposes. Its short top and rapid growth especially fit it for growing under glass in frames or boxes, hence its name. Often fit to pull before the leaves are large enough to tie. Pkt., 5 cents; ounce, 10 cents; ¼ pound, 30 cents; lb., $1.00.

**ROUND DARK RED.**—The market-gardener's favorite Radish, as it sells everywhere at a better price and ahead of all other red radishes. Its rapid growth, beautiful shape and its truly magnificent color at once recommend it. **Sow Dark Red once, you sow it always;** as great an improvement on the Scarlet Turnip as it is possible to make. Pkt., 10c.; oz., 20c.; ¼ lb., 40c.; lb., $1.15.

**MAULE'S LONG SCARLET.**—**Short top.**—This is undoubtedly the very best Long Red. It is very early, grows half out of the ground. Root bright red, very brittle. **I really think I have the best strain of this Radish on the market. Certainly no other can surpass it.** Packet, 10 cents; ounce, 20 cents; ¼ pound, 40 cents; pound, $1.15.

**WHITE LADY-FINGER.**—Unquestionably the finest **Long White.** It is of very rapid growth, and **remarkably crisp, brittle and tender.** Packet, 10 cents; ounce, 15 cents; ¼ pound, 30 cents; pound, 90 cents.

**CHARTIERS.**—A new variety that has met with great popularity. It is a long radish, red at the top and shading off to a fine white at the tip. Grows to a good size and is also brittle and tender. Pkt., 5 cts.; oz., 10 cts.; ¼ lb., 25cts.; lb., 75c.

**WHITE STRASBURG.**—It is of pure white skin and flesh; firm and brittle; a quick grower rapidly attaining a large size, and withstands severe heat. Packet, 5 cents; ounce, 10 cents; ¼ pound, 20 cents; pound, 30 cents.

**GOLDEN SUMMER TURNIP.**—Of good size; it withstands heat and drouth wonderfully well; of most excellent shape and flavor. It is often fit for use four weeks from sowing. **As far ahead of the old Yellow Summer as Dark Red is ahead of Scarlet Turnip.** Pkt., 5c.; oz., 10c.; ¼ lb., 20c.; lb., 50c.

**GIANT STUTTGART.**—There is no question that this mammoth radish **is the largest of all;** at the same time it is of remarkably quick growth. Packet, 5 cents; ounce, 10 cents; ¼ pound, 20 cents; pound, 50 cents.

B. F. Hoyt, Manchester, Iowa, sent me in 1889 a Giant Stuttgart Radish weighing 14 lbs. This monster radish secured Mr. H. the $25 premium.

**CHINA ROSE WINTER.**—One of the very best for winter use. Packet 5 cents; ounce, 10 cents; ¼ pound, 20 cents; pound, 50 cents.

**BLACK SPANISH WINTER.**—Of large size, firm and keeps well until Spring. Packet, 5 cents; ounce, 10 cents; ¼ pound, 25 cents; pound, 75 cents.

**WHITE SPANISH WINTER.**—Solid, pungent flavor, but milder than the black. Packet, 5 cents; ounce, 10 cents; ¼ pound, 25 cents; pound, 75 cents.

**CALIFORNIA MAMMOTH WINTER.**—Sometimes a foot long. Packet, 5 cents; ounce, 10 cents; ¼ pound, 25 cents; pound, 75 cents.

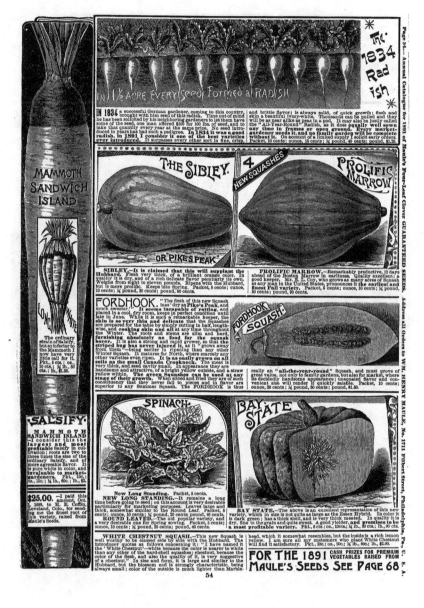

**THE 1834 Radish**

IN 1½ ACRE EVERY SEED Formed a RADISH

IN 1834 a successful German gardener, coming to this country, brought with him seed of this radish. Time out of mind he has been solicited by his neighboring gardeners to let them have some of the seed, one man offered $100 for 100 lbs. of seed, and to take that quantity every year at the same price. No seed introduced in years has had such a pedigree. **In 1834 it was a good radish. In 1891 I consider it one of the best varieties ever introduced.** It surpasses every other sort in fine, crisp, and brittle flavor; is always solid, of quick growth; flesh and skin a beautiful ivory-white. Thousands can be pulled and they will be as near alike as peas in a pod. It may also be justly called the "All-Year-Round" Radish, as it does **equally well sown any time in frames or open ground. Every market-gardener needs it, and no family garden will be complete without it.** On account of a limited supply I solicit early orders. Packet, 10 cents; ounce, 15 cents; ¼ pound, 40 cents; pound, $1.25.

**THE SIBLEY. 4 NEW SQUASHES PROLIFIC MARROW**

**OR PIKE'S PEAK**

**SIBLEY.**—It is claimed that this will supplant the Hubbard. Flesh very thick, of a brilliant orange color. In quality it is dry, and of a rich delicate flavor peculiarly its own. Weighs from eight to eleven pounds. Ripens with the Hubbard, but is more prolific. Keeps into Spring. Packet, 5 cents; ounce, 10 cents; ¼ pound, 30 cents; pound, 90 cents.

**PROLIFIC MARROW.**—Remarkably productive, 12 days ahead of the Boston Marrow in earliness. Quality excellent; a good keeper. Mr. E. L. Coy, who grows as many acres of Squash as any man in the United States, pronounces it **the earliest and finest Fall variety.** Packet, 5 cents; ounce, 10 cents; ¼ pound, 30 cents; pound, 90 cents.

**FORDHOOK SQUASH.**

**FORDHOOK.** "The flesh of this new Squash much sweeter." **It seems incapable of rotting,** and placed in a cool, dry room, keeps in perfect condition until late in June. While it is such a remarkable keeper, the skin is so very thin and delicate that the Squashes are prepared for the table by simply cutting in half, lengthwise, and **cooking skin and all** at any time throughout the Winter. The roots and stems are slim and hard, **furnishing absolutely no food for the squash borer.** It is also a strong and rapid grower, so that the striped bug has never injured it, as it "grows away from them"—being earlier in ripening than any other Winter Squash. It matures far North, where scarcely any other varieties even ripen. **It is as easily grown on all soils as the small Canada Crookneck.** The meat is very thick, and seed cavity small. In appearance they are handsome and attractive, of a bright yellow outside, and a straw yellow within. **The green Squashes can be used at any stage of their growth.** When sliced and fried they are of such constituency that they never fall to pieces and in flavor are superior to any Summer Squash. The FORDHOOK is thus really an **"all-the-year-round"** Squash, and must prove of great value, not only to family gardens, but also for market, where its decidedly handsome appearance; unequaled flavor and convenient size will render it quickly salable. Packet, 10 cents; ounce, 20 cents; ¼ pound, 50 cents; pound, $1.50.

**SPINACH.**

New Long Standing. Packet, 5 cents.

**NEW LONG STANDING.**—It remains a long time before going to seed; on this account is very desirable particularly for marketing purposes. Leaves large and thick, somewhat similar to the Round Leaf. Packet, 5 cents; ounce, 10 cents; ¼ pound, 20 cents; pound, 40 cents.

**ROUND LEAVED.**—The old popular variety, and a very desirable one for Spring sowing. Packet, 5 cents; ounce, 10 cents; ¼ pound, 20 cents; pound, 40 cents.

**BAY STATE.**

**BAY STATE.**—The above is an excellent representation of this new variety, which in size is not quite as large as the Essex Hybrid. In color it is dark green; has a thick shell, and is very thick meated. In quality it is dry, fine in the grain and quite sweet. A good yielder, **and promises to be a most profitable variety.** Pkt., 5 cts.; oz., 10 cts.; ¼ lb., 30 cts.; lb., 90 cts.

**WHITE CHESTNUT SQUASH.**—This new Squash is well worthy to be classed side by side with the Hubbard. The introducer quotes as follows concerning it: "I have named it the 'White Chestnut'—white because the color is nearer to white than any other of the hard-shell squashes; chestnut, because the color of the flesh, and also the quality of it, is very suggestive of a chestnut." In size and form, it is large and similar to the Hubbard, but the blossom end is strongly characteristic, being always small; color of the outside is much lighter than Marblehead, which it somewhat resembles, but the inside is a rich lemon yellow. I am sure all my customers who plant White Chestnut will find it satisfactory. Pkt., 10c.; oz., 20c.; ¼ lb., 60c.; lb., $2.00.

**FOR THE 1891 MAULE'S SEEDS SEE PAGE 68.** CASH PRIZES FOR PREMIUM VEGETABLES RAISED FROM

**MAMMOTH SANDWICH ISLAND**

**LONG WHITE**

The ordinary strain of Salsify, but so inferior to the Mammoth I now have very little call for it. Pkt., 5 cts.; oz., 10 cts.; ¼ lb., 50 cts.; lb., $1.35.

**SALSIFY.**

**MAMMOTH SANDWICH ISLAND**—I consider this the largest and most profitable Salsify in cultivation; roots are two to three times the size of the ordinary Salsify, and of more agreeable flavor. It is pure white in color, and invaluable to market-gardeners. Pkt., 10c.; oz., 15c.; ¼ lb., 60c.; lb., $2.

**$25.00.**—I paid this amount, Oct. 1, 1889, to H. E. Coffin, Loveland, Colo., for sending me the finest root of this variety, raised from Maule's Seeds.

54

**EARLY WHITE BUSH.**—The Bush or Patty Pan Squashes are earlier than any other Summer variety. The shape well shown in illustration; skin is white; and they are always tender when ready for use. They are very hardy, of dwarf habit and very productive. Pkt., 5 cts.; oz., 10 cts.; ¼ lb., 20 cts.; lb., 50 cts.

**EARLY YELLOW BUSH.**—Similar to the above except in color. Packet, 5 cents; ounce, 10 cents; ¼ pound, 20 cents; pound, 50 cents.

**GOLDEN SUMMER CROOKNECK.**—This is one of the very best of Summer Squashes, and **I can particularly recommend my selected stock to the attention of all market growers.** Of bushy dwarf habit, they are very productive. Flesh is greenish-yellow, dry, and of a most agreeable flavor, so much so that it is the most highly esteemed of all the Summer varieties. Packet, 5 cts.; ounce, 10 cts.; ¼ pound, 20 cts.; pound, 50 cents.

**BRAZIL SUGAR.**—This distinct new variety for Summer and Autumn use, is the *richest flavored* and *sweetest* of all squashes. It is liked for table use in every stage of its growth. During the months of August, September and October it has no equal. It is *enormously productive.* A single plant has yielded as many as *twelve perfectly ripened squashes.* The flesh is yellow, slightly tinged with green. They ripen as early as the Boston Marrow. Pkt., 5 cts.; oz., 10 cts.; ¼ lb., 20 cts.; lb., 50 cts.

**PERFECT GEM.**—This variety is a vigorous grower, on a single vine have been counted 2½ perfect squashes within a distance of 3 feet. Packet, 5 cents; ounce, 10 cents; ¼ pound, 30 cents; pound 90 cents.

**PINEAPPLE.**—As a Winter Squash, ahead of every other variety for making pies or custards, which in flavor remarkably resemble cocoanut. Can also be sliced and fried same as egg plant; it keeps wonderfully till late in the Spring, **and I have seen them kept in perfect condition for over one year.** Combine wonderful productiveness, with a desirable selling size and shape. A pure white color, unusually thick flesh, good both for Summer or Winter. Packet, 5 cents; ounce, 10 cents; ¼ pound, 30 cents; pound, 90 cents.

**BOSTON MARROW.**—Oval in form; thin skin; outer color, orange. Flesh sweet and fine grained. A good keeper. Pkt., 5 cts.; oz., 10 cts.; ¼ lb., 28 cts.; lb., 70 cts.

**MARBLEHEAD.—THE BEST KEEPER of all.** Very fine grained, possessing a **sweet and delicious flavor.** This is an old variety, but is so good that it should be more largely grown than it is. Packet, 5 cents; ounce, 10 cents; ¼ pound, 25 cts.; pound; 70 cts.

**COCOANUT.—Very desirable.** Is fine grained and well flavored. 8 to 12 grow on a vine: **is the most beautiful of all squashes.** Bear in mind also that the Cocoanut will give a crop when other varieties fail. Packet, 5 cts.; ounce, 10 cts.; ¼ pound, 25 cts.; pound, 70 cts.

**ESSEX HYBRID.**—It is not only one of the richest flavored, finest grained, and sweetest of all the squash family, but one of the very best keepers I know of. The flesh is thick, rich colored, and solid; it is also **one of the most productive squashes** ever introduced. On a vine 3½ feet long, 3 squashes, weighing collectively, 39 pounds, have been counted, all about the same size and well ripened. Pkt., 10 cts.; oz., 15 cts.; ¼ lb., 40 cts.; lb., $1.00.

**NEW RED CHINA.**—It is a good grower, matures early, and keeps in fine condition until late in the Spring. Its immense productiveness, handsome appearance, fine quality, and convenient size, make it one of the most desirable Squashes ever introduced. Pkt., 5 cts.; oz., 10 cts.; ¼ lb., 30 cts.; lb., 90 cts.

**OLIVE.**—Resembles an olive in shape and color. It is a little larger than the Hubbard. Skin extremely smooth and thin; flesh very thick, rich, golden yellow color, firm, mealy, sweet and good. Packet, 5 cents; ounce, 10 cents; ¼ pound, 30 cts; pound, $1.00.

RED CHINA.

**HUBBARD.—Decidedly one of the best squashes ever introduced.** Flesh, bright orange, very dry, sweet and rich flavored. **I recommend this variety** as superior for Winter use. It keeps perfectly through the Winter three months later than the Marrows, and has long been one of the most popular varieties in cultivation. Pkt., 10 cts.; oz., 15 cts.; ¼ lb., 40 cts.: lb., 1.10.

**ALL GARDEN SEEDS** are delivered free at prices ———— quoted in this book, except peas, beans and sweet corn, by peck and bushel, at prices quoted on page 12.

55

## • Mansfield Tree Tomato •

THERE ARE NO CHICKENS UP HERE

MANSFIELD TREE TOMATO.

I cannot do better in describing this variety than to quote as follows from a letter written by Mr. Mansfield, the originator: "I will state facts, and nothing but facts. The Mansfield Tree Tomato has been originated by me after eighteen years of careful selections and special methods of cultivation, until it has attained the height of 10 feet and 7 inches for the tree, and a weight for a single Tomato of 34 ounces, and a diameter of 6 inches, with testimonials of over 60 pounds of ripe fruit to a single tree, of a quality that surpasses all others. Fruit ripens from July 4th until frost. I have one tree laid by for a sample, to show you or any of your customers, which measures 10 feet and 7 inches, and can show testimonials to back all my statements, and you can stake any money on them on my account, and come on for the vouchers. I had my first ripe Tomato July 4th, and a fine one it was. My best trees, July 25th, stood 7 feet high, and I had Tomatoes on them that were five inches in diameter at that time and still growing. They were then all liberally loaded with fruit from the blossom up to five inches, and run up as high as seventeen on one stem, and always of superior quality. They are as solid all the way through as a hard boiled egg, and but very few seeds in a Tomato. There are several other Tomatoes that have been called "Tree Tomato," but have all proven to be poor, worthless and sour Tomatoes; but the Mansfield Tree Tomato has proved to be all that is claimed for it, and sends back to me from sample seed sent out, most wonderful accounts from Dakota to Vermont, and from the Lakes to Florida and California." My supply of seed of this Tomato is very limited, consequently regret to say, I can offer it by the packet only. Packet, 15 cents.

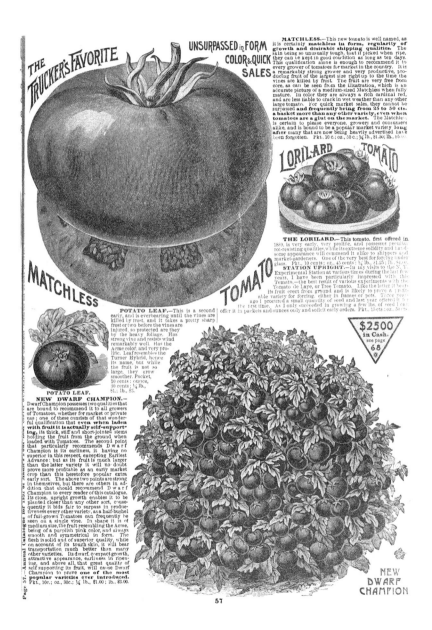

**THE TRUCKER'S FAVORITE**

**UNSURPASSED in FORM COLOR & QUICK SALES**

**MATCHLESS.**—This new tomato is well named, as it is certainly **matchless in form, regularity of growth and desirable shipping qualities.** The skin being so unusually tough, that if picked when ripe, they can be kept in good condition as long as ten days. This qualification alone is enough to recommend it to every grower of tomatoes for market in the country. It is a remarkably strong grower and very productive, producing fruit of the largest size right up to the time the vines are killed by frost. The fruit are very free from core, as can be seen from the illustration, which is an accurate picture of a medium-sized Matchless when fully mature. In color they are always a rich cardinal red, and are less liable to crack in wet weather than any other large tomato. For quick market sales, they cannot be surpassed **and frequently bring from 25 to 50 cts. a basket more than any other variety, even when tomatoes are a glut on the market.** The Matchless is certain to please everyone, growers and consumers alike, and is bound to be a popular market variety long after many that are now being heavily advertised have been forgotten. Pkt. 10 c.; oz., 50 c.; ¼ lb., $1.50; lb., $5.00

**LORILARD TOMATO**

**THE LORILARD.**—This tomato, first offered in 1889, is very early, very prolific, and possesses peculiar rot-resisting qualities, while its extreme solidity and handsome appearance will commend it alike to shippers and market-gardeners. One of the very best for forcing under glass. Pkt., 10 cents; oz., 45 cents; ¼ lb., $1.25; lb., $4.00

**STATION UPRIGHT.**—In my visits to the N. Y. Experimental Station at various times during the last few years, I have been particularly impressed with this Tomato,—the best result of various experiments with the Tomato de Laye, or Tree Tomato. Like the latter, it bears its fruit erect from ground and is likely to prove a profitable variety for forcing, either in frames or pots. Three years ago I procured a small quantity of seed and last year offered it for the first time. As I only succeeded in growing a few lbs. of seed I can offer it in packets and ounces only and solicit early orders. Pkt., 15 cts.; oz., 50 cts.

**TOMATO**

**MATCHLESS**

**POTATO LEAF.**—This is a second early, and is everbearing until the vines are killed by frost, and it takes a pretty sharp frost or two before the vines are injured, so protected are they by the heavy foliage. Has strong vine and resists wind remarkably well. Has the Acme color, and very prolific. Leaf resembles the Turner Hybrid, hence its name, but while the fruit is not so large, they grow smoother. Packet, 10 cents; ounce, 30 cents; ¼ lb., $1.; lb., $3.

**POTATO LEAF.**

**NEW DWARF CHAMPION.**—Dwarf Champion possesses two qualities that are bound to recommend it to all growers of Tomatoes, whether for market or private use; one of these consists of that wonderful qualification that **even when laden with fruit is actually self-supporting,** its thick, stiff and short-jointed stems holding the fruit from the ground when loaded with Tomatoes. The second point that particularly recommends D w a r f Champion is its earliness, it having no superior in this respect, excepting Earliest Advance; but as its fruit is much larger than the latter variety it will no doubt prove more profitable as an early market crop than this heretofore popular extra early sort. The above two points are strong in themselves, but there are others in addition that should recommend D w a r f Champion to every reader of this catalogue. Its close, upright growth enables it to be planted closer than any other sort, consequently it bids fair to surpass in productiveness every other variety, as a half-bushel of full-grown Tomatoes can frequently be seen on a single vine. In shape it is of medium size, the fruit resembling the Acme, being of a purplish pink color, and always smooth and symmetrical in form. The flesh is solid and of superior quality, while on account of its tough skin, it will bear transportation much better than many other varieties. Its dwarf, compact growth, attractive appearance, earliness in ripening, and above all, that great quality of self supporting its fruit, will cause Dwarf Champion to prove **one of the most popular varieties ever introduced.** Pkt., 10c.; oz., 30c.; ¼ lb., $1.00; lb., $3.00.

**$2500 in Cash, see page 68.**

**NEW DWARF CHAMPION**

**EARLIEST ADVANCE.**—This fine new variety is unquestionably the earliest by from 2 weeks to 10 days. If you sow Advance you will have, with favorable weather, fine tomatoes in 90 days from sowing of the seed. A cross between Alpha and perfection, it surpasses the former in wonderful early ripening qualities and equals the latter in beautiful form and productiveness. It is as excellent shipper, being exempt from rot or cracking, ripens all over at once and is wonderfully smooth—none smoother. No matter how many sorts you have lately tried, you need it. Packet, 10 cts.; ounce, 30 cts.; ¼ lb., $1.00.

**BEAUTY.**—A hard sort to surpass and after Turner Hybrid should be classed among the very best. Certainly it stands at the head of Mr. Livingston's introductions. It grows in clusters of 4 or 5 large fruits. Color, a rich glossy crimson. For shipping and early market it cannot be excelled for solidity, toughness of skin, and especially on account of color, as it can be picked when quite green and will ripen up nicely. Pkt., 10c.; oz., 25c.; ¼ lb., 75c.; lb., $2.25.

**MAYFLOWER.**—Of a glossy, bright red color, ripens evenly and perfectly up to stem. Shape round, slightly flattened, unusually smooth; flesh solid, rich flavor, and seedless. Not excelled in productiveness, bearing full crops until frost. Excellent shipper. Pkt., 5c.; oz., 20c.; ¼ lb., 60c.; lb., $2.00.

**VOLUNTEER.**—Popular among L. I. growers. Large, round, smooth, bright red; no core; ripens early. Pkt., 10c.; oz., 30c.

**OPTIMUS.**—Comes highly spoken of and promises to take place among the best. Smooth, good color, excellent shipper. Pkt., 5c.; oz., 20c.; ¼ lb., 60c.; lb., $2.

**PEAR-SHAPED.** Red or yellow, either variety. Packet, 10 cts.; ounce, 25 cts.; ¼ lb., 75 cts.; lb., $2.25.

**FAVORITE.**—It is smoother than Paragon; does not crack like Acme; after ripe it is a darker red than Perfection and is larger than either. Has few seeds, weighs heavier than any of its size. Ripens evenly all at once; no hard core. Pkt., 5c.; oz., 20c.; ¼ lb., 80c; lb., $1.75.

**CARDINAL.**—Discovered in a field of Acme. Color is a most brilliant cardinal-red, very glossy, looking, when ripe, almost as if varnished, making it the most beautiful of all. Flesh is of same color, being scarcely any lighter, absolutely no green core. Shape perfect; smooth as a ball; none equal to it in evenness of ripening; uniformly of the same large size throughout the entire season; solid and of superior flavor. Ripe fruit, picked in mid-summer has kept in fine condition 10 days to 2 weeks. Pkt. 10c.; oz. 25c.; ¼ lb. 75c.; lb. $2.25.

**PERFECTION.**—Shaped like the Acme but larger, same flavor; fully as early, blood-red color, perfectly smooth with more flesh, fewer seeds. A heavy cropper. Pkt. 5c.; oz. 20c.; ¼ lb. 60c.; lb. $2.00.

**ESSEX HYBRID.**—A valuable new variety, rapidly gaining great popularity. Very solid, rich flavor, perfectly smooth, large size, very productive. Ripens all over alike, flesh is very hard and solid. A vigorous grower; fruits evenly on the vines. Just the sort for shipping. All progressive growers should plant the Essex variety largely. Pkt., 10 cts.; oz., 25 cts.; ¼ lb. 75 cts.; lb., $2.25.

**MAULE'S TROPHY.**—My strain of this old favorite has been very carefully selected for years and produces the most perfect fruit of very large size. Pkt. 10c.; oz. 25c.; ¼ lb. 75c.; lb. $2.25.

**PARAGON.**—Color, dark red; flesh, solid, of excellent flavor. Ripens very evenly. Very desirable and largely used for canning. Packet, 5 cts.; ounce, 20 cts.; ¼ pound, 60 cts.; pound, $1.75.

**SELECTED ACME.**—Very productive, form round, smooth; delicious in flavor. My strain of this famous Tomato is surpassed by none. Pkt., 5 cts.; oz., 20 cts.; ¼ lb., 60 cts.; lb., 1.75.

**GOLDEN QUEEN.**—The perfection of Yellow Tomatoes. There is no question it is the very best. In size, smoothness, solidity and productiveness the equal of the Paragon. In color a beautiful yellow, and there is none better suited for preserving. Pkt., 10c.; oz., 25c.; ¼ lb., 75c.; lb., $2.50.

ADVANCE

EARLY MAYFLOWER

VOLUNTEER

OPTIMUS

BEAUTY

COPYRIGHTED BY W. HENRY MAULE

Essex Hybrid

THE CARDINAL.

GOLDEN QUEEN

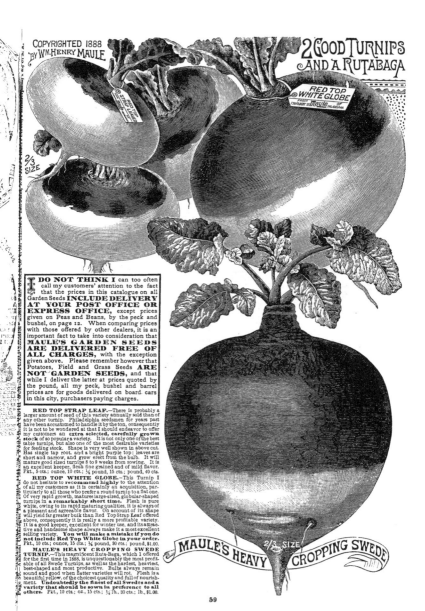

# 2 GOOD TURNIPS AND A RUTABAGA

RED TOP WHITE GLOBE

2/3 SIZE

MAULE'S HEAVY CROPPING SWEDE 2/3 SIZE

**I DO NOT THINK I** can too often call my customers' attention to the fact that the prices in this catalogue on all Garden Seeds **INCLUDE DELIVERY AT YOUR POST OFFICE OR EXPRESS OFFICE,** except prices given on Peas and Beans, by the peck and bushel, on page 12. When comparing prices with those offered by other dealers, it is an important fact to take into consideration that **MAULE'S GARDEN SEEDS ARE DELIVERED FREE OF ALL CHARGES,** with the exception given above. Please remember however that Potatoes, Field and Grass Seeds **ARE NOT GARDEN SEEDS,** and that while I deliver the latter at prices quoted by the pound, all my peck, bushel and barrel prices are for goods delivered on board cars in this city, purchasers paying charges.

**RED TOP STRAP LEAF.**—There is probably a larger amount of seed of this variety annually sold than of any other turnip. Philadelphia seedsmen for years past have been accustomed to handle it by the ton, consequently it is not to be wondered at that I should endeavor to offer my customers an **extra selected, carefully grown stock** of so popular a variety. It is not only one of the best table turnips, but also one of the most desirable varieties for feeding stock. Shape is very well shown in above cut. Has single tap root, and a bright purple top; leaves are short and narrow, and grow erect from the bulb. It will mature good sized turnips 8 to 9 weeks from sowing. It is an excellent keeper, flesh fine grained and of mild flavor. Pkt., 5 cts.; ounce, 10 cts.; ¼ pound, 15 cts.; pound, 40 cts.

**RED TOP WHITE GLOBE.**—This Turnip I do not hesitate to **recommend highly** to the attention of all my customers as it is certainly an acquisition, particularly to all those who prefer a round turnip to a flat one. Of very rapid growth, matures large-sized, globular-shaped turnips in **a remarkably short time.** Flesh is pure white, owing to its rapid maturing qualities, it is always of a pleasant and agreeable flavor. On account of its shape will yield far greater bulk than Red Top Strap Leaf offered above, consequently it is really a more profitable variety. It is a good keeper, excellent for winter use, and its attractive and handsome shape always make it a most excellent selling variety. **You will make a mistake if you do not include Red Top White Globe in your order.** Pkt., 10 cts.; ounce, 15 cts.; ¼ pound, 30 cts.; pound, $1.00.

**MAULE'S HEAVY CROPPING SWEDE TURNIP.**—This magnificent Ruta-Baga, which I offered for the first time in 1888, is unquestionably the most profitable of all Swede Turnips, as well as the hardest, heaviest, best-shaped and most productive. Bulbs always remain sound and good when flatter varieties will rot. Flesh is a beautiful yellow, of the choicest quality and full of nourishment. **Undoubtedly the finest of all Swedes and a variety that should be sown in preference to all others.** Pkt., 10 cts.; oz., 15 cts.; ¼ lb., 30 cts.; lb., $1.00.

# TURNIPS

**FLAT DUTCH**

**EXTRA EARLY MUNICH.**

**EXTRA EARLY MILAN.**

**EARLY FLAT DUTCH.**—For many years this has been the most profitable white flat garden turnip in cultivation, and is held in high esteem by all growers. I have always paid particular attention to my strain of this variety, and can safely say that while there may be as good seed offered by other seedsmen, I **do not think there can be any better.** It grows to a medium size very quickly, has clear white skin, is always juicy and extra choice for table use, and bulbs are entirely free from small roots, the long narrow strap leaves growing erect which permits close culture. **One of the very best, if not the best variety for Spring sowing.** Pkt. 5 cts.; oz. 10 cts.; ¼ lb. 15 cts.; lb. 45 cts.

**EXTRA EARLY MUNICH.**—Sown alongside of many other varieties it has proved one week earlier than any of them. Has formed turnips 6 inches in diameter within three months. It is white, with purplish-red top; very productive. Pkt. 5 cts.; oz., 10 cts.; ¼ lb., 15 cts.; lb., 45 cts.

**NEW JERSEY LILY.**—One of the very earliest white turnips. In shape it is as perfect as an orange, and in flavor always mild and pleasant. Has a single tap root and also very small top; has given unusual satisfaction wherever tried, and is **undoubtedly a most excellent round, white garden turnip.** Pkt., 10c.; oz., 20c.; ¼ lb 40c.; lb., $1.00.

**EXTRA EARLY MILAN.**—The earliest in cultivation. It is fully one week earlier than the Munich, and of much better quality. The bulb is very flat, of medium size, quite smooth with a bright purple top; leaves few, short and of light color, growing very compact, and making an exceedingly small and neat top. The pure white flesh is of the choicest quality, hard, solid and fine grained. It is an excellent **GOLDEN BALL.**— Rich, sweet, unsurpassed for quick growth and excellent table qualities. Keeps well. Pkt., 5 cts.; oz., 10 cts.; ¼ lb., 15 cts.; lb., 45 cts.

**YELLOW ABERDEEN.**—Tender and sugary; very solid; in color, purple above, deep yellow below. Pkt., 5 cts.; oz., 10 cts.; ¼ lb., 15 cents; lb., 45 cents.

**WHITE GLOBE.**—The roots in rich ground will often attain the weight of 12 pounds. An extra good Fall turnip, skin white and smooth, roots grow quickly and form a perfect globe. Pkt., 5 cts.; oz.,10 cts.; ¼ lb., 20 cts.; lb., 45 cts.

**COW HORN.**—Fine flavored, of quick growth, good

size, stands half out of the ground. Pkt., 5 c.; oz., 10 c.; ¼ lb., 20.; lb., 50c.

**LARGE YELLOW GLOBE.**—One of the best standard yellow turnips, both for table and stock feeding; keeps well until Spring. Pkt., 5c.; oz., 10c.; ¼ lb., 20c.; lb. 50c.

**LARGE WHITE NORFOLK.**—The standard variety for field culture for feeding stock. Very large size. Pkt., 5 cts.; oz., 10 cts.; ¼ lb., 15 cts.; lb., 40 cts.

**EARLY WHITE SIX WEEKS.**—This is a new very early turnip, that matures rapidly; fine, large, handsome bulbs, free from side roots. Pkt. 5 cts.; oz., 10 cts.; ¼ lb., 20 cts.; lb., 55 cts.

**EARLY SIX WEEKS.**

**WHITE EGG.**—This comparatively new variety produces beautiful egg-shaped roots, with thin white skin; they are always firm, solid, and of sweet and agreeable flavor. It is a good keeper, and excellent either for early or late sowing; its attractive appearance makes it very desirable for table use. Pkt., 5 cents; oz., 10 cents; ¼ lb., 20 cents, lb., 60 cents.

## BEAR IN MIND

I DO NOT FURNISH MAULE'S SEEDS FOR RETAILING BY DEALERS ON ANY TERMS WHATEVER. IF WANTED THEY CAN ONLY BE OBTAINED BY ORDERING THEM DIRECT FROM PHILADELPHIA.

## Ruta Bagas or Swede Turnips

**IMPROVED PURPLE TOP.**—One of the best standard varieties. Of fine quality, keeps hard and brittle until summer. Unsurpassed both for the table and stock feeding. My extra choice stock I consider unequaled. Try it. Pkt., 5 cts.; oz., 10 cts.; ¼ lb., 15 cts.; lb., 40 cts.

**SUTTON'S CHAMPION.**—Has produced 38 to 43 tons per acre. One of **the very best grown.** Pkt., 5c.; oz., 10c.; ¼ lb., 15c.; lb. 40c.

**WHITE ROCK.**—This extra choice American Ruta Baga is little known outside of the New England States. There it has an enviable reputation as an **extra good cropper, an excellent keeper,** and for being equally desirable for the table or for stock feeding. Pkt. 5c.; oz. 10c.; ¼ lb. 20c.; lb. 60c.

**LARGE WHITE FRENCH.**—Grows to a large size, and is most excellent for either table or stock. Flesh firm, rich and sweet flavor. Pkt., 5 cts.; oz., 10 cts.; ¼ lb., 15 cts.; lb., 40 cts.

**IMPERIAL HARDY SWEDE.**—A very heavy yielder, a good keeper and one of the best, has a small top and a single tap root. Pkt., 5 cents; oz., 10 cents; ¼ lb., 15 cents.; lb., 40 cents.

**IMPROVED PURPLE TOP**

**REMEMBER** $1.00 buys seeds in packets to the value of $1.30. $2.00 buys $2.75, and $10 will buy $15 worth.

**GOLDEN BALL**

**YELLOW ABERDEEN**

**WHITE NORFOLK**

**COW HORN**

**WHITE ROCK**

61

# THE PEOPLE'S POTATO

THE PEOPLE'S JUNE 1st AS COMPARED WITH OTHER VARIETIES AT SAME DATE

4.93 TO THE ACRE WITH ORDINARY CULTIVATION IN THE MOST UNFAVORABLE SEASON IN YEARS

A POTATO THAT COMBINES MORE GOOD QUALITIES THAN ANY OTHER VARIETY, EXCEPTING THE FREEMAN.

—This new seedling comes to me from one of the largest potato growers in Illinois, a man who has experimented and tried every new variety introduced in the last twenty years. It is a cross between the Minnesota Seedling, and Pearl of Savoy. The Minnesota Seedling is Burbank crossed with the good old Ohio. Hence the parents and ancestors of People's are a grand union of the very best blood in the country. The originator in describing it, writes me as follows: "In shape the People's is a beautiful, oval, oblong to round; skin a russet white or tan color, some being splashed with pink, eyes shallow, flesh white, of fine pure flavor, cooking perfectly dry and mealy through, not falling to waste. The vines are heavy, and strong, and the yield of handsome tubers of great uniformity of size is unusually large. Tubers in size are from large to very large, and growing mostly under the hill vine. It was originated in 1885, and is the best keeper I know of. A number being kept in the past season until June without showing any signs of sprouting. Last year planted in June on old unmanured land, a coating of ashes only being used, they produced a good fair crop, when all others planted at that time with only one exception failed almost entirely; and this splendid showing was made with a dry, hot July and August. In the season of '88 they averaged 8 to 10 large to very large tubers to the hill, showing but very few small ones, and the last two seasons in Minnesota and Illinois they have surpassed all the novelties. Their season is medium and I regard them as the most valuable potato in existence. In Minnesota, where nearly everything failed the past season, on account of drought, the People's made a good fair crop, and in Illinois where we had a hot, dry July and August, they produced a beautiful crop nearly all being of marketable size, as high as 17 marketable tubers being taken from one hill."

I send the People's out with the full conviction that it will take the same position among the late varieties as the Polaris has already secured among the early sorts, namely, the very head of the list. With Polaris for early and the People's for late, you will have two most profitable varieties. Lb., 50 cents; 3 lbs., $1.25 postpaid. By express or freight, peck, $1.50; bushel, $3.50; bbl., $7.00.

THE POTENTATE POTATO.—In describing this magnificent variety, I cannot do better than repeat what I said of it in last year's catalogue. For the last three years, on my trips through New York State, inspecting my seed crops, a large grower of choice seed potatoes has always called my attention to a potato he called the Potentate, as being particularly fine, and worthy of a good notice in my Seed Catalogue. Out of some 30 or 40 sorts, embracing all the new varieties, as well as the good old stand-bys, he, as well as his entire family, has used it in preference to all others for their own table. Even as late as July or 1st of August, the Potentate from the year before, cooked better and was preferred to many of the early potatoes that were then ready for use. From this, its two particular strong points—good keeping and good eating qualities—can readily be seen. Potentate originated in the State of Iowa, and matures about the same time as Magnum Bonum. They stand out even or smooth. It is the smoothest and more nearly round than any potato I have ever seen. The tubers are uniformly of a good size, and grow closely together in the hill. For a late Winter or Spring Potato I doubt if it can be equaled. In seasons like last year, Potentate will and has proved the most profitable to grow. Yields better, rots less, under adverse circumstances than any other variety. $10 invested in Potentates ought to return every purchaser one thousand per cent. profit next Fall. Pound, 50 cents; 3 pounds, $1.25, postpaid. By express or freight, purchaser paying charges, peck, $1.25; bushel, $3.00; barrel, $6.00.

SUPERIOR.—(Coy's Seedling, No. 88,) First introduced in 1889, originated from a seed ball found in a field of White Star. In shape it somewhat resembles its parent but is more compact in form. Pound, 30 cts.; 3 pounds, 75 cts., by mail, postpaid. By express or freight, pk., $1; bus., $2.50; bbl., $5.00.

GREEN MOUNTAIN.—Superior comes to us from New York, while Green Mountain, as its name implies, comes from the excellent potato-growing State, Vermont. It is a late intermediate variety, of large size, white and handsome form. The Rural New Yorker reports that in 1887 it gave the largest yield ever harvested on their grounds. Quality good and especially recommended for late keeping. Pound, 30 cents ; 3 pounds, 75 cents, postpaid. Peck, $1; bushel, $3; barrel, $5.50.

ARIZONA.—This originated in Arizona from a cross of the Early Rose with a native Wild Mountain Potato. It is second early, very hardy, an extra cropper and a vigorous grower. It comes to me highly recommended and I think will be sure to please my customers. Pound, 30 cents; 3 pounds, 75 cents, postpaid. Peck, $1.00; bushel, $2.50; barrel, $5.00.

POTATO SEED. I have a quantity of very choice potato seed from the flower-ball (the true seed), which I am pleased to offer to my customers who would try to raise a new kind of potato. Growing new sorts from the seed-ball seed is a very interesting employment for old or young. There is the widest range of difference in color, shape, and general characteristics between the different seedlings; every one is more or less unlike every other. The tubers rarely grow to be more than a half-inch in diameter the first year, but the second, they get to be quite respectable potatoes, so that we may judge pretty nearly of their value, though they do not get out for all they are worth until the third year. Plant in fairly rich soil when it is time to plant Indian corn; keep clear of weeds, and give them good cultivation. Pkt., 25 cts.

Mr. T. Wend, Shoup, Idaho.: "I ship you to-day six of the largest People's Potatoes raised from seed purchased of you last spring, and hope they will reach the top of the ladder and entitle me to the premium. I have raised from one peck of seed potatoes 49 bushels, and they average 2 pounds each : there are no small potatoes among them. They are as fine as I ever harvested or ever saw in the Rocky mountains. All your seeds are first-class."

M. E. Schwindel, Stockton, Ills.: "We are well pleased with your seeds, they have given perfect satisfaction, especially the Potentate Potato. We value it far beyond its price, and would advise any one wanting an A1 potato, to try it; they are a grand eating potato, besides being an abundant yielder."

J. B. Trimble, Ogden, Utah : "The potatoes I got of you last spring proved to be good, especially the People's. I have dug some of them and they turn out fully better than I expected : six of them weighed 8 pounds net, and I am confident I can find some still larger when I dig the rest of them."

M. E. Sammis, Huntington, N. Y.: "I consider your People's the most productive potato I ever saw. I planted the four tubers whole; when the sprouts were about 4 inches high I broke them off and planted in rather poor soil; they made about half as much top as the planted tubers but when I dug them I was greatly surprised to find potatoes that weighed fully one pound under the transplanted vines, while some in the other hills reached 1¾ pounds. I raised six June Jumbo Watermelons on one vine, the largest weighing 50 pounds.

SPECIAL PRICES Will be given by letter to any one desiring to purchase ten or more bbls. at one time, either of one variety or assorted lots. GOOD SEED POTATOES HAVE NOT BEEN SO SCARCE IN YEARS. MY PRESENT SUPPLY IS LARGER THAN EVER, BUT AS I EXPECT AN ENORMOUS DEMAND REGULAR CUSTOMERS SHOULD ENGAGE THEIR SUPPLY AT AN EARLY DATE.

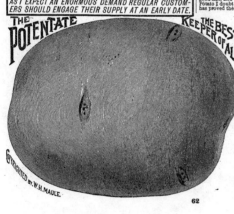

THE POTENTATE THE BEST KEEPER OF ALL

COPYRIGHTED BY W.H. MAULE.

62

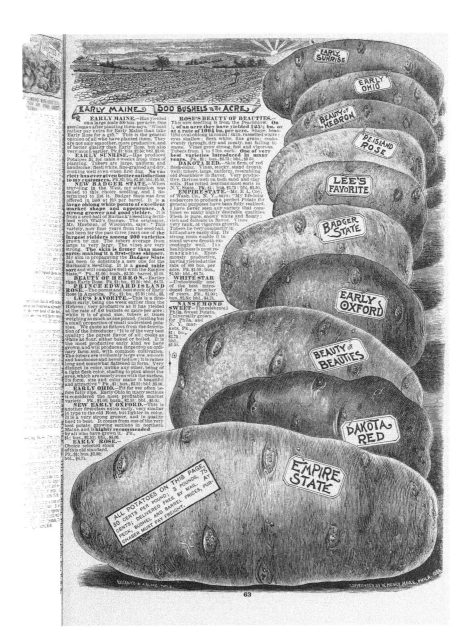

**EARLY MAINE.**—500 BUSHELS ᴛᴏ ᴛʜᴇ ACRE.

**EARLY MAINE.**—Has yielded on a large scale 500 bus. per acre. One gentleman after planting them says, "Would rather pay extra for Early Maine than take Early Rose for a gift." This is the general opinion of all who have planted them. They are not only smoother, more productive, and of better quality than Early Rose, but also very much earlier. Pk. $1; bus, $2.50; bbl, $5.00.

**EARLY SUNRISE.**—Has produced Potatoes fit for table 8 weeks from time of planting. Tubers are large, uniform, and handsome; flesh white, fine-grained and dry, cooking well even when first dug. No variety has ever given better satisfaction to my customers. Pk. $1; bus, $2.50; bbl, $5.00.

**NEW BADGER STATE.**—When traveling in the West, my attention was called to this choice seedling, and I determined to list it. Badger State was first offered in 1889 at $10 per barrel. It is a **large oblong white potato of excellent market shape and good yielder.** It is from a seed-ball of Burbank's Seedling fertilized with Wall's Orange. The originator, Mr. Huebner, of Wisconsin, says: "This variety, now four years from the seed-ball, has been for the past three years one of the **largest yielders among 200 varieties** grown by me. The tubers average from large to very large. The vines are very strong. **The skin is firmer than most sorts, making it a first-class shipper.** My aim in propagating the Badger State has been to substitute a new one for the Burbank's Seedling. It is a **good table sort** and will compare well with the Empire State." Pk., $1.00; bush, $2.50; barrel, $5.00.

**BEAUTY OF HEBRON.**—Earlier than Early Rose. Pk. $1; bu., $2.50; bbl, $4.75.

**PRINCE EDWARD ISLAND ROSE.**—The purest and best stock of Early Rose in America. Pk., $1; bu., $2.50; bbl., $5.

**LEE'S FAVORITE.**—This is a first-class early, being one week earlier than the Hebron; very productive as it has yielded at the rate of 400 bushels or more per acre; while it is of good size, tubers at times weighing as much as one pound, yielding but a small proportion of small undersized potatoes. We quote as follows from the description of the introducer: "It is of the very best quality; the purest flavor of all; cooks as white as flour, either baked or boiled. It is the most productive early kind we have grown, and will produce a large crop on ordinary farm soil, with common cultivation. The tubers are uniformly large size, smooth and handsome and never hollow; it is rather long and somewhat flattened in form. Very distinct in color, unlike any other, being of a light flesh color, shading to pink about the eyes, which are nearly even with the surface. Its form, size and color make it beautiful and attractive." Pk., $1; bus., $2.50; bbl, $5.00.

**EARLY OHIO.**—Fit for use often before fully ripe. Early Ohio in many sections is considered the most profitable market variety. Pk., $1.00; bush., $2.50; bbl, $5.00.

**NEW EARLY OXFORD.**—This is another first-class extra early, very similar in type to the old Rose, but lighter in color. It is a very strong grower, and in quality hard to beat. It comes from one of the very best potato growing sections in northern Maine, and is **highly recommended** by all who have grown it. Pk., $1; bus., $2.50; bbl., $5.00.

**EARLY ROSE.**—Choice selected stock of this old standard. Pk., $1; bus, $2.40; bbl., $4.75.

**ROSE'S BEAUTY OF BEAUTIES.**—This new seedling is from the Peachblow. **On 1½ of an acre they have yielded 125¼ bu. or at a rate of 100¼ bu. per acre.** Shape, beautiful oval-oblong to round; skin russeted white; eyes shallow; flesh white, fine grain; cooks evenly through dry and mealy, not falling to waste. Vines grow strong, fast and vigorous. Tubers from 1 to 2 lbs. each. **One of very best varieties introduced in many years.** Pk. $1; bus., $2.75; bbl., $5.50.

**DAKOTA RED.**—Skin firm, of red flesh-color. Vines, stocky, stand drouth well; tubers, large, uniform, resembling old Peachblow in flavor. Very productive, thrives well on both sand and clay soils. Has rotted less than most sorts in N. Y. State. PK. $1; bus, $2.75; bbl, $5.50.

**EMPIRE STATE.**—Mr. E. L. Coy, of Wash. Co., N. Y., says: "My life-long endeavors to produce a perfect Potato for general purposes have been fully realized. I have never seen any variety that combines so many highly desirable qualities. Flesh is pure, snowy white and floury; rich and delicate in flavor. Vines very rank, of vigorous growth. Tubers lie very compactly in hill and are easily dug. Its strong roots enable it to stand severe drouth exceedingly well. Its healthiness is most remarkable. Enormously productive, having yielded at the rate of 400 bus. per acre. PK. $1.00; bus., $2.50; bbl, $4.75.

**WHITE STAR.**—Undoubtedly one of the best, introduced for a number of years. PK., $1.00; bus.,$2.50; bbl., $4.75.

**NANSEMOND SWEET.**—The celebrated Phila. Sweet Potato. Universally grown for Phila. and N. Y. market. Pk., $1; bu., $2.75; bbl, $5.50.

**ALL POTATOES ON THIS PAGE, 30 CENTS PER POUND; 3 POUNDS, 75 CENTS; DELIVERED FREE BY MAIL. AT PECK, BUSHEL AND BARREL PRICES, PURCHASER MUST PAY FREIGHT.**

# THE POLARIS POTATO

## North, South, East and West, from the Pacific to the Atlantic, the Polaris Potato has made a Name for Itself Unsurpassed by any other in Cultivation. ✳ ✳

### FOR YEARS THE DEMAND HAS BEEN SO GREAT FOR THIS SUPERB POTATO AS TO EARLY EXHAUST THE SUPPLY; MY SALES ANNUALLY RUNNING INTO THE CARLOADS, WHERE OTHER SORTS SELL BY THE 100 BARRELS. IN ALL SECTIONS OF THE COUNTRY, DURING THE TRYING SEASON OF 1890, THE POLARIS POTATO SURPASSED ALL OTHER SORTS IN YIELD, KEEPING QUALITIES AND FREENESS FROM ROT. EVERY READER OF THIS BOOK WHO HAS NOT PLANTED THE POLARIS POTATO SHOULD DO SO IN 1891.

In presenting this Potato to my customers, I did it knowing that it **combined more essential qualities than any other first-class Potato Not EXCEPTING ANY VARIETY.** It is of long oval shape, and a creamy-white in color, cooking as white as the finest flour. It originated by nature's own processes; is hardy, prolific, handsome, early, and a good keeper, and as a table variety has no superior. With the originator it has yielded at the rate of 600 bushels per acre. It has certainly made for itself a wonderful record during the last few years wherever grown.

**THERE is no question in my mind but that the Polaris is the best early potato after The Freeman,** and not one of my customers investing in this new variety will regret his purchase. My stock comes to me direct from the originator in Vermont, and I would respectfully solicit early orders. If you desire Simon-pure stock of the Polaris Potato, you should send direct to headquarters. This year my supply is limited to but little over 1000 barrels, and as many of my customers are already corresponding for large quantities (one in California for a car-load) I would respectfully solicit early orders.

Mr. H. F. Smith, the originator of the Polaris, writes as follows concerning the claim of a certain seedsman that the Polaris and Early Puritan are identical: "The Polaris was introduced at least three years before the Puritan was named. It was named as early as 1884, at which time it was publicly noticed by the New England press, and had gained quite a local reputation in Vermont, having been exhibited at local fairs, etc. In 1886 its merits were recognized by the U.S. Dept. of Agriculture, and a bid made by the department for a quantity for testing purposes. Now all this occurring prior to the introduction of the Puritan, conclusively disproves the fact of the Polaris being identical with the Puritan Potato. Also, during 1887, the year the Puritan was introduced, and was of course, selling at a high price by a prominent New York seedsman, the Polaris were being offered and sold at almost the same prices as those at which it is offered this year. While the two potatoes have a white skin, and when bulked somewhat resemble each other, I consider there is no similarity between the two; and if they are identical, certainly the Puritan must be the Polaris, if there is anything in priority of introduction." H. F. SMITH.

In view of the fact that the introducer of the Puritan and myself, who have been largely instrumental in putting the Polaris before the public, both consider these varieties distinct, further comment seems hardly necessary. WM. HENRY MAULE.

**PRICE OF POLARIS POTATO FOR 1891, lb., 50 cts.; 3 lbs. $1.00, postpaid. By express or freight, purchaser paying freight, pk., $1.00; bus., $4.50; bbl., $5.00.**

R. W. Rogers, McVill, Pa.: "I am, after a year's trial with Polaris Potatoes purchased of you, very much pleased with it. They are worthy all the praise they have ever got. This year, Potatoes have rotted badly with me, while I have not got one rotten one of Polaris, Magnum Bonum planted side by side has rotted very badly."

Orin Smith, Pawtucket, R. I.: "I received last spring 40 pounds of your Polaris Potatoes. I planted about the 20th of May, and dug part of them the 5th of August, and the remainder the 12th of August. I raised 1630 pounds from the 40 pounds of seed; my neighbors said they were the finest they had ever seen. All the small potatoes I had was 18 pounds."

J. N. Vansant, Galena, Md.: "I have a prospect of a very fine crop of Polaris Potatoes which I bought of you last spring. They are doing splendid; I have them, alongside of Burbank's and White Star, which are doing finely, but the Polaris are away ahead of them."

Abraham Culler, Columbiana, Ohio: "Last Spring I bought one pound of your Early Polaris Potatoes from which I raised 1135 pounds of very choice potatoes. They are the talk of the whole neighborhood."

S. C. Downing, Richville, N. Y.: "All varieties have rotted badly here, and the Polaris did not escape, though they stood the test better, and rotted least of any of the 8 varieties I planted this season, and I have the satisfaction of knowing that I have secured the best early potato in existence. They were planted May 8th, and were largest enough for cooking July 3d. They proved to be of the best quality. I dug a few bushels for early market, and found they yielded at the rate of 400 bushels per acre, which was ahead of any variety I planted."

**NEW EARLY WHITE PRIZE.**—Early Prize is one of a lot of seedlings raised in 1880, since which time it has been carefully grown and selected, until it is simply the perfection of all early potatoes. In the words of its originator, a large grower in the northern part of this State, it is the smoothest, handsomest, and best yielding early potato in cultivation. In shape it resembles the Early Beauty of Hebron, skin of a russety appearance shaded creamy white; they are very smooth, eyes being even with the surface. In table qualities it is especially fine, flesh is white, always cook dry and mealy. At the experimental grounds of The Rural New Yorker it yielded at the rate of 726 bushels per acre. In conclusion: I will only say there are few better early potatoes, in my opinion, in existence. Pound, 40 cents; 3 pounds, $1.00, postpaid. By express or freight, purchaser paying charges, peck, $1.00; bushel, $2.50; barrel, $5.00.

**EARLY PURITAN.**—I quote as follows from the introducer's description: "The skin and flesh are very white, it cooks dry and floury, and is equal in

quality to that of the Snowflake. But the great value of Early Puritan Potato lies in its great productiveness; planted under exactly the same conditions, it has thus far yielded nearly double that of the Early Rose, and the Beauty of Hebron. It ripens as early as the Early Rose, but unlike that variety, the tubers when half grown are wonderfully dry and fit for the table." Pound, 40 cents; 3 pounds, $1.00, postpaid. By express or freight purchaser paying charges, peck, $1.00; bushel, $2.50; barrel, $5.00.

**THE CHAS. DOWNING POTATO.**—Claimed to be the most productive and finest table potato yet disseminated. The introducer says: "They are beauties. Our farmers are crazy for them. I think they are perfect, and predict that in a short time they will become one of the most popular varieties in America. Tested at the Ohio Experimental Station with over 100 other sorts, the average yield was given at 375 1-10 bushels per acre." Lb., 40 cts.; 3 lbs., $1.00, postpaid. By express or freight, peck, $1.00; bushel, $2.50; barrel, $5.00.

# The Polaris Potato.

ORIGINATED BY MR H. F. SMITH OF VT. IN 1881.

ALTHOUGH 10 YEARS OLD THE DEMAND HAS ALWAYS EXCEEDED THE SUPPLY.

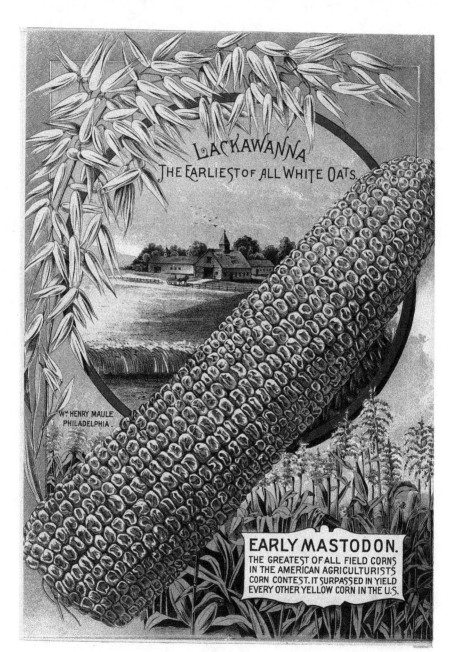

LACKAWANNA
THE EARLIEST OF ALL WHITE OATS.

Wᵐ HENRY MAULE
PHILADELPHIA

EARLY MASTODON.
THE GREATEST OF ALL FIELD CORNS
IN THE AMERICAN AGRICULTURISTS
CORN CONTEST. IT SURPASSED IN YIELD
EVERY OTHER YELLOW CORN IN THE U.S.

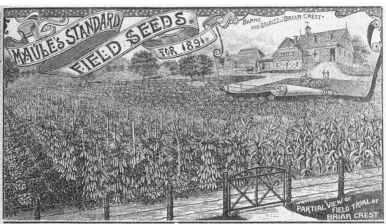

## MAULE'S STANDARD FIELD SEEDS FOR 1891

BARNS AND STABLES at BRIAR CREST

PARTIAL VIEW of FIELD TRIAL at BRIAR CREST

### Early Mastodon Corn

### THE GREATEST OF ALL YELLOW FIELD-CORNS

*IN the celebrated American Agriculturist corn contest, it far outyielded every other Yellow Corn in America. Alfred Rose, Yates Co., N.Y., from seed purchased of me, raising on one acre 15,898 lbs. of corn on the ear, which made 213 bus. of shelled corn. Another of my customers, George Gartner, Pawnee Co., Neb., reporting next best yield on one acre, 11,380 lbs. on ear, or 171 bushels of shelled corn. See full detailed reports in the March, 1890, issue of the American Agriculturist.*

### IS NOT THIS THE CHAMPION OF ALL ?

Last year my entire supply, amounting to almost 2,000 bushels, sold out early in the season, and hundreds of dollars had to be returned to disappointed customers. The demand for 1891 for Mastodon promises to surpass all previous records. Be sure to purchase direct from headquarters, as thousands of bushels of corn —Mastodon only in name—will be sold by unprincipled dealers.

Early Mastodon will be found to combine large yield, large grains and extra earliness to a remarkable degree, better than any other variety. It originated with Mr. C. S. Clark, of Ohio, probably the largest grower of field and sweet corn for seed purposes in America, as Mr. Clark ships annually seed corn by the hundred car-loads. Mr Clark grows every variety of corn known to the American public, and in Mastodon he claims to have THE BEST OF ALL. In describing Mastodon, I cannot do better than quote as follows from a letter from Mr. Clark.

" The Early Mastodon Corn, named Mastodon, because of its large ears, is a cross between the White Cap and the Early Roe Dent Corn, and has been brought to its present standard by careful selection. The seed trade and large growers of field corn have for many years been anxiously inquiring for a large-eared, yet early, Dent Corn, and to supply their wants I have for years been studying it up, and until I got up this corn was not fully satisfied. Many seris have been tried and found wanting. In the Mastodon your customers will find a high-bred corn, of beautiful color, and one which will please them. I claim for this corn the largest number of rows on cob, and the deepest, longest grains of any corn ever originated. It makes the finest appearing shelled corn I have ever seen, being a cast of two colors, and such corn as brings the highest price in market. It fully withstands the vigor of our Northern climate, and grows very rapid, strong and rank, at a medium height, and will out-yield any corn ever grown in this section. To convince your customers of its earliness, tell them it was grown and ripened in from 96 to 100 days within eight miles of Lake Erie. Field planted June 1st were cut up September 15th. You cannot too highly recommend this corn to your customers. My reputation as the largest grower of seed corn in this country is at stake, when I say to you, as I have said before, that the Mastodon Corn is the earliest corn in the world, taking its size and number of rows on the cob. I have grown thousands of bushels of Golden Beauty and now have many fields under contract; the Mastodon is from three weeks to one month earlier, growing side by side and planted the same week; and again Mastodon Corn is from one week to ten days earlier than the J. 8. or any other Leaming Corn grown, and with us ripened up in some cases earlier than Pride of the North.' How can it be otherwise, when it is crossed with two of the earliest corns ever grown in the North—the White Cap and Early Roe Dent.' I love the seed trade as well as any man, and I expect to follow its calling as long as I live, and to do so successfully must recommend things just as they are. Now I want you to push this corn. Mr. Sibley said before he died, ' I made a great mistake in not contracting for all of that corn.' Seedsmen who have visited me this Summer, one and all congratulate you upon getting hold of this corn first, and I am afraid I will not have half enough to supply your trade."

---

If you wish to be abreast of the times you must put in a few acres of Mastodon in 1891. Not a corn grower who reads this catalogue should miss this opportunity of planting the most improved Yellow Dent Corn in America—a corn sure to outclass any other variety at present grown.

### PRICES OF EARLY MASTODON FOR 1891 : Packet, 10c.; lb., 50c.; 3 lbs., $1, by mail postpaid. By express or freight, peck, $1.00 ; bus. $2.50 ; 2 bus., $4 ; 10 bus., $18.75.

As I was a contestant for the Agriculturist Corn Prize in 1889, will say my yield was 213 bushels shelled corn, grown on one measured acre of the Early Mastodon corn. I have grown nearly all of the improved high-class field corn and find Early Mastodon is the most wonderful of all Dent corn, and the handsomest. It grows quick, strong and powerful, has broad heavy leaves, and large ears, 20 to 26 rows on a cob. Longer grains than any other variety. Ears generally 9 to 11 inches long, with the stalks 15 to 17 feet high. For ensilage it will grow more fodder than any other now known, many stalks bearing 3 to 5 large ears, some weighing 2 lbs. each and some with 1600 kernels on a cob. My prize acre was grown on a sandy, loam soil, was planted 3 feet by 1 in the row, 2 kernels to each hill. When plowed, 1/2 lbs. of Mape's Corn Manure was broadcasted on the acre and 400 lbs. scattered between the rows and sides. When the corn was earing, then cultivated and hoed and the few bastard stalks and many others then setting for ears were cut out and many others cut off above the oat sets. This was to let in more sun and air; all the stalks then had ears set on. We had too much rain for best results, as it rained nearly every day or night from June to November. When husked, the Agriculturist agent measured the acre and weighed most of the corn, the three witnesses the balance. The net weight was 15,898 lbs. When the corn was in milk some unknown persons picked over 500 ears and carried them off. These were not counted ; if they could have been would have made over 225 bushels of shelled corn to the acre. There were 25 loads of dry fodder. The acre cost $200. Interest on the same $12. Manure $17.50. Plowing, planting, seed, cultivating, hoeing, topping, husking, etc., and witnesses and affidavits, etc., cost $61 ; an average cost of 28 cents per bushel.

ALFRED ROSE, of N.Y.,
in The Practical Farmer, March 8, 1890.

---

### EXTRA EARLY

### Lackawanna

### OATS

In 1889 I took pleasure in offering my customers for the first time, this new extra early Oats, not with that it would come up so very thin made for it, and knowing that every customer who planted Early Lackawanna would find it by ALL ODDS THE EARLIEST OAT THEY HAVE EVER SOWN. It not only made good every promise made, but far surpassed the expectations of my most sanguine customers. Such heads as were sent me in competition for the $100 premiums were never seen before. Most of my customers have planted Welcome Oats during the last five or six years, and have written me that they consider that variety the earliest oat they have ever sown. Early Lackawanna will be found to mature fully eight to ten days earlier than the Welcome, and at the same time will surpass this popular and profitable variety in yield. I am fully aware this is a broad claim to make for any oat, but I am sure that all who plant Lackawanna this year will bear me out next Fall in what I say. While these claims of earliness and great productiveness are great recommendations in themselves and ought to make it a desirable sort for every one of my customers to plant, still there are other characteristics that might recommend Early Lackawanna almost as strongly to our farmers in America. In addition to being so wonderfully early and prolific, the straw is always stout and stiff and not liable to lodge, and above all is entirely free from rust. They grow four to five feet high, heads being large and well-filled, with fine plump heavy grain. It weighs 52 pounds to the measured bushel, which, while not so heavy as the Welcome, still stamps it as being an extra heavy variety. Finally I would add one more strong point and that is while it responds most liberally to high cultivation, it has always succeeded wonderfully well on common or poor soil. Supply so very limited, so would advise every orders for it in every one desiring to sow Lackawanna. Pkt. 10c.; lb. 50c.; 3 lbs. $1. By express at expense of purchaser, peck $2 : bus. $5.

65

# A PAGE OF FIELD-CORN

**HICKORY KING**

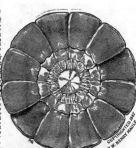

**IMPROVED GOLDEN BEAUT'**
BY HENRY MAULE

COPYRIGHTED 1891

**IMPROVED GOLDEN BEAUTY.**—The ears are of perfect shape, with from ten to fourteen straight rows of brightest golden yellow grains, of **remarkable size, and filled out completely to the extreme end of the cob. THE COBS ARE UNUSUALLY SMALL, when broken in half the grains will always reach across.** The illustration is an exact representation of half an ear. The richness of color and fine quality of grain make it very superior for grinding into meal. The grains are not of a hard, flinty type, neither are they so soft as to be greatly shriveled, as is the Golden Dent. The ears are easily shelled, although the kernels are firm on the ear, and in **every respect presents as perfect a type as could be desired.** The stalk takes a strong hold in the ground; grows vigorously to a height of eight to ten feet. **This year I offer seed grown for me by the originator of Golden Beauty. For the last six years he has continued by careful selection to greatly improve this magnificent variety until it is now far better than ever it was before, and my seed is certainly worthy the name Improved.** Pkt., 10c.; lb., 30c.; 3 lbs., 75c., by mail, postpaid. Peck, 75 cents; bushel, $2; 10 bushels, $18.75.

**HICKORY KING.**—**Has the smallest cob and largest grains and is the most valuable and reliable White Corn in cultivation.** It will shell more and weigh more to a given measure, make more ears to a stalk and bear planting closer than any other field variety of white corn in the world. As the stalks are never barren, no matter how thin the soil, you are always sure to get a crop of the **Hickory King.** It ripens in from 100 to 120 days from planting, shells and husks easily, and makes as much fodder to the acre as other kinds. It is unusually productive, nearly always 2 and very often 3 good ears to a stalk. The ears have a thin husk, uncommonly **small cob.** By breaking an ear in half, one grain will cover the entire end of the cob. Both ends filled full out to the end of the cob. Pkt. 10 cts.; lb., 30 cts.; 3 lbs., 75 cts., postpaid. By express or freight, peck, 75 cts.; bus., $2.25; 2 bus. sack, $4.00.

**CHAMPION WHITE PEARL.**—Originated in Illinois and is enormously productive, a strong grower, matures in about 100 days. The stalk is stout and thick, and ears are set low. I offer the direct headquarters stock. Pkt., 10c.; lb., 30c.; 3 lbs., 75c., postpaid; by ex. or freight, pk., $1; bu., $2.25; 2 bu., $4.

**PRIDE OF THE NORTH.**—One of the earliest Dents in cultivation, and has been grown farther North than any other Golden Dent I know of, and matured a crop. Planted on the fourth day of July, it has fully matured before frost, and it also has been planted as a second crop after wheat harvest, and yielded a full, well-ripened crop. It is very prolific, 100 bushels per acre having been grown; will grow wonderfully well on poor soil, and makes no suckers. I can safely recommend it as earlier than any other variety of Yellow Dent Corn. Mastodon is the nearest of the large eared Dent varieties; but Pride of the North, growing a smaller ear and stalk, is even earlier. It is just the variety for all my customers to plant who desire a first-class extra early. Packet, 10 cents; pound, 30 cents; 3 pounds, 75 cents, postpaid. By express or freight, peck, 75 cents; bushel, $2.00; 2 bushels, $3.50.

LEAMING CORN

**FLOUR CORN.**—This southern variety will produce from three to five times as much per acre as wheat (owing to climate and soil), makes Bread, Cakes, Rolls, Biscuits, Waffles, etc., as light and good as those made from the best wheat flour. It will yield twice as many bushels as common varieties of field corn, and four times as much fodder. Makes fine roasting ears, hominy, and beautiful starch. The same process is used as in grinding and boiling wheat. It should be planted same as other corn, 2 grains to the hill, and grows well on any land where Indian Corn is grown. It must, however, to mature in this latitude, be planted by the 1st to the 20th of May, as it requires all the time as long a season as Chester County Mammoth to mature. **The stalks stool from the ground like sorghum,** and grow 7 to 8 feet high, each grain producing four to six stalks, as when it is 8 to 10 inches high it begins to tiller up like wheat, one hill making an armful of fodder. This one quality is sufficient to recommend it, for it makes it yield more and better fodder than any corn in cultivation. It averages 10 ears to the hill; ears from 5 to 7 inches in circumference, and from 8 to 12 inches long; grain very white. Stooling from the ground like sorghum, as stated above, suckers should not be pulled off. Cultivate same as other corn. Flour Corn is worthy of a trial, at least, by every corn or wheat-grower who reads this catalogue. There is not a county in the same latitude as Philadelphia or south of it, where it should not be at least experimented with. **Large** packets 10 cts. each; pound, 40 cts.; 3 pounds, $1.00, postpaid.

**LEAMING.**—Is in character somewhat of a Dent variety, nearly always two good ears to the stalk. **In good soil, well manured, has produced by actual measurement 134 bushels of shelled corn per acre.** Stalks grow to a medium size, and produce but few suckers, ears large and handsome, of a deep orange color and small red cob. Some dealers offer an Improved Leaming, the Leaming I offer needs no improvement. It is perfection itself. Pkt. 10 cts.; lb. 30 cts.; 3 lbs., 75c., postpaid. Peck, 75c.; bus., $2; 2 bus. $3.50.

D. H. Logan, Fisher, Texas: " Our drouth in June and July both done us up generally on a corn crop; but I had some Maule's Mastodon that I raised last year from seed bought of you, which beat the drouth and got here first, and was made before the dry hurt it much. I will plant nothing else next year, and from fresh seed from you."

Jesse Sharp, Buckhannon, W. Va.: " The Mastodon Corn I got from you proved to be a success. I have the finest corn from it this season that I ever saw grown."

E. C. Patrick, Fulton, Ky.: " I consider the Mastodon the best corn I have ever seen. On account of the drouth here, it has not done as much as it would otherwise, but I think I had a very good yield. I counted 7850 good ears of corn on one acre.

W. P. McKinney, Blanket, Texas: " Mastodon Corn is the corn for dry western Texas, and don't you forget it."

Henry Barber, Raney, Wis.: " Your Mastodon Corn has done well here. It took first premium at the Racine Fair."

J. E. Meade, Smith Creek, Va.: " I have corn from Post Oak Island, Tenn., and French Broad River Bottoms, and Chucky River corn; but Early Mastodon beats them all with me. I am highly pleased with it, and wouldn't take any reasonable sum for what I have if I could not procure any more."

Howard Radcliff, Pepper, W. Va.: " I got the best price for corn in this county from seed purchased of you. Other corn patches are in very bad condition."

**CHESTER CO. MAMMOTH CORN.**—There have been hundreds of thousands of bushels of worthless stuff, Chester County Mammoth only in name, distributed all over the country. If you want the genuine, send direct **to headquarters.** The Chester County Mammoth Corn, wherever introduced, has given universal satisfaction, both on account of its **large yield, fine quality of grain and superb fodder.** The strain of Chester County Mammoth Corn I offer for sale has been brought to its present perfection by untiring care and judicious skill of several of the most scientific corn growers of Chester County, being strictly pure, and saved only from the finest ears of the most productive fields. Packet, 10 cents; pound, 30 cents; 3 pounds, 75 cents, postpaid. Peck, 75 cents; bushel, $2.00; 2 bushel sack, $3.50.

**FARMERS' FAVORITE GOLDEN DENT CORN.**—This variety, produced after eight years' skillful selection and careful cultivation by one of our most scientific and practical corn-growers, was first introduced by us to public notice, being confident that it would prove worthy of a place in the front rank of the best and most popular varieties of field corn. The grains are very deep, the cobs bright red, extremely small and well-filled. It is easily shelled. The corn does not get too hard for feeding, but is easily digested, and nutritious. 70 pounds of ears of this variety will average 6 to 8 quarts more than a measured bus. Farmers who desire an early and prolific corn **cannot fail to be suited with the "Farmers' Favorite."** Pkt., 10c.; lb., 30c.; 3 lbs., 75c. postpaid. By express or freight, pk.,.75c.; bus., $2.00; 2 bus. sack, $3.50.

CHESTER CO. MAMMOTH

**DON'T fail to read what I have to say on the last page of the order sheet enclosed with this catalogue.**

FARMERS' FAVORITE

GOLDEN DENT

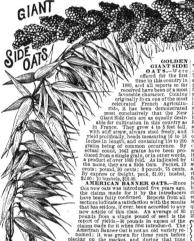

### GOLDEN GIANT SIDE OATS

GOLDEN GIANT SIDE OATS.—Were offered for the first time in this country in 1889, and all reports so far received have been of a most favorable character. Coming originally from one of the most celebrated French Agriculturist, it has been demonstrated most conclusively that the New Giant Side Oats are as equally desirable for cultivation in this country as in France. They grow 4 to 5 feet tall, with stiff straw, always stool freely, and yield prolifically, heads measuring 16 to 18 inches in length, and containing 150 to 200 grains being of common occurrence. By actual count, 1642 grains have been produced from a single grain, or in other words, a product of over 1600 fold. As indicated by the name, they are a Side Oats. Packet, 10 cents; pound, 20 cents; 3 pounds, 75 cents. By express or freight, peck, $1.00; bushel, $2.00; 10 bushels, $18.00.

AMERICAN BANNER OATS.—Since this new oats was introduced five years ago, the claims made for it by the introducers have been fully confirmed. Reports from all sections indicate a satisfaction with the results that has seldom, if ever, been accorded to any new article of this class. An average of 80 pounds from a single pound of seed is the report of yields—30 pounds in excess of the claims made for it when first introduced. The American Banner Oat is not an old variety re-named; it was grown for three years before placing on the market, and during that time showed no tendency to rust, and has invariably yielded very large crops. The grain is white, large and plump, ripens early, and has stiff straw of good strength. It tillers freely, so it can be sown thinner than is customary. Every customer who raises grain should try the American Banner Oats. Large pkt., 10c.; lb., 30c.; 3 lbs., 75c., postpaid. By express or freight, peck, 50c.; bu., $1.50; 10 bu.,$12.50.

WIDE AWAKE OATS, (also called Clydesdale.)—Claimed by the originator an improvement on most of the heavy sorts, superior in yielding qualities, hardiness and vigor; the straw is very long and stiff, attaining an average growth of four to six feet, and is less liable to rust than any other varieties; has long branching heads, filled with good plump oats, weighing 38 lbs. per bushel. Large packet, 10 cents; pound, 30 cents; 3 pounds, 75 cents, postpaid. By express or freight, peck, 80 cents; bushel, $1.50; 10 bushels, $12.50.

BADGER QUEEN OATS.—A Wisconsin variety of which the grower makes the following claims: "A new and distinct variety, tested in all sections and offered to the public with the assurance that it will prove in all points as represented. It is one of the earliest oats in cultivation. being in advance of the Welcome. A rank grower, with stout stiff straw, not liable to lodge; heads long, thickly set, and filled with plump, heavy grain. Remarkably free from rust and blight. At the Illinois State Fair, these oats were awarded a special $75 prize in competition with nearly all known varieties over twenty-five samples. This, we believe, is the largest premium ever awarded a bushel of oats. At the Western Experimental Station, they led the Welcome by nearly ten bushels." Large pkt., 10c.; lb., 30c.; 3 lbs., 75c., postpaid. By express or freight, pk., 50c.; bu., $1.50.

PRINGLE'S PROGRESS OATS.—This new and distinct variety of oats was made by Mr. Pringle several years ago, by crossing the Excelsior with the Chinese Hulless. In it we have a combination of good qualities which cannot fail to please—a short, stiff straw, and a long, full head or panicle. In the Progress we have a head averaging as large as the largest of the taller varieties, well-filled, and being so much shorter, it does not lodge. In our trial plot of about 20 varieties of Oats, the Progress matured next to the Early Lackawanna. In the spring of 1886, from one and three-fourths bushels drilled in on a rather poor soil, 162 bushels, threshers measure, were harvested. We believe if the farmer prefers grain to straw, the Progress will suit every time. Horses seem to like these Oats much better than most sorts, probably because of the thin and tender shuck. The annexed illustration shows a cluster of the heads grown with ordinary cultivation. Pkt., 10c.; lb., 30c.; 3 lbs., 77c., postpaid. By express or freight, pk., 60c.; bu., $1.50.

**PRINGLE'S PROGRESS.**

### GOLDEN WONDER MILLET

GOLDEN WONDER MILLET.—This is a Hybrid Millet. The combination was brought about by one of Minnesota's experimental farmers. This is the fourth year of its growth, each succeeding year showing marked improvements. Heads eighteen inches in length, containing 18,000 seeds, are not at all rare. The average length of heads is about 15 inches; height from ground to top of head, six feet. The yield is enormous. The stalk at butt measures about one-fourth of an inch, full of broad leaves, resembling those of corn, yielding from ten to twelve tons of fodder per acre, which is as easily cured as clover hay. A splendid ensilage plant, the same as other millets, the advantage being that it will yield, under equal circumstances, three times as much seed and twice as much fodder per acre. "Golden Wonder Millet" can be grown and matured in high latitudes, where corn will not ripen. One of the best crops known for cutting and feeding green and for soiling purposes. Its yield is large, its leaves juicy and tender, and much relished by milch cows and other stock, making a palatable change from hay. When labor is more of a consideration than acreage, "Golden Wonder Millet" is an especially economical crop. Another good quality is, it leaves the land clean, its vigorous growth crowding out the weeds. Pkt., 10 cents.; ¼ lb., 25 cents; one lb., 50 cents; 3 lbs., $1.00.

RACEHORSE OATS.—A handsome English oat, grown from stock imported direct. A heavy cropper, two weeks earlier than the common varieties, with grains almost as plump as well-filled barley. At the Ohio State Experimental Station, it excelled all other varieties in yield and weight of straw. Large pkt., 10c.; lb., 30c.; 75c., postpaid. By express or freight, pk., 50c.; bu., $1.50.

WELCOME OATS.—No oats have ever been so extensively advertised as Welcome, nor been distributed more extensively in all sections of the country. Weighing as high as 56 lbs. per level bushel, it surpasses all others, while it is also remarkably productive, over 10 bushels having been grown in 1883 from 2 ozs. of seed. It is unusually handsome, straw standing almost 6 ft. and I have seen heads over 24 inches in length. The grain is very large and handsome, very plump and full, with thin, white, close-fitting husks. The Welcome Oat stool heavily, with strong, straight straw of good height; stand up well, and crowded with long, beautiful, branching, well-filled heads. With good cultivation, they will yield 80 to 125 legal bushels per acre. This may seem almost beyond belief, but will be easily understood when it is considered that each measured bushel weighs more than one and one-half bushels of any ordinary oats. I offer direct headquarters' stock. Pkt., 10 cts.; lb. 30 cts.; 3 lbs., 75 cts., postpaid. By express or freight, pk., 50 cts., 50 bus., $12.50.

AMERICAN BEAUTY OATS.—Tested at the experimental station at Geneva, N. Y., the report concerning American Beauty is as follows: It is long and taper-pointed; average height 3 feet 3 inches, straw very erect and stout leaves often exceeding 16 inches in length; averaging length of panicle 9 inches; berry large. This variety is destined to become very popular, and is one of the most prolific varieties known. This sort we can confidently recommend as being a reliable new Oat. It is a heavy cropper and does not lodge. The straw is excellent for fodder. Peck, 50 cents; bushel, $1.75; 10 bushels $13.50.

HIGHLAND CHIEF BARLEY.—This is an entirely new and distinct two-rowed variety of Barley. It is very robust, a vigorous grower, and the size of the grain when compared with any other is immense. It is less liable to be damaged by wet than other kinds, inasmuch as it is more closely covered with broad awns or spikelets consequently it is less liable to lose color by the wet weather. Its strong, upright straw, yields from fifty to sixty bushels per acre, and usually weighs over fifty pounds to the measured bushel. The stock we offer this season, has been examined by eminent agriculturists in bulk, and pronounced the finest quality of barley they had ever seen. The very few practical farmers in this country who do not raise barley, and nearly all have experimented with two, four and six-rowed varieties, and experience tells that the two-rowed for this climate is far preferable. It yields better, and can stand longer after it is fit to cut. Packet, 10 cents; pound, 33 cents; 3 pounds, 90 cents, postpaid. By express or freight, peck, 75 cents; bushel, $2.50.

**Highland Chief Barley.**

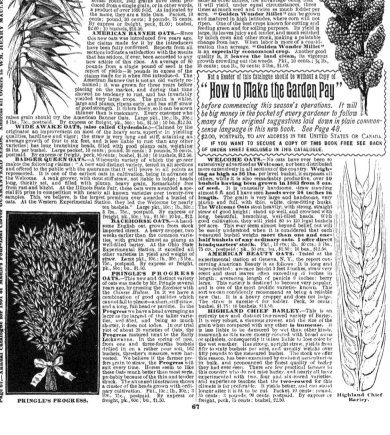

# 1891 ✻ Cash Prizes ✻ 1891

FOR years the premiums annually awarded for prize crops of vegetables, etc., raised from Maule's seeds have been a **striking** feature of my business. Thousands upon thousands of dollars have been distributed in all sections of the country, from Maine to California, with the most satisfactory results to all concerned. Last year Mr. Jas. E. Way, Postmaster, Clove, N. Y., from an investment of $3.10 in Maule's seeds in the spring of the year, secured $200 in cash, Oct. last, while in 1889, J. Polk Heivner, Augusta, Ia., from an investment of $3.55, received $175, and Mr. A. Fuller, East Ashford, N. Y., from an order amounting to 65 cents, secured a $100 premium in the Fall of the year. In 1888, Michael Crowley, Muskegon, Mich., from an investment of $1.50, secured $150 in cash premiums. The same year forty-eight customers in Arroyo Grande, Cal., sent me during the Spring and Winter, $188.55 ; in October, 1888, three of these forty-eight customers received my checks for $475 for premium vegetables. Consequently, my Arroyo Grande customers, from a remittance of $188.55 in the Spring of the year, had $475 returned to them in the Fall. It is an established fact that while some of my competitors have been promising to pay premiums amounting to a few hundred dollars, thousands of dollars in cash have been paid and distributed all over the United States among customers of Maule's seeds. I would only add that this system of awarding cash prizes has certainly incited my customers to raise extra good vegetables that have surpassed anything ever produced in their respective neighborhoods.

### For the Season of 1891 I Offer $2,500 in CASH PRIZES to be Divided as Follows :

**$50** For the largest pod of Bush Lima Beans sent me, and raised by one of my customers from seed purchased of me this season.

**$50** For the largest head of Prize Wakefield Cabbage sent me, and raised by one of my customers from seed purchased of me this season.

**$50** For the largest and heaviest Oxheart Carrot sent me, and raised by one of my customers from seed purchased of me this season.

**$50** For the six best stalks of Golden Self Blanching Celery sent me, and raised by one of my customers from seed purchased of me.

**$50** For the largest and best-shaped Maule's Extra Early Cucumber sent me, raised by one of my customers from seed purchased of me.

**$50** For the longest ear of New Cory Sweet Corn sent me, and raised by one of my customers from seed purchased of me this season.

**$50** For the heaviest head of Large White Passion Lettuce sent me, and raised by one of my customers from seed purchased of me this season.

**$50** For the largest Frame's Prize—The Jumbo of all Watermelons—sent me, and raised by one of my customers from seed purchased of me.

**$50** For the largest Procopp's Giant Pepper sent me, and raised by one of my customers from seed purchased of me this season.

**$50** For the vine containing the most pods of Early Prize Peas sent me by one of my customers from seed purchased of me this season.

**$50** For the six best Early Scarlet Erfurt Radishes sent me, and raised by one of my customers from seed purchased of me this season.

**$50** For the best six white Strasburg Radishes sent me, and raised by one of my customers from seed purchased of me this season.

**$50** For the heaviest Sibley or Pike's Peak Squash sent me and raised by one of my customers from seed purchased of me this season.

**$50** For the heaviest Matchless Tomato sent me, and raised by one of my customers from seed purchased of me this season.

**$50** For the longest ear of Early Mastodon Field Corn sent me, and raised by one of my customers from seed purchased of me this season.

**$25** For the longest ear of Mapledale Popcorn sent me, and raised by one of my customers from seed purchased of me this season.

**$25** For the largest head of Mammoth Russian Sun Flower sent me, and raised by one of my customers from seed purchased of me this season.

The above eighteen varieties of seed represent a combination of as choice sorts of their respective varieties as could be collected from any seed catalogue published in America this year.
**One packet of each of the above premium seeds, eighteen packets in all, will be mailed to any customer on receipt of $1.00.**
All the above premiums will be awarded October 1st, 1891, and all specimens in competition for the prizes must reach me on or before that date.

In addition to the above, I will award, **JULY 1st, 1891, $1000 IN CASH** for the largest club orders of packets and ounces of Maule's seeds sent me this season. See page 4.

### $450 IN ONION PRIZES WILL BE PAID NOV. 1, 1891. See page 40.

**$150** for the largest yield from five pounds of seed sown of Maule's Large Red Wethersfield.
**$150** for the largest yield from one pound of seed sown of Maule's Prizetaker Onion.
**$150** for the largest yield from five pounds of seed sown of Maule's Yellow Danvers Onion.

**$100,** October 1st, 1891, will be paid to the customer sending the largest Pumpkin or Mammoth Squash raised from seed purchased of me. See page 52.

**FOR ALL VEGETABLES** not required to be sent me, charges prepaid, a report, signed by two well-known and thoroughly reliable witnesses and sworn before a Justice of Peace is necessary. By well-known witnesses, I mean country storekeepers in good standing in the community. Competition is open to all, excepting those to whom I have paid $100 or more in prizes within the last three years. I think that anyone who has been so successful as to secure as much as $100, should be satisfied to withdraw for a time from the competition, as I do not propose to offer premiums and pay a large share every year to the same people, who, by reason of an unusually favorable soil or location, may be better situated to raise premium vegetables than others.

**$100** Oct. 1st, 1891, will also be paid to the customer sending me in the largest and best shaped Freeman Potato, raised from seed purchased of me this season. See page 61.

**MAKING A GRAND TOTAL FOR**
===1891===
**$2,500 CASH**

**AN EXTRA PREMIUM.** I now have customers at 33,631 different post-offices. There are still, however, a large number of post-offices where I have not as yet a single customer. Whoever first sends me an order from one of these last-named offices will receive a liberal extra premium over and above the amount of order.

# A Page of Grasses

**ESPARCET CLOVER.**—A New Forage Plant; **Esparcet or Sanfoin Clover**, as it is sometimes called, is grown very extensively in every part of Europe on land where it is impossible to secure a stand of other grasses, but as yet this most excellent Clover is but little known in this country. In England, sown on land that could be only rented for $1.00 per acre, it has within a period of 20 years so enhanced the fertility of the soil that the same ground can be readily rented for $7.50 per annum. One writer going so far as to say "There are many parts of the United Kingdom in which a farmer could not pay his rent without the use of this Clover." In Norfolk, on the poorest sandy lands, it has produced, the second year, as high as 2½ tons of cured hay per acre on soil that was worthless for any thing else. Esparcet is a perennial, usually sown in the Spring; it equals any clover in nutrition and flesh-forming qualities, and no grass grown requires so little pains to cure. The seed being much larger than other varieties of clover, it should be covered deeper. It can be sown with Oats, and harrowed in at the rate of 4 bushels to the acre. Thrives best on dry, chalky and sandy soil. On heretofore barren wastes, when once thoroughly established, it has produced two abundant crops in a season. There is no doubt that in this country, as soon as the merits of Esparcet become known, that it will prove the most valuable of our heat-resisting clovers. Seed weighs 26 pounds to the bushel. Packet, 10 cents; pound, 30 cents; 3 pounds, 75 cents, postpaid. By express or freight 15 cents per pound; $10.00 per 100 pounds.

**LUCERNE.**—I can give no better description of this most excellent Clover than the following written by a correspondent of *The Farm and Garden.* "Lucerne will grow on any land that will produce wheat, corn or potatoes and will thrive on very light sand or gravel, and does well on clay. But will not grow on land that the water stands within 1 ft. of the surface. Although particular about wet land, it will stand any amount of wet in the summer provided there is plenty of drainage; also will stand all the water that may fall in the Winter. Will yield about on average of six tons per acre, although it has yielded twice this amount. It is a perennial. The best method is to sow broadcast 15 pounds per acre where land is in good condition, on weedy land, or clear gravel, or sand that is very poor, about 3 pounds more. You cannot get a crop from it the first year; but don't get discouraged if the plants are on an average of ten inches apart—little, thin, single stems, about four or six inches high. Your prospect is good that you will have four tons per acre next year, and the next year will be as good as ever it will be and stand that way for ten years. It is best to sow in the Spring with oats. When rain is plenty no cultivation is needed; do not manure it, as it thrives as well on washed sand as it does on the best garden spot. In a few years it will convert a clear sand into a rich land, this is owing to the decay of its roots. Cut when in full bloom, a little old is better than too young; try to cure without getting it wet. Rake into winrows if cut with a machine, let it dry until leaves fall off when roughly handled, put it in piles of about a fork-full to cure. Not many animals take to it when dry, without having it in their manger for two or three days with other hay, then you will see them eat the Lucerne in preference to any other. Do not let hungry cattle get it while green, especially it wet. If you wish to pasture them on it, first feed them all they can eat and then turn them on the green Lucerne and no harm will come to them. It is the best thing to renew old worn out lands that I ever saw, and there is not a weed in this country that can stand before it." Pkt., 10c. lb., 30c.; 3 lbs., 75c.; by mail, postpaid. By express or freight. 20c. per lb.; $15 per 100 lbs.

**RED CLOVER.**—Lb., 30c.; 3 lbs., 75c. postpaid. By express or freight, pk., $1.75; bus., $6.00.

**MAMMOTH OR PEA VINE CLOVER.**—Lasts longer than most varieties; grows 5 to 6 feet high. Lb., 30c.; 3 lbs., 75c.; postpaid. By express or freight, pk., $2.00; bus., $7.00.

**ALSIKE CLOVER.**—This is a very hardy perennial and thrives equally well on wet or dry land; an excellent clover for land that is clover sick. Lb., 30 cts.; 3 lbs., 75c., postpaid. By express or freight, 100 lbs., $16.00.

**WHITE CLOVER.**—Very valuable when mixed with other grasses for lawns, etc. Lb., 40 cts.; 3 lbs., $1.00, postpaid. By express or freight, 100 lbs., $30.

**TIMOTHY.**—Well known and extensively grown in all parts of the country. 45 lbs. per bus. Lb., 30c.; 3 lbs., 75c., postpaid. By express or freight, pk., $1.00; bus., $2.25.

**RED TOP OR HERD GRASS.**—Grows well on almost any soil or in any climate, very valuable for a permanent pasture. 12 lbs. per bus. Qt., 20 cts., postpaid. By ex., or ft., bus., $1.00; 50 lb. sack, $3.75.

**ORCHARD GRASS.**—A very desirable variety for stock, also grows well under trees. 12 lbs. per bus. Qt., 30 cts., postpaid. By express or freight, bus., $2.00.

**GERMAN OR GOLDEN MILLET.**—Yields more hay and seed per acre than any other variety. Lb., 30 cts.; 3 lbs., 75 cts., postpaid. By express or freight, pk., 60 cts.; bus., $2.00.

**MEADOW FESCUE.**—Thrives on any soil. Lb., 40 cts.; 3 lbs., $1.00, postpaid.

**ENGLISH RYE GRASS.**—Very nutritious; a good grass for permanent pastures and meadows. Qt., 25 cts., postpaid. By express or freight. pk., $1; bus., $3.

**KENTUCKY BLUE GRASS.**—Excellent for lawns; also valuable for pasture mixed with other grasses and retains its verdure in the hottest weather. Qt., 30 cts., postpaid. By express or freight, bus., $3.75.

**HUNGARIAN MILLET.**—Valuable soiling plant Grows on light soil, stands heat and drouth. Lb., 30 cts.; 3 lbs., 75 cts., postpaid. By ex. or ft, pk., 50 cts.; bus., $1.50.

**SWEET VERNAL GRASS.**—Used extensively to mix with other grasses for lawns, etc. Lb., 40 cts.; 3 lbs., $1.00, postpaid.

**MEADOW FOXTAIL.**—Early and of rapid growth. Lb., 45 cts.; 3 lbs., $1.10, postpaid.

ESPARCET THE GREAT DROUGHT RESISTING CLOVER

LUCERNE

LAWN AT BRIAR CREST

## M. EX. LAWN GRASS.

A country place, now-a-days, without its lawn of from one to five or, ten acres, is seldom seen, and it is no wonder, for what more beautiful sight is there than a well-kept, carefully mown lawn? But although a good lawn may be beautiful, a poor one is about as ugly a sight as one cares to see. Appreciating this point, I have taken unusual pains with my Lawn Grass Mixture, selecting nothing but the most desirable grasses, that will give a luxuriant growth, Spring, Summer and Autumn, always presenting the same green velvety appearance. With the ground carefully prepared, graded and rolled, seed sown at the rate of a bus. per acre, and the lawn then frequently mown and rolled, it is within the reach of everyone, at trifling trouble and expense by sowing Maule's Lawn Grass, to have as fine a lawn as one desires. Qt. 20c; 2 qt. 40c. postpaid. Pk. $1.50; bu., $4.50; 4 bu. $16, purchaser to pay expressage.

## MAULE'S SPECIAL MIXTURE FOR PERMANENT PASTURE.

This mixture of standard grasses is particularly recommended to every farmer receiving this catalogue who desires to lay any portion of his farm to permanent pasture. I have prepared a mixture of grasses for this purpose which I consider unequaled. It contains nothing but the most desirable varieties, such as will insure a heavy stand for a number of years. Four bushels should be sown to the acre. Bus. $3.00; 4 bus., enough for 1 acre, $10.00. With this mixture, when intended for either mowing lands or pasture, should be also sown 10 pounds of mixed clover per acre, comprising White Mammoth, Alsike, etc. 10 pounds of this mixed clover, with a bus. of Permanent Pasture Seed, is worth $12.00, thus making a 5cost, for 5 or 6 years lay, the trifling amount of $42 per acre. The clover being much the heavier seed, it should be sown separately. Please state when ordering if land is thin or heavy.

69

# A PAGE of FODDER PLANTS

**RED COB ENSILAGE CORN.—A pure white Corn, cropping as high as 45 tons per acre.** In introducing this variety of Ensilage Corn to my customers, I consider I offer them the very best grown. It is sweet, tender and juicy, furnishes more nourishment than any other variety, has short joints, abundance of leaves and grows to a great height. It is adapted to every section of the country, (see testimonials below). Hundreds of dairy farmers use it, and are never disappointed. Do not fail to give this corn a trial this season, for I know if once grown, you will plant it every season. **PRICE: Pk., 50 cts.; bus., $1.50; 10 bus., $12.50.**
What is said by a few customers: By mail, pkt., 10c.; lb., 30c.; 3 lbs., 75c.

**MAINE.** "It is very much liked and is the only corn we can get that is sure to grow."

**MASSACHUSETTS.** "Red Cob gives splendid satisfaction. It has more leaves and stands the storms better than any other kind I have been able to obtain."

**NEW YORK.** "We think it the best fodder corn we have ever seen. It looked to us as though every kernel grew. It has more fodder on a stalk than any other kind; grows very rapidly, is fine color, and the stalk is extra sweet."

**OHIO.** "Red Cob Ensilage Corn is excellent, very large and juicy. Think one-third more can be produced to the acre than any other kind."

**ILLINOIS.** "Planted under very unfavorable circumstances, June 28th, still it yielded better than other Ensilage planted at the same time. Some stalks grew 14 feet high."

**MICHIGAN.** "Any one who has stock to winter in this State, the more of this corn he plants, the better. Some stalks grew sixteen feet high."

**MINNESOTA.** "In no case has anything but praise been said of Red Cob."

**CANADA.** "Ensilage Corn grew to great height, and produced very fine sweet fodder."

**KAFFIR CORN.— A New Forage Plant from the South.**—Kaffir Corn produces two to four heads from a single stalk, and in Georgia has yielded in a single season, by the middle of October, two crops of green fodder, and a full crop of grain (50 to 60 bus. per acre). The whole stalk if cut down as soon as seed heads appear, at once starts a second growth from the roots. It also stands drought wonderfully. If growth is checked for want of moisture the plant waits for rain, and when it comes, at once resumes its growth. On very thin or worn-out lands it yields paying crops of grain or forage even in dry seasons when corn has utterly failed. The whole stalk, as well as blades, makes excellent fodder, and all stock eat it greedily. It is as early or quick in growth as Minnesota Amber Cane, and is therefore reliable in any latitude where Amber Cane has been found useful as a fodder crop. Should be sown in drills and cultivated same as Indian Corn. Compared with other sorghums Kaffir Corn has proved itself to be early, abundant in yield, reliable in all seasons, and a superior crop for both quantity and quality of its product. It keeps green, and stalk is brittle and juicy to the last; is not a hard and cane-like growth such as other sorghums. Flour made from Kaffir Corn is excellent for batter cakes, muffins, etc., has a slightly sweetish taste, otherwise is not distinguished from wheat. Large pkt., 10c.; lb., 40c.; 3 lbs., $1, postpaid.

**SUGAR CORN FOR GREEN FODDER.**—Profitable as green feed for milch cows. It is sweeter and more nutritious and eaten more readily than fodder from Field Corn. Peck, 75 cents; Bushel, $1.75.

**KAFFIR CORN. Packet, 10 cents.**

**YELLOW MILO MAIZE.**—This is another variety of the sorghum family, and I cannot do better in describing it than by giving the experience one of my customers (Judge Hudson, of Mississippi,) had with it. "I planted it in my Irish potato patch, four by two feet, three stalks to the hill, and about 200 hills, and cultivated as corn. It was a bold, vigorous grower and deep-green color and continues so yet from bottom to top; grows eight to ten feet. About half-way up the stalk and on the top are numerous large shoots with fine large blades on them like those of the main stalk, and on which shoots are other shoots or suckers, all bearing fine heads like the main head or stalk, but not quite so large until from mid-way the stalk up is a large mass of heads and fodder. Some stalks have as high as twenty heads, weighing from one-fourth to one pound per head, and as fine heavy blades as the best common corn. One stalk will make a good, rich feed or meal for a horse. It makes a beautiful, delicious, rich meal for pop-corn. There is no use to raise anything else for horses, cattle, chickens or pop-corn. Fertilize and cultivate well; nothing of its kind will pay as well. It will mature its main head in 100 days, and still grow on and mature others and fodder until frost." Pkt., 10c.; lb., 40c.; 3 lbs, $1.00, postpaid.

**Yellow Milo Maize.**

**TEOSINTE.**—So many have spoken to me of this magnificent forage plant that I am glad I have at last been able to secure a small quantity of seed. In this latitude, planted July 3d, it produced from one seed, twenty-seven stalks, and attained a height of seven feet by Sept. 10th, making a luxuriant growth of leaves, which the horses and cattle ate as freely as young sugar corn. In appearance somewhat resembles Indian Corn, but the leaves are much longer and broader, and the stalk contains sweeter sap. In its perfection it produces a great number of shoots, growing twelve feet high, very thickly covered with leaves, yielding such an abundance of forage that one plant is considered to be sufficient to feed a pair of cattle for 24 hours. In the South it surpasses either Corn or Sorghum as a soiling or fodder-plant. 85 stalks have been grown from one seed, attaining a height of 11 feet. Packet, 15 cents; ¼ pound, 60 cents; pound, $2.20.

**TEOSINTE. Packet, 15 cents.**

All prices on Field and Grass Seeds (except when quoted by mail, postpaid,) include delivery free on board cars in this city. No charge for bags. Customer to pay freight or express charges.

# A PAGE OF MISCELLANEOUS FARM SEEDS

**JAPANESE BUCKWHEAT.**—I would advise all who grow Buckwheat to give Japanese a trial. It is not only the very best, but by far the most productive and profitable variety in cultivation. From ½ bushel of seed sown, 40 bushels of good seed have been harvested. A glance at the illustration will show the peculiar shape of kernels, and also that they are nearly twice the size of any other variety. In color the kernel is a rich dark brown. Straw is heavier, and branches more than the Silver Hull, while it need not be sown as thickly as other varieties. Flour made from the Japanese is fully equal if not superior to any other sort. It ripens a week earlier than Silver Hull, and yields two to three times as much. Can be planted as far north as New Hampshire. It is also an excellent variety for bees. Pkt., 10 cents; lb., 30 cents; 3 lbs., 75 cents, by mail postpaid. By express or freight, pk., 60 cents; bus., $1.75; 10 bus., $12.50.

**SILVER HULL BUCKWHEAT.**—This variety continues in bloom days sooner, and under the same conditions yields much better per acre. The flour is whiter and more nutritious, while on account of the thinner husks 15 to 20 per cent. waste is saved in grinding. Pkt., 10 cts.; lb., 30 cts.; 3 lbs., 75 cts.; by mail postpaid. By express or freight, peck, 60 cts.; bushel, $1.75; 10 bushels $12.50.

**NEW AUSTRALIAN BROOM CORN.**—This Australian variety, is without doubt one of the most profitable varieties for the Am. grower of Broom Corn. Imported from Australia a few years ago, it has only been grown in this country to a limited extent, but all who have ever seen or examined the brush, consider that it makes **far better brooms than any variety they have** ever grown. Some few of its producing qualities can be had from the fact that it has readily produced in this State 500 brooms to an acre, and 50 bushels of seed. The brush does not get crooked or tangled, like many other varieties, and the gentleman who grew the seeds I have to sell this season could not find 25 tangled brush in an entire field of more than an acre. The brush, in addition to being so straight and fine, is nearly as long again as the ordinary evergreen variety, and will invariably bring better prices, when put on the market, than any other sort. I have ever seen. My supply of seed is still limited. Packet, 10 cents; pound, 50 cents; 3 pounds, $1.25. By express or freight, peck, $1.00.

**IMPROVED EVERGREEN BROOM CORN.**—The best for general cultivation, and is more largely grown than any other variety; brush firm, of good length and bright green color; never gets red, and brings the highest market price. By express or freight, peck, $1.00; bushel, $3.00.

**CALIFORNIA GOLDEN BROOM CORN.**—A strong growing variety, much resembling the Evergreen, but longer in brush; a bright golden color when ripe. Good for making hurl brooms. By express or freight, peck, $1.00; bu., $3.50. By mail, both the above varieties, large pkt., 10 cts.; lb., 30 cts.; 3 lbs., 75 cts.

**SUGAR CANE—EARLY AMBER.**—This is by far the best variety for sugar, as it matures quickly, and has been cultivated as far North as St. Paul, Minn. The seed is valuable also as food for horses and cattle, and is greedily eaten by poultry, increasing the egg production. For ensilage or fodder, it possesses important advantages. By mail, postpaid, lb., 30c.; 3 lbs., 75c.; by express or freight, pk., $1.; bus. of 56 lbs., $2.50; 10 bus. or over, $2.25 per bus.

**SUGAR CANE—EARLY ORANGE.**—The favorite Southern variety. Yields an abundance of syrup, does not grow quite as tall as Early Amber, but is heavier by mail, postpaid, lb. 30c.; 3 lb. 75c.; by express or freight bu. of 56 lbs. $3.

**WILD RICE.**—It grows very rapidly in 1 to 8 feet of water, ripens late in Aug. or early in Sept. Should be planted broadcast from a boat, in 2 or 3 feet of water, having a hard bottom. As an attraction for wild fowl it cannot be equaled. In large ponds and lakes it purifies the water. Does well in marshes, and makes good hay. At the South two crops can be cut; all cattle are very fond of it. Pkt., 10 cts.; lb., 40 cts., postpaid. By express, per bushel of 15 pounds, $4.00.

The line running down the side of the different pages of this catalogue always contains my full address; but should you mislay this book a letter addressed simply **MAULE'S SEEDS, PHILADELPHIA,** would be sure to reach me, as my name is well-known at almost every post-office in the United States.

## The Two Best Sunflowers

**MAMMOTH RUSSIAN.**—Sunflower seed is one of the best egg-producing foods known for poultry, keeping them in fine condition and largely increasing the supply of eggs. It can be sown any time up to the middle of July. It should be grown by every poultry breeder who has the opportunity to raise only a few stalks even. It may be set in any soil where other fruits and vegetables cannot be conveniently raised or anywhere where the soil is not easily cultivated. The flowers are double the size of the common variety, and as a food it far excels the latter. Pkt., 10 cts.; pt. 25 cts.; qt. 40 cts.; postpaid; by express, $1.00 per peck.

**BLACK GIANT.**—This magnificent Sunflower produces even larger heads than the Mammoth Russian. Seeds are short, unusually plump, and filled full of meat, while on account of the thinness of the shell it is of course more easily eaten by the fowls than other varieties. Another good quality is that the seeds are held very tightly in the flower, and are not as easily shelled or as readily eaten by birds as other sorts. There is nothing more healthy for poultry or that will so much increase egg production. Packet, 15 cents; pint, 30 cents; quart, 50 cents; postpaid.

## TREE SEEDS

Apple, oz., 15 cts., lb., 55 cts.
Cherry Mazard, oz., 15 c., lb., 45c.
Peach, oz., 10 cts., lb., 35 cts.
Pear, oz., 30 cts., lb., $2.70.
Quince, oz., 30 cts., lb., $2.70.
Arbor Vitæ, American, oz., 40 cts., lb., $3.60.
Silver Fir, oz., 15 cts., lb., $1.35.
Hemlock, oz., 50 cts., lb., $4.50.
Scotch Pine, oz., 20 cts., lb., $1.80.
White Pine, oz., 30cts., lb., $2.70.
Norway Spruce, oz., 15 cts., lb., $1.35.
White Ash, oz., 15 cts., lb., $1.35.

White Birch, oz., 15c., lb., $1.35.
Box Elder, oz., 15 cts., lb., $1.35.
Hardy Catalpa, oz., 15 cts., lb., $1.15.
European Larch, oz., 15 cts., lb., $1.35.
European Linden, oz., 15 cts., lb., $1.35.
Honey Locust, oz., 10c., lb., 55c.
Yellow Locust, oz., 10c., lb., 55c.
White Mulberry, oz., 25 cts., lb., $2.00.
Russian Mulberry, oz., 60 cts., lb., $5.40.

**OSAGE ORANGE.**—This will produce, with proper cultivation, a good hedge in from 3 to 4 years, from the seed, that will turn all kinds of stock. Oz., 15 cts.; lb., 65 cts. Bushel, by express or freight, purchaser paying charges, $7.50.

**PEACH PITS. Natural.**—By express or freight, $3.00 per bushel.

71

1. VERBENA NEW GIANT STRIPED.
2. NEW YELLOW ASTER, AUREALIN BEAUTY.
3. NEW LARGE FLOWERING PYRAMIDAL STOCKS AZURE QUEEN.
4. PANSY, MAULE'S PRIZE MIXED.
5. NEW DOUBLE PAEONY FLOWERED POPPY "FIREBALL".
6. NEW PHLOX DRUMMONDII GRANDIFLORA "MONARCH".

ONE PACKET OF EACH OF THE ABOVE SIX NEW AND TRULY HANDSOME NOVELTIES SENT POST PAID FOR $1.00. SINGLE PACKET 25 CTS.

Address
W<sup>m</sup> HENRY MAULE,
PHILADELPHIA.

MARGUERITE CARNATIONS

SEED 15 CENTS PER PACKET
2 PACKETS 25 CENTS.

The
FLORAL
NOVELTY
OF THE
SEASON.

BLOOMS 4 MONTHS
FROM SOWING
THE SEED.

WM. HENRY MAULE, Philadelphia.

## VERBENA COMPACTA "DEFIANCE"

**NEW STRIPED DOUBLE LARKSPUR**

**VERBENA COMPACTA DEFIANCE.**—An exceedingly dwarf and compact Verbena, only growing about 5 inches high, and spreading itself fully 15 inches, forming a dense mass of dark green foliage, which produce their beautiful large trusses of most graceful, glowing scarlet flowers, a color quite distinct from any other variety. For bedding purposes no Verbena can equal the beautiful Compacta Defiance, which on account of its dwarf compact, spreading growth forms a solid mass of green, covered the whole summer with their bright scarlet blooms, the effect being most pleasing. A bed of Snowball Phlox and Defiance Verbena will be found very attractive. Packet, 15 cts.; 2 packets, 25 cts.

**NEW STRIPED DOUBLE LARKSPUR.**—This handsome novelty which I offer this year for the first time, is certain to be appreciated by all lovers of flowers The above illustration is quite accurate, yet it gives you but a faint idea of their extreme beauty. Many years of careful selection and improvement have brought this Larkspur to perfection, and is without a doubt the most distinct variety ever offered. The colors range through many pretty shades of pink, carmine dark blue, purple, and white, striped and blotched, delicately and beautifully blended, the handsome double flowers being produced in the greatest profusion, making it **one of the finest annuals in cultivation.** For border decoration no plant is more valuable than the Larkspur, and my customers should not fail to plant this beautiful and distinct novelty this season. Packet, 25 cents; 3 packets 50 cents.

### The Marguerite Carnation

SEE COLORED PLATE OPPOSITE

Many new, exceedingly valuable and beautiful novelties in Flower Seeds have lately been introduced, but I feel confident that none of them will excite such widespread admiration as will the Beautiful Marguerite Carnations. In the first place, any one growing these beautiful Carnations can secure the greatest possible perfection with the most ordinary care. In the second place, it is hardly possible that they will ever be excelled as to size of flowers, which equal, if indeed they do not surpass, the Malmaison Carnations, which were before considered perfection. But above all they will bloom within 4 months after sowing the seed. The vigorous stalks grow usually 6 to 8 inches high, the buds and flowers, much crowded together, forming many large tufts. The flowers are of brilliant colors, ranging through all shades of red, pink, and white, many handsomely variegated, and are always, as stated above, of enormous size. They are most valuable for pot culture, bedding, groups and borders; and in conclusion would say that any one in want of fine flowering plants is offered in the beautiful Marguerite Carnations a new race that cannot be excelled, all the more remarkable is the fact that they can be planted at any season of the year **AND WILL BLOOM IN FOUR MONTHS AFTER SOWING THE SEED.** Sown in March they require but little different cultivation other than that given to the ordinary Annual. Packet, 15 cents; 2 packets, 25c.

**SOLANUM GUINEENSE.**

**SOLANUM GUINEENSE.**—A bold plant, which if sown early and planted out will readily grow 6 to 8 feet in height in a season; it can also be kept dwarfer if grown in pots The flowers, which are small and violet in color, are succeeded by an abundance of fruit early in August. The fruit is borne in grape-like bunches and jet black, but cannot be eaten. It is sure to produce a singular effect. As an ornamental plant, for decorative display, etc., I know of no plant more desirable than the beautiful Solanum Guineense. Packet, 15 cents; 2 packets, 25 cents.

**SCABIOSA HYBRIDA VICTORIA**

**LOBELIA CARDINALIS**

**SCABIOSA HYBRIDA VICTORIA.**—This pretty new dwarf plant obtained by hybridization is a decided acquisition; it is almost constantly in bloom and its beautiful flowers, ranging in all shades of rose, red and violet are delightfully fragrant, being produced on long stems they will therefore be valuable for all purposes where cut flowers can be used. I consider the Scabiosa Hybrida Victoria one of my best novelties for this season, and as the Scabiosa has been largely grown of late for cut flowers, I predict a large demand for this the handsomest variety ever introduced. Packet, 15 cents; 2 packets, 25 cents.

**LOBELIA CARDINALIS.** (**Cardinal Flower**).—This is undoubtedly the most distinct Lobelia yet introduced and one of the handsomest of all open-air flowers, for none can surpass it in the brilliancy of its rich vermilion flowers; its bold, erect habit and striking effect. It is especially adapted for situations where bright colors are desirable, and I feel confident that it would be hard to surpass Lobelia Cardinalis in this respect. It is moreover a profuse bloomer, flowering until late in the Fall. Packet, 10 cents; 3 packets, 25 cents.

THE 3 BEST PANSIES

SUPERB CAMELLIA FLOWERED BALSAMS

GLOBE PYRAMIDAL STOCKS

**BALSAM.— Maule's Superb Camellia Flowered.—**This is the finest strain of large-flowered, perfectly double Balsam in cultivation, producing its gorgeous masses of beautiful, brilliant-colored double flowers in the greatest profusion. It embraces varied and brilliant self-colors, and also superbly mottled and striped varieties. In this mixture will be found such desirable colors as pure white, rosy pink, brilliant scarlet, scarlet spotted with white, white striped with scarlet and purple, flesh color solid purple, new light lemon and many other shades, well worthy of a place in any flower garden. Packet, 10 cents.

**STOCKS.—Globe Pyramidal Mixed.** In the New Large Flowering Globe Pyramidal, I **have the most magnificent race yet perfected.** Both the spikes and flowers are very large, individual blooms frequently measuring from 2 to 2½ inches in diameter. The large double and perfect flowers are produced in great profusion, the spikes being compactly pyramidal in shape, and the plants of neat habit of growth. I offer the Globe Pyramidal Stocks in a very fine mixture of twenty beautiful and distinct shades and colors. Packet, 10 cents.

**PANSY.—No. 1. Odier or Five Blotched.—**A beautiful strain of various colored, very large, fine, perfect formed flowers, each petal distinctly and handsomely spotted with rich and varied darker shades. The large and brilliant flowers are produced in great numbers and borne well above the foliage on strong stems. **Certain to please every lover of this popular flower.** Packet, 20 cents; 3 packets, 50 cents.

**No. 2. New Imperial German.—**In the New Imperial German Pansies the labor of years of careful cultivation and constant selection has resulted in **an almost endless variety of charming shades of colors united** with **extra large size.** They bloom throughout the entire summer, and embrace all the solid or self-colors; large spotted; dark and light marbled varieties; with clear distinct eyes; striped flowers of striking beauty, and vividly colored fancy varieties, blotched, veined, mottled and margined in combinations that would be thought impossible until the flowers are actually seen. All my customers who plant this strain of pansy will be delighted with the endless variety and wonderful combinations of colors, and enormous size of its handsome flowers. Packet, 10 cents; 3 packets, 25 cents.

**No. 3. Giant Trimardeau.—**An altogether distinct and beautiful new class of pansy, the flowers of which are of a very large size, **in fact larger than anything hitherto attained.** They carry their blooms well above the foliage, which in itself is a desirable feature. The plants are of strong, compact habit, and are marked with three large blotches. The seed has been carefully saved from the finest flowers of enormous size. Packet, 20 cents; 3 packets, 50 cents.

ESCHSCHOLTZIA MANDARIN

NICOTIANA AFFINIS

NASTURTIUM EMPRESS OF INDIA

VIOLET THE CZAR

**ESCHSCHOLTZIA.—Mandarin (Cal. Poppy).—**The handsomest variety of this favorite flower; the inside of the petals are of a rich orange color, the outside dazzling dark crimson. Is very attractive in beds or borders; hardy annual; 1 ft. Pkt. 5c.

**NICOTIANA.—Affinis.—**Produces handsome pure white Bouvardia like flowers, 2 or 3 in. long, and as much in diameter; are delightfully sweet-scented, a small bed filling a large garden with fragrance. The plants can be taken up in the fall, cut back and potted for the house, and will bloom freely all winter. Pkt., 5 cents.

**NASTURTIUM.—Empress of India.—**The plant is of dwarf bushy habit, with dark tinted foliage, while the flowers are of the most brilliant crimson color, **so freely produced that no other annual in cultivation can approach it in effectiveness.** Its dazzling colors are remarkable. Packet, 5 cents.

**VIOLET.—The Czar.—**This beautiful new, perpetual bloomer is the **largest flowering and richest colored** deep-blue, sweet Violet in cultivation. In delicious perfume it stands unequaled. Seed slow to germinate. Packet, 10 cents.

74

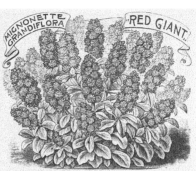

**CLEOME PUNGENS—The Giant Spider Plant.**—Although this is one of our Native Annuals, it is but little known. The flowers are a deep purplish pink when they first open, but fade to light pink so that the lower part of the panicle is a different color from the upper. The stamens are several inches long, from which it derives the name—spider flower. It is a strong, robust grower, 4 to 5 feet high with great panicles of bloom as large as a Hydrangea and unaffected by wind or weather. Seed sown in the open ground in May will flower in July and continue in flower uninterruptedly until frost. Packet, 10 cents, 3 packets, 25 cents.

**MIGNONETTE—Grandiflora Red Giant.**—This grand novelty now introduced for the first time, is of perfect form, growing vigorously, and forming a compact pyramid of elegant appearance. The flower spikes are of enormous unequaled size the single blossoms of an intense red color. The plant attains a height of from 12 to 16 inches, producing its large spikes of rich red flowers most profusely. This handsome Mignonette is the result of many years' careful selection, and is without a doubt the most distinct variety ever offered. Packet 25 cents ; 3 packets, 50 cents.

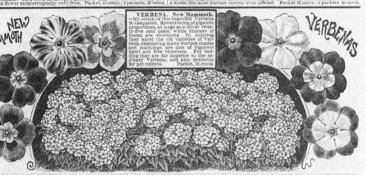

**VERBENA, New Mammoth.**—My strain of this beautiful Verbena is unequaled, flowers being of gigantic proportions, as large as a silver twenty-five cent piece, while clusters of bloom are enormous. In coloring they excel the old varieties of Verbena, embracing many distinct shades and markings, are also of vigorous habit and free bloomers. For bedding they are far superior to the ordinary Verbena, and also desirable for pot culture. Packet, 15 cents.

**THE PEACOCK POPPY.**—A new and exceedingly pretty Poppy, growing about 2 feet high and blooming freely. The most striking feature of the flower is the conspicuous glossy black zone near the centre, which brings out the vivid scarlet and cherry crimson of the rest of the flower. The buds are of a drooping habit, which adds greatly to their beauty. Packet, 10 cents.

**POPPY SNOWDRIFT.**—In the last 3 or 4 years many new varieties of Poppy have been introduced, but with the exception of Fireball, none of them can approach the Snowdrift for neat and compact habit of growth or immense size of flowers, frequently measuring 2½ to 3 inches in diameter. It is a profuse bloomer, covering its foliage with pure white flowers, round, double, with finely imbricated petals. Produces an abundance of bloom all Summer. Pkt., 10 cts.

**THE MIKADO.**—One of the most charming sorts of the Poppy family has been sent to this country from Japan, and is in form and character essentially a Japanese flower in its quaint —yet artistic—beauty. Flowers pure white at the back, its fringed edges crimson scarlet. It is one of the most effective Annuals in existence, and can be highly recommended. Packet, 10 cts.

75

**EUPHORBIA HETEROPHYLLA.—Fire on the Mountain.** A pretty hardy annual of the easiest culture, forming bushy plants 3 to 4 feet high, with smooth glossy branches, at first entirely green, but as the season advances each branch becomes tipped with greenish white flowers, enveloped in unique orange-scarlet bracts, the whole surrounding leaves becoming blazed with dark scarlet tipped with green. Desirable for garden or pot culture. Packet. 15 cents.

**NEW IMPERIAL HIBISCUS.—**The flowers of this grand and handsome Hibiscus are of a lovely shade of rich yellow, and from their large size and handsome shape make a novel appearance, and from their large great profusion from July until the end of September. They are produced in which these beautiful flowers can be raised for. The easy most season should induce every one to give the New Imperial Hibiscus a place in their garden. Packet, 15 cents.

COPYRIGHT 1890 BY WM. HENRY MAULE

### SCARLET BALSAM APPLE— ✳ —PRIDE of CALIFORNIA.

**SCARLET BALSAM APPLE.—Momordica Involucrata.—**A growing luxuriant climber from the mountains of Natal, of strong vigorous, covering trellises, arbors, etc., with vivid green, deeply-cut large flowers are borne in lavish profusion; some creamy white others pure white with red pistils. The flowers are succeeded by sulphur-yellow fruits 3 in. long, changing to rich carmine-scarlet; burst and show the seeds of blood-red color. Packet. 20 cents.

**PRIDE OF CALIFORNIA.—Lathyrus Splendens.—**A Sweet Pea, and is considered in the far west the handsomest of all. They produce immense large clusters of brilliant deep rose flowers fusely, being loaded down in season with their handsome blooms. most desirable trailers for covering a porch or trellis, and being perf will produce a wealth of graceful and brilliant deep rose blossoms which time the effect is wonderful. Packet, 15 cents; 2 packets, 25 cents

### 2 NEW GRAND NICOTIANAS

RED FLOWERED NICOTIANA.

NICOTIANA DECURRENS.

**NICOTIANA MACROPHYLLA.—Red-flowered Nicotiana.—**One most brilliant Nicotianas ever introduced, growing from 3 to 4 feet high, and a profuse bloomer. Flowers are in color a rich cardinal red, inches in length, and borne in large numbers on stiff stems, standing above the foliage, producing a fine effect. I do not think any annual more beautiful Nicotiana, in habit of growth, or brilliancy of its cardinal flowers. Packet. 10 cents.

**NICOTIANA.—Decurrens.—**This handsome new Nicotiana form, branching freely from the ground, giving a great number branches, thus making it a profuse bloomer. The flowers are large tubes pure white, and deliciously fragrant, opening before sundown very late the following morning to re-open again towards evening flowering seed should be started in the house, although if sown in the first of May will flower in July. Packet, 10 cents.

76

**NEW ANNUAL CHRYSANTHEMUMS.**—During the last few years many new and beautiful forms of this æsthetic annual, have been introduced, which I now offer in a mixture, thus giving my customers a chance of securing all the new varieties for the price of one. The varied markings of bronze, crimson, maroon, and gold, alternating with pure white and deep purple, are strikingly beautiful, whether as pot plants or conservatory or for growing out of doors. For cutting they are invaluable.  Packet, 10 cents.

**RARE CACTUS.**—These wonderful plants are admired by everyone who sees them. Their curious forms and wonderfully brilliant flowers are sure to make them attractive. Illustration conveys but a faint idea of what can be obtained with proper attention from one of my packets of seeds, affording untold interest and pleasure. For growing in the garden or for sitting-room decoration nothing can be more effective. Seed should be sown under glass in light sandy soil, germinating readily.  Packet, 15 cents ; 2 packets, 25 cents.

of
s in
eat
ney
ers
the
nts.
a

**DANTHE.** Manglesi
m.—A New Dwarf White
g Rhodanthe, blooming in
fusion, bearing pure silvery
ers that are bound to charm
e them. It may be sown in
round, and had in flower in
e. For cutting purposes it
ound extremely useful for
mediate use, or for various
ecorative purposes during
a dried state.  Packet, 10c.

**CLARKIA. Mrs. Langtry.**—An exceedingly bea
form of Clarkia. The petals have an even edge, the col
the flower being purest white, with an evenly defined di
centre, of brilliant carmine-crimson. It is remarkably free
ering, of dwarf compact habit ; as a pot-plant or for be
purposes, it will be most welcome, and its easy cultiv
specially recommends its use for children's gardens and amo
generally.  Packet, 5 c

77

## NEW SWEET PEAS

**ORANGE PRINCE.**—Standard bright orange pink, flushed with scarlet, wings clear bright rose, pink-veined, handsome and distinct. Packet, 15c.

**THE QUEEN.**—Wings light mauve, standard light rosy pink, delicately handsome. Packet, 10c.

**IMPERIAL BLUE.**—Rich purplish crimson, wings bright blue, shaded mauve, very rich. Pkt., 10c.

**ISA ECKFORD.**—Handsome creamy white, shaded rosy pink, very large flower. Pkt., 15c.

**BLACK WARRIOR.**—Dark black purple, striped with lighter shades. Pkt., 10c.

**APPLE BLOSSOM.**—Standards bright pinkish rose, wings apple blossom, quite distinct. Packet, 15c.

**VESUVIUS.**—Standard rose color, veined and spotted with brown, wings clear blue, shaded rose and lilac distinct. Pkt., 10c.

**CARDINAL.**—Rich shining crimson scarlet, the brightest of all Sweet Peas, very robust habit and free flowering. Packet, 10c.

**PRINCESS OF WALES.**—A showy variety, shaded and flaked mauve on a white ground. Pkt., 10c.

**BRONZE PRINCE.**—Rich bronzy maroon, lower petals deep purple, large and handsome. Pkt., 10c.

**NEW SWEET PEAS.**—Superb mixture, all the above and many others, various shades and colors. Pkt., 10c.

## COSMOS HYBRIDUS

**COSMOS. Hybridus.**—An exceedingly beautiful Autumn flowering plant, requiring treatment similar to the Dahlia. The flowers are borne profusely in loose clusters and present a charming appearance. The Hybridus, or New Hybrids embrace all shades of Red, White, Blue, Lavender, and are indeed beautiful. Seed should be sown early in the spring and transplanted in the open border when all danger of frost is past. They will commence blooming in July, and continue to bloom profusely until cut down by frost. Packet, 10 cents.

## ZEBRA ZINNIAS

This strain presents a new departure in Zinnias, bearing large, perfectly double flowers as evenly imbricated as a Camellia. The flowers are variously striped and mottled, presenting all colors and shades known in the Zinnia, such as crimson, pink, orange, yellow, violet, rose, white, etc. An interesting characteristic of the New Zebra Zinnia is a tendency shown by some of the plants, to throw out a branch on which the flowers are self-colored, while all the other blooms are variegated or striped, making a striking and unique contrast. Packet, 10 cents.

## NEW GIANT MIMULUS

**MIMULUS, New Giant.**—This magnificent strain of Mimulus is unequaled for beauty, and size of its large and variously colored flowers, some beautifully spotted, and others richly blotched with rose, carmine, crimson, etc. These plants have beautiful specimens for pot culture, and although the seed is small it is not difficult to grow. Sure to please all my customers. Packet, 10 cents.

## "GIANT" LARKSPUR

**"GIANT" LARKSPUR.**—I here offer a much improved type of these well-known free-blooming garden favorites. The flowers are much larger than the old varieties, and the mixture I offer contains some beautiful and distinct colors such as rose, red, striped, azure blue, violet, white, flesh, etc. They are very showy for garden culture. Mixed colors. Packet, 10 cents.

**ALYSSUM. Little Gem.**—A new variety, of compact, spreading growth, 3 to 4 inches high. A single plant will cover a circle 10 to 12 inches in diameter. 300 perfect spikes of flowers in full bloom at one time have been counted on one plant. For edgings it has no superior. Packet, 10 cents.

**MIGNONETTE. Giant White Spiral.**—Grows 2 or 3 feet high, perfectly erect, and spikes of bloom have been seen measuring 10 in. Its color is pure snow-white. The grand spikes of bloom can be seen for a long distance, and being so beautiful in form and color, much unlike anything else in cultivation, it attracts the attention of every one. Its fragrance is rich and powerful, and it will produce twice as much bloom as any other variety. Seed can be sown in open ground in April or May, where it will grow rapidly and bloom profusely early in June. Packet, 10 cents.

**DAISY, Longfellow.**—The flowers are of large size, of a beautiful dark rose color and are borne abundantly on long and stiff stalks. Of unusual merit, and deserves to be largely grown. May be easily raised from seed and bad in flower in a few weeks. Packet, 15 cents; 2 Packets, 25 cents.

78

**DWARF SCARLET ZINNIA**

**Zinnia. Nana Compacta Coccinea.**—A very attractive dwarf compact variety, producing its large, double fiery-scarlet flowers in great abundance. Especially suited for edgings, groups and pot culture, and a bed set with them produces a beautiful and most striking effect, being an elegant substitute for Scarlet Geraniums. Packet, 10 cents.

**THE CRUEL PLANT**

**CRUEL PLANT. Physianthus Albens.** A beautiful and rapid growing climber. It bears an immense number of pure white bell-shaped fragrant flowers, and derives its name from the fact that various insects, sucking honey from its sweet blooms, are caught and securely held until death overtakes them. They thrive best in a compost of sandy loam and fibry peat and are more sure of germination if started in hot-bed or a shallow box in the house. Half hardy Perennial. 20 feet. Packet, 15c; 2 Packets, 25c.

**PHLOX ECLIPSE**

**PHLOX DRUMMONDII GRANDIFLORA. Eclipse.** The two great points on which I can recommend this handsome sort, are the large size of the individual flowers and the enormous size of its beautiful heads. When the flowers first open they are of a bright rosy purple, deepening to rich imperial purple or violet. It is a very free bloomer which, with the size of the flowers and richness of coloring, make it a most striking and handsome variety of the ever popular Phlox Drummondii Grandiflora. Packet, 10 cents.

**RICINUS CAMBOGIENSIS.**

**RICINUS CAMBOGIENSIS. The Cambodian Palma Christi.** The most handsome Ricinus ever introduced, which for tropical effects in masses on the lawn, or singly in the garden is highly effective. A vigorous grower, 5 to 6 ft. high, with large palm-like leaves of a bronzy red maroon color, while the stalks are of a the shining ebony black. Packet of 6 seed, 10c.

**CUP & SAUCER CAMPANULA**

**SHIRLEY POPPIES**

**CAMPANULA. Cup and Saucer.**—A new, entirely distinct and exceedingly beautiful variety of Canterbury Bells, and is quite an acquisition to this class of hardy perennials, which are at present receiving a great deal of attention, both at home and abroad. The bell or trumpet of the flower is quite three inches in diameter, presenting the form of a cup and saucer, as shown in illustration above. Colors are blue, rose, lilac and white, and also includes the new striped sorts which are entirely new and distinct and as yet very scarce and expensive. The plants are of strong growth and their beautiful blooms almost completely hide the foliage from view. Packet, 15 cents; 2 packets, 25 cents.

**SHIRLEY POPPY.**—These charming Poppies represent an entirely new strain of the Ranunculus-flowered family. They range in color from pure white, through many shades of pale pink, rose and carmine, ending in the deepest crimson, many delicately edged, blotched, and striped, which add greatly to their loveliness. The form of the flower is most beautiful, generally single or semi-double, and will be found very valuable for table decorations, where its charming colors, shades and markings, cannot fail to attract the attention of all who behold them. The seed I offer has been most carefully saved from a grand collection, embracing only the best colors and forms. Perfectly hardy and flowers the first season from seed. Packet, 10 cents.

"VERBENA ODORATA"
FLOWERS ½ NATURAL SIZE

**NEW DWARF TOM THUMB NASTURTIUM. Cloth of Gold.**—A new distinct and handsome Golden Leaved Nasturtium. The plant is of dwarf habit, forming a handsome pyramid, the deep scarlet flowers intermingled among its compact golden foliage, adding to its beauty. It is a shy bloomer, but if they did not bloom at all, would be desirable, their distinct foliage not being found in any other Nasturtium. Packet, 10 cents.

DOUBLE YELLOW

## VERBENA ODORATA

**VERBENA ODORATA.**—The Verbena as it stands to-day is one of our prettiest garden favorites, its only drawback being that it has no fragrance. In the Odorata this obstacle is overcome, and I now offer a sweet-scented variety, knowing that it will soon become a favorite. The flowers do not grow in clusters like other sorts, but run up into spikes about 3 inches long, which become very fragrant in the evening. Colors. white and pinkish-white. They bloom profusely all summer, are easy to germinate in the open ground, and can be had in flower in a few weeks. Packet, 10 cents; 3 packets, 25 cents.

## LARKSPUR "ZALIL"

**NEW DOUBLE YELLOW LARKSPUR. Zalil.**—A new, distinct and handsome hardy perennial, being the only known yellow-flowering variety of this species in cultivation. Its dark green and finely lacinated leaves cover the lower part of the main stem, each branch of which bears a spike of bloom 8 to 16 inches in length. The flowers are of most lovely and delicate shade of sulphur-yellow, the color of a Marechal Neil Rose, and as they expand almost simultaneously from the base to the summit of the spike, the beauty of this attractive plant is seen to full advantage. Packet, 25 cents.

## SALVIA LACTEA

**SALVIA, COCCINEA LACTEA. A pure white Salvia.**—This is the first pure white ornamental Salvia ever introduced, and is therefore a decided novelty. Like the old specimen Salvia Coccinea Scarlet, it is one of the most handsome summer and autumn flowering plants, bearing its beautiful snow-white flowers in abundance, on long stems 8 to 10 inches long. It is very effective for ribboning or enlivening shrubberies, and particularly desirable for massing on the lawn, where a round or oval bed of this pretty flower alone is at once attractive, but is made more so if edged or centered with the Salvia Coccinea Scarlet, making one mass of white and red on a deep green base, which is strikingly handsome, in fact I know of nothing more attractive than the Salvia. Packet, 15 cents. To those wishing to plant both the Salvia Coccinea, Lactea White and the Splendens Scarlet, I will send 1 packet of each for 20 cents.

1891

WHITE QUEEN ASTER GODETIA "PRINCESS HENRY"

**ASTER, NEW WHITE QUEEN.**—A distinct and decidedly handsome White Aster, resembling in height, form and habit the Victoria race, but is a more profuse bloomer. Habit very dwarf and bushy, only growing about 8 to 10 inches high, each plant bearing from 20 to 30 beautifully formed and exceedingly large and perfect double flowers, almost completely hiding the foliage. For massing, bedding bordering, and more particularly for pot-culture the New White Queen cannot be excelled if equaled. Packet, 15 cents.

**GODETIA. Princess Henry.**—A new and pretty addition to that popular garden favorite, the Godetia. Its distinctness over all others is clearly established by its dwarf, compact habit, and beautiful colorings of its large flowers. They are of a most delicate satiny rose, each petal marked with a broad and shining carmine spot, contrasting beautifully with its rich ground color. I can only say that if every reader of this catalogue knew how beautiful Godetia Princess Henry really is, not one would fail to plant it. Packet. 10 cents.

**CAMELLIA FLOWERED BALSAM**

**BALSAM CAMELLIA FLOWERED Perfection.**—Pink.—Perfectly double. Each plant a beautiful specimen, producing a mass of bloom. The centre of the flower is rich, deep pink, shading to a very bright rosy tinge at the extreme edge. Has to be seen to be appreciated. Packet, 10 cents.

**CRIMSON KING ASTER**

**ASTER, Crimson King.**—A fine Aster for lines or masses of bedding, and borders exceedingly dwarf and compact, producing immense clusters of rich crimson flowers, as many as 40 being counted on a single plant. It also makes a charming Aster for pot culture. Packet, 15 cents.

**STRIPED DAHLIA**

**NEW STRIPED SINGLE DAHLIAS.**—It is impossible to describe the wonderful and striking beauty of the New Striped Single Dahlias. Flowers are very large, measuring from 3 to 4 inches in diameter, beautifully striped and mottled, single plants producing both self-colored, and striped and spotted flowers, which is in itself odd and pleasing. They are easy to cultivate, and begin to bloom much earlier than the double, and ordinary single sorts, coming into bloom early in July and are covered with an abundance of their beautiful large flowers until killed by frost. Packet, 10 cents.

**M. CROSY CANNA**

**NEW DWARF FRENCH CANNAS.**—A new class, introduced by Crosy, of France, not over 3 to 4 feet in height. They resemble but far excel the Gladiolus in brilliancy, ranging through all shades of yellow and orange to the richest crimson, scarlet and vermilion; some are also beautifully striped. Seed sown in the house or hot-bed from Jan. to April will produce flowering plants in July. Mixed varieties. Pkt., 15 cts.

**NEW ORNAMENTAL FOLIAGE BEETS.**—The most effective plant in existence; its leaves producing a wealth of tropical beauty. In England they have been highly appreciated as a decorative plant for years. Leaves have a glistening, varnish-like surface, beautifully ribbed with scarlet and yellow. Packet, 10 cents.

**JAPANESE HOP**

**JAPANESE HOPS, Humulus Japonicus.**—This new annual Hop from Japan is a very ornamental and extremely fast-growing, climbing plant. A most valuable feature of this new variety is that it can be sown in the open ground in spring, and will attain enormous dimensions in a very short time. Excellent for covering verandas. Packet, 10 cents.

81

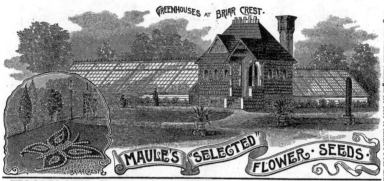

*GREENHOUSES AT BRIAR CREST.*

*MAULE'S "SELECTED" FLOWER SEEDS.*

# ANNUALS

**And others that bloom the first season from seed.**

Under this head I class the true Annuals, that is, flowers that bloom the first year then die. Also Biennials and Perennials that flower freely from seed the first year. **In this list will be found many new varieties, together with the old and well-tried favorites, having been selected with great care, with a view of offering only the most desirable sorts.**

**ABRONIA.**—A charming trailer, with beautiful Verbena-like clusters of sweet-scented flowers; continues in bloom a long time; very effective for rock-work, or hanging-baskets.
—**Umbellata.** Rosy lilac, white eye. Packet 5c.
**ADONIS.**—Also known as Pheasant's Eye. A showy, hardy annual of easy culture, with pretty, fine-cut foliage, and lasting a long time in bloom.
—**Estivalis.** Bright scarlet. 1 foot. 5c
**AGERATUM.**—Valuable plants for large beds or borders, and very useful where cut-flowers are in demand; in bloom the whole summer.
—**Finest Varieties Mixed.** 5c.
**AGROSTEMMA.**—*Rose of Heaven.* Handsome, free-flowering, attractive border plants, at home in any garden.
—**Finest Mixed.** All colors. 5c.
**ALYSSUM.**—Free-flowering, pretty little plants for beds, edgings, or rock-work.
—**Sweet, white, fragrant.** 5c.
**AMARANTHUS.**—Ornamental foliaged plants, extremely graceful and interesting, producing a striking effect, whether grown for conservatory or out-door flower garden.
—**Gibbosus.** Long drooping panicles, 1½ to 2 feet long, color, purplish red.
—**Caudatus.** *Love Lies Bleeding.* Blood red. 5c.
—**Tricolor.** *Joseph's Coat.* Leaves red, yellow, and green. Very attractive. 5c.
—**Mixed.** All varieties. 5c.

**Aster Pæony Perfection Dwarf.**

**AMARANTHUS GIBBOSUS.**

**ASTERS.**—Chrysanthemum Flowered—*(Dwarf).* Fine large double flowers, resembling chrysanthemums, and valuable on account of its profuse flowering when others are done. All colors, mixed. 12 inches. 10c.
—**Cocardeau or Crown.** A very showy variety, centre petals being pure white and outside petals bright colors. All colors, mixed. 1½ ft. 10c.
—**Shakespeare or Dwarf Pompon.** Exquisitely formed small flowers; very dwarf, and continues in bloom a long time. Mixed, all colors. 10c.
—**New Victoria.** Flowers large, and distinguished by an elegant and regular overlapping of the petals. The plants bear from 10 to 20 flowers, with the appearance of an elegant pyramid. Quite distinct. All colors, mixed. 1½ feet. 15c.
—**New Washington.** Without exception the largest Aster in cultivation; flowers frequently measuring 4 to 5 inches in diameter, and of perfect form. All colors, mixed. 2 feet. 10c.
—**Large Rose Flowered.** Pyramidal, robust habit, regularly imbricated; variously-colored, large, very double, brilliant flowers. All colors, mixed. 2 feet. 10c.

**ANTIRRHINUM.**—*Snap Dragon.* Beautiful spikes of gay colored flowers produced the first summer until after frost, also flowering well the second season.
—**Tom Thumb.** Finest dwarf. Mixed. 1 foot. 5c.
—**Majus.** Tall. Mixed. 2 feet. 5c.
**ASTERS.**—Queen Margaret. One of the most popular and effective of our garden favorites, producing in profusion flowers in which richness and variety of colors are combined, with the most perfect and beautiful form. It is indispensable in every garden or pleasure ground where an autumnal display is desired. My seed has been grown by the leading German flower seed growers, and has no superior.
—**Comet.** Quite distinct from other sorts in shape of flowers. Grows from 12 to 15 inches high, and covered with large double flowers 3 to 4 inches across, their long wavy and twisted petals forming a loose yet dense half globe, resembling a large flowered Japanese Chrysanthemum, each petal a delicate pink margined with white. Packet, 15c.
—**Pæony Perfection Dwarf.** Grows only 11 inches high, of very neat, compact habit, and blooms most profusely. Flowers large, and perfectly double. The colors are peculiarly rich and brilliant. Strongly recommended for planting either in beds or masses. All colors, mixed. 10c.
—**Zirngiebel's Double White.** Finest White Aster in cultivation. The plant is about 18 inches high, of good habit, and covered with large flowers which are of globular form, full and double to the centre, with finely imbricated petals. 15c.
—**Improved Quilled German.** Finest mixed. 5c.
—**Choice Varieties Mixed.** About 20 sorts. 10c.

*Comet Aster*

CANDYTUFT—WHITE ROCKET.

**ASPERULA.**—A hardy annual with clusters of small sweet-scented flowers, bloom profusely and continuously; a beautiful bouquet flower.
—**Odorata.**—*Sweet Woodruff.* Flowers have a delicious odor when dried that imparts an agreeable perfume to clothes when kept among them. Color of flower white. 8 to 12 inches. Packet, 5c.

**BALSAM.**—*Lady Slippers.* An old and favorite garden flower, producing its gorgeous masses of beautiful, brilliant colored double flowers in the greatest profusion; of easy culture; succeeds in a good, rich soil; also fine for pot culture and conservatory decorations. My strain cannot be equaled.
—**Double Dwarf Mixed.** Very dwarf. 1½ feet. 10c.
—**German Double Mixed.** All colors. Very fine. 10c.

**CACALIA.**—*Tassel Flower.* Very handsome, profuse blooming plants, covered with beautiful tassel-shaped flowers, and of remarkably easy culture. 1½ feet.
—**Fine Mixed.** 5c.

**CALENDULA.**—*Cape Marigold.* Profuse flowering plants, making a fine show in beds or borders.
—**Meteor.** Light golden yellow. 1 foot. 5c.

**CALLIOPSIS.**—Few, if any, annuals are more useful than this; the colors are rich and striking, flowers numerous and beautiful, and produce a fine effect in mixed borders.—**Fine Mixed.** 5c.

**CANDYTUFT.**—A beautiful and useful plant of the earliest culture, for growing in beds or masses, the white varieties are extensively grown by florists for bouquets.
—**White Rocket.** Large trusses. 1 foot. Pkt. 5c.
—**Hybrid Dwarf Mixed.** ½ foot. 10c.

**CANNA.**—*Indian Shot Plant.* Stately and highly ornamental foliage plants; growing from 5 to 10 feet high, and forming a most beautiful object for the lawn or for large circular beds. Some have light green leaves and others of a brownish red color. The flowers are of scarlet and yellow colors and very showy. Soak the seed well in warm water before sowing. Take up the roots before frost and preserve in a warm cellar or room.
—**Mixed, all colors.** 5c.

**CATCHFLY.**—*Silene.* An easy growing, free-flowering plant, producing dense umbels of white, red and rose pink-like blossoms. The plant is covered with a glutinous moisture, from which flies cannot disengage themselves, hence the name Catchfly. After having been once grown, the seed will sow itself in the ground.
—**Choice Mixed.** 5c.

**CELOSIA.**—*Cockscomb.* Most peculiar, and attractive; producing spikes of beautiful feathery flowers.
—**Cristata.** Extra fine, mixed. 5c.

**CHRYSANTHEMUM.**—Showy and effective garden favorites, extensively grown for cut flowers.
—**Coronarium.** Finest double mixed. 5c.

**CONVOLVULUS.**
—**Minor.**—*Dwarf Morning Glory.* Remarkably showy plants, with exceedingly handsome, rich-colored flowers, producing in beds and mixed borders and unusually brilliant effect. 1 foot.
—**Tricolor.** All colors, mixed. 5c.

**CYANUS.**—*Centaurea, Corn Flower or Ragged Sailor.* Ornamental plants for shrubberies and mixed borders, and exceedingly useful where cut flowers are in demand; growing in any common garden soil.
—**Cyanus Minor.** Mixed. 5c.

**DAHLIA.**—Few are aware that Dahlia plants from seed sown in the spring, will bloom beautifully the first summer, and give quite as good, if not better satisfaction than bulbs. I offer seed that, if started under glass and transplanted to the garden in good rich soil the last of May, will give a magnificent display of the brightest colors in August and bloom continuously until cut by frost.
—**Extra Choice Large Flowering.** Double Mixed. Seed saved from largest flowered and most double sorts, embracing all the new varieties. Pkt. 10c.
—**Double Extra Fine Mixed.** Very fine; about twenty varieties. 10c.
—**Superb New Single.** Fine, mixed. Probably no new flower of modern times is more beautiful or brilliant than the new single Dahlia. They begin to flower in July, and continue until October, and in sheltered places as late as November. The seed I offer is saved from large, fine flowers, all the choicest varieties. Pkt., 10c.

**DAISY.**—*Bellis.* A favorite plant for beds or pot culture, or for edging in shady situations. In bloom from April to June. ¼ foot.
—**Double Mixed.** 10c.

**DATURA.**—*Trumpet, or Ghost Flower.* Grows several feet high and branches freely, producing large trumpet-shaped flowers, a foot or more in length.
—**Meteloides Wrightii.** White, bordered with lilac; very fragrant. 5c.

**DIANTHUS.**—*Pinks.* A magnificent genus, embracing some of the most popular flowers in cultivation, producing a great variety of brilliant colors and profusion of bloom.
—**Chinensis.** *China, or Indian Pink.* Finest double mixed. 5c.
—**Heddewigii.** Flore Pleno. *Double Japan Pink.* Seed saved from the best double flowers only. Fine collection of colors. 10c.
—**Imperialis.** fl. pl. *Double Imperial Pink.* Fine mixture of all colors. 5c.
—**Diadematus.** fl. pl. *Diadem Pink.* True, fine extra double mixed. My strain of this beautiful pink is unrivaled in size of flowers and variety of colors. 10c.

**ESCHSCHOLTZIA.**—*California Poppy.* Very attractive plants for beds, edgings, or masses; profuse flowering and fine cut foliage, in bloom from June till frost. 1 ft.
—**Mixed, all Colors.** 5c.

**EUPHORBIA.**—*Snow on the Mountain.* A showy border plant, with foliage veined and margined with white; very attractive.
—**Variegata.** 5c.

**EVENING PRIMROSE.**—*Œnothera. Sundrops.* These splendid plants are of the easiest culture and deserve a place in every collection. The flowers open in the latter part of the day, making a most brilliant display during the evening and early morning.
—**Fine Mixed.** 5c.

**FEVERFEW.**—*Matricaria Eximia.* Free flowering plants, succeeding in any garden soil. A fine bedding plant or for pot culture; blooms until frost.
—**Double White.** 5c.

**GAILLARDIA.**—Showy and admirable perennials, flowering the first year, and among the gayest ornaments of summer flowering beds. Choice mixed. 5c.

**GODETIA.** Beautiful garden plants, of easy cultivation in any good garden soil, and remarkable for the delicacy of their very fine, large blossoms.
—**Lady Satin Rose.** Deep rose pink, the surface shining like satin. 5c.
—**Extra Fine Mixed.** 5c.

**GOLDEN FEATHER.**—*Pyrethrum Aureum.* Golden yellow foliage, very ornamental for ribbon gardening or borders. 6 in. 10c.

**ICE PLANT.**—*Mesembryanthemum crystallinum.* A pretty little trailer for baskets or massing. ½ foot.
—**White. Very effective.** 5c.

**LARKSPUR.**—Pretty blooming plants, flowers being noted for profusion and duration. Thrives in a deep rich soil. 1½ feet.

ESCHSCHOLTZIA.

LOBELIA.

—**Finest Mixed Varieties.**—*Scarlet Flax.* One of the most effective and showy bedding plants, of long duration having fine foliage and delicate stems.
—**Grandiflorum Coccineum.** Scarlet. 5c.

**LOBELIA.**—Charming little plants, of great value and importance to the flower garden and hanging basket.
—**Fancy Varieties Mixed.** Packet, 5c.

**MARVEL OF PERU.**—The well-known Four O'Clock. Beautiful summer-blooming plants; producing large azalea-like flowers, white, yellow, crimson, striped, etc. The roots may be preserved through the winter. 2 feet.
—**Hybrid Fine Mixed.** Mixture of many sorts. All the most desirable varieties in a single packet. 5c.

LARKSPUR.

CELOSIA CRISTATA.

CYANUS MINOR.

DIANTHUS HEDDEWIGII FLORE PLENO.

MARVEL OF PERU.

**MARIGOLD.**—*Tagetes.* Well-known, free-flowering plants, with handsome double flowers of rich and beautiful colors. The African, the tallest, is also the most striking in large beds, mixed flower, and shrubbery borders. The dwarf French is used as foreground to taller plants and makes splendid compact edgings to beds or borders.

—**Eldorado.** Large, bushy plants of brilliant colors, many single plants having from 75 to 100 flowers in full bloom at one time. The colors run through all shades of yellow, from very light primrose to the deepest orange. 5c.

—**New French Compact Gold Striped.** Very compact, and dwarf in growth, attaining a height of only 6 to 8 inches. It forms a veritable bouquet, as each plant is thickly studded with large, handsome flowers, generally striped regularly with chestnut brown on a bright yellow ground. 5c.

**MIGNONETTE.**—*Reseda Odorata.* A well-known, fragrant favorite; fine for pot or garden culture, and can be had during the whole year by sowing at intervals.

—**Parson's New White.** Large spikes, pure white, very fragrant. 5c.

—**Golden Queen.** A very attractive and quite distinct variety, spikes bright golden yellow, very fragrant. 5c.

—**Sweet Scented.** Small spikes. 5c.

—**Machet.** A variety of very dwarf, vigorous growth with massive spikes of deliciously scented red flowers; the best of all sorts for pots. 10c.

**MIMOSA.**—*Sensitive Plant.* A curious plant, so called because the leaves close and droop when touched.

—**Sensitiva.** Pinked white flowers. 5c.

**MIMULUS.**—*Monkey Flower.* Showy, profuse-flowering plants, comprising numerous varieties with white, sulphur and yellow grounds, spotted with crimson, scarlet and pink; fine for the greenhouse, or moist, shady situations.

—**Mixed Varieties.** All colors and markings. 10c.

**MYOSOTIS.**—*Forget-me-not.* Neat and beautiful little plants, with star-like flowers, succeeding best in shady, moist situations.

—**Palustris.** True blue, white and yellow eyes. 5c

ATOMARIA ATRO CŒRULEA.

**NEW NEMOPHILA**

NASTURTIUM—TOM THUMB—LADY BIRD.

**PANSY—Azure Blue.** Beautiful light blue. 10c.

—**Bronze Colored.** A rich bright bronze shade. 5c.

—**Extra Fine Mixed.**—All the popular costly European varieties. 15c.

—**Choice Mixed.** A very superior mixture. 10c.

**PETUNIA.**—For outdoor decoration or house culture few plants are equal to this class. They commence flowering early, and continue a mass of bloom throughout the whole season, until killed by frost. Easily cultivated, requiring rich soil and a sunny situation. Some varieties are of a trailing habit.

—**Inimitable Nana Compacta.** Beautifully blotched and striped; dwarf, ⅓ foot. 10c.

—**Single Fringed Varieties.** Superb mixture. 10c.

—**Single Large Flowered.** Superb mixture. 10c.

—**Belle Etoile.** Beautiful large-flowered strain of striped and blotched Petunias of the most symmetrical shape and form, sure to please. 15c.

—**New Hybrids Mixed.** Fine. 5c.

—**Double Large Flowering.** For the most perfect strain ever offered. *See page.*

**PHLOX DRUMMONDII.**—Remarkable for the brilliancy and abundance of their large flowers, completely hiding the foliage. The blossoms are of many colors, from pure white to deepest purple, eyed and striped. For masses or separate colors and for cutting for bouquets they are unsurpassed.

—**New Dwarf Phlox. Fireball.** Brilliant scarlet. 8 inches. 10c.

—**New Dwarf Phlox. Snowball.** Pure white. 8 inches. 10c.

—**New Dwarf Phlox. Superb Mixture,** all shades, colors and markings. 6 to 8 inches. 10c.

—**Grandiflora Mixed.** Best varieties in superb mixture. 10c.

—**Splendid Mixed.** Very fine mixture. 10c.

**POPPY.**—A showy and easily cultivated hardy annual; with large brilliant colored flowers, growing freely in any garden soil, and producing a fine effect in large clumps or mixed beds. 2 feet.

—**Fairy Blush.**—Petals beautifully fringed, pure white, tipped with rosy cream, shaded at the base with a light lemon color. Flowers very double, and immense size, some measuring from 10 to 12 inches in circumference. Quite distinct. 10c.

—**Crimson King.** Large double flowers, intense crimson. 5c.

—**Carnation.** Double mixed, very fine, large double sorts. 5c.

**PORTULACA.**—A favorite for beds, edgings, rock-work, etc. Thrives best in a rather rich, light loam, or sandy soil. ½ foot.

—**Large Flowered Mixed.** All colors. 5c.

—**Grandiflora. Fl. pl. Double Flowering Portulaca.** Colors of most brilliant shades. Seed saved from perfect double flowers. 10c.

**RICINUS.**—*Castor Oil Bean.* A tree-like plant, effective at points where plants of stately growth are desirable. 6 to 10 feet.

—**Fine Mixed.** 5c.

**SALPIGLOSSIS.**—An Autumn bloomer, effective in beds and borders. Succeeds best in light rich soil. 1½ ft.

—**Hybrid Mixed.** 5c.

—**Very fine.** 5c.

PETUNIA—INIMITABLE NANA COMPACTA.

**NASTURTIUM.**—*Tom Thumb Varieties.* The dwarf varieties are all desirable, and are among our most popular plants, standing any amount of heat and drought, growing vigorously and flowering freely all summer and fall. Excellent for massing and ribboning, doing well even in poor soil. 1 foot.

—**Tom Thumb Pearl.** Light cream color, the nearest approach to a white Nasturtium yet obtained, quite odd and beautiful. 10c.

—**Tom Thumb—Lady Bird.** Rich golden with a flame of ruby crimson on each petal, very attractive. 10c.

—**Tom Thumb—Ruby King.** Pink shaded with carmine. Very rich and attractive. 5c.

—**Tom Thumb—Spotted.** Bright spotted flowers. A most handsome sort. 5c.

—**Tom Thumb—King Theodore.** Dark green foliage; flowers almost black. 5c.

—**Tom Thumb—Golden King.** Deep yellow. 5c.

—**Tom Thumb—Finest Mixed.** 5c.

**NEMOPHILA.**—*Love Grove.* Of neat, compact habit; blooms freely all Summer if planted in a rather cool, shaded place, and not too rich a soil. 1 foot.

—**Fine Mixed.** All colors. 5c.

—**Atomaria Atro Cerulea.**—It has a compact, spreading growth, and is of a rich, deep hue of blue, in fact, no colored illustration could do justice to its shade of color, a hue of glorious blue wanted in flower gardens and which is so in way impaired by the presence of a beautiful zone of black-purple round the small white centre. 5c.

**NIGELLA.**—*Love in a Mist, or Devil in a Bush.* A compact, free-flowering plant with finely cut foliage, curious looking flowers and seed-pods; of easy-culture, growing in any garden soil. 1 foot.

—**Damescena Mixed.** Blue and white flowers. 5c.

**PANSY.**—*Viola Tricolor Maxima.* This attractive plant is too well-known to need any description, as it is a favorite with all. My strain is unrivaled.

—**Snowflake.** Satiny white, quite distinct. 1 15c.

—**Lord Beaconsfield.** Large flowers of deep purple-violet, shading off in the top petals only, to a white hue. Attractive and beautiful. 10c.

—**Emperor William.** Brilliant ultramarine color, with a purple-violet eye. 10c.

—**Belgian Striped or Variegated.** 10c.

—**Faust or King of the Blacks.** Black. 10c.

—**Pure White.** Very striking. 10c.

—**Violet.** Margined with white. 10c.

—**Mahogany Colored.** Desirable variety. 10c.

—**Golden Yellow.** Very remarkable. 10c.

—**Gold Margined.** Dark shade, yellow edge. 10c.

—**Black Blue.** Another beautiful blue. 10c.

—**Brown Red.** Handsome, desirable. 10c.

SALPIGLOSSIS.

POPPY—FAIRY BLUSH.

A BED OF PHLOX DRUMMONDII-GRANDIFLORA, MIXED.

84

STOCKS—GERMAN—TEN WEEKS.

SALVIA COCCINEA SPLENDENS SCARLET.

# PERENNIALS.

In the following will be found Biennials and Perennials, which live over Winter and flower in the following Spring and Summer. Seed can be sown in Spring or early Autumn; in the latter case the beds should be shaded and watered until the plants appear.
**ACONITUM.**—*Monk's Hood.* A hardy perennial, producing in abundance its curiously-shaped flowers, succeed in any good garden soil.
—**Napellus.** White and blue flowers 3 feet. 5c.
**ALYSSUM.**—*Gold Dust.* Alyssum Compactum, popularly known as Gold Dust, is well adapted for rockwork; it is compact habit, with golden yellow flowers in masses.
—**Saxatile Compactum.** 5c.
**AQUILEGIA.**—*Double Columbine.* This plant produces beautiful, curiously formed and variously colored flowers, blooms freely early in the Spring.
—**Finest Double Mixed.** All sorts and shades. 5c.
**CAMPANULA.**—*Canterbury Bells.* Beautiful, large bell-shaped flowers; effective plants for the border or pot culture.
—**Medium.** Splendid mixed. Single and double varieties. 5c.
**CARNATIONS AND PICOTEES.**—Well known to all. The seed I offer has been imported from the best European growers, and will produce many splendid varieties in double and semi-double flowers. All sorts and colors mixed, including many new sorts and handsome colors. 10c.
**CHAMÆPEUCE.**—*Ivory Thistle.* A beautiful perennial thistle, and quite an ornament for garden decoration, the midrib and spines are ivory white, the leaves green, shaded by a snowy down. 2 feet.
—**Diacantha.** True Ivory Thistle. 5c.
**DIGITALIS.**—*Foxglove.* Especially useful among shrubbery and half shady places. Long racemes of beautiful flowers. 3 feet.
—**Gloxinoides.** Mixed. All shades and markings. 5c.
**GLADIOLUS.**—Beautiful summer and autumn flowering plants, producing long spikes of pretty flowers, marked, striped, blotched and shaded in various colors, half hardy perennial bulbs.
—**Lemoini Hybrids, Mixed.** New types with large round, open bell-shaped flowers, colors new and strikingly beautiful. 15c.
—**Finest Mixed Hybrids.** All shades and colors. 10c.
**HOLLYHOCK.**—This splendid plant now ranks with the Dahlia for Summer decoration and, from its stately growth and the varied colors of its magnificent large spikes of flowers, may justly claim a place in every garden or pleasure ground. Seed sown in July will flower the following Spring. Hardy.
—**Double Fine Mixed.** All colors. 10c.
**PHLOX PERENNIAL.** The varieties of Perennial Phlox are among the choicest of our flowers for bedding and border plants. They are perfectly hardy, and need no protection; will flourish in any soil, succeeding better, however, in deep, rich, moist ground.
—**Fine Mixed.** 8c.
**PRIMULA.**—Favorite early free flowering plants, should be extensively grown for filling the beds and borders of the Spring-flower-garden; succeed best in rich soil.—**Elatior.** *Cowslip.* Fine mixed. 5c.

NEW SILVER LEAVED SUNFLOWER.

**PRIMULA**—**Auricula.** The Auricula is a beautiful hardy Primrose blooming early in Spring, and often in Summer. The colors are exceedingly odd and beautiful. 15c.
**SWEET WILLIAM.**—*Dianthus Barbatus.* A well-known free-flowering plant, which has been greatly improved of late years, producing a splendid effect in beds and shrubbery with their rich and varied flowers.
—**Auricula Flowered Perfection.** A handsome class of single varieties in many striking shades each flower having a clearly defined eye, mixed. 10c.
—**Fine Double Mixed.** All colors, splendid strain. 10c.
—**Single Finest Mixed.** 5c.
**TRITOMA.**—*Red Hot Poker.* Flowers grow upon spikes 3 feet long, used in beds or masses.
—**Uvaria.** Varies from yellow to scarlet. 5c.
**VALERIANA.**—*Hardy Heliotrope.* Showy border plants, or for mixing in shrubbery, producing large corymbs of beautiful flowers, which are very desirable for bouquets, or floral decoration. 2 feet.
—**Mixed.** Rose, red and white. 5c.
**VIOLA.**—*Violet.* The popular sweet Violet, flowers very early in the Spring and can be grown easily from seed.
—**Fine Mixed.** 10c.
**WALLFLOWER.**—Massive spikes of fragrant flowers. Ornamental in forming groups, etc.
—**Double Mixed.** 12 colors. 10c.

VIOLA.

AQUILEGIA.

DIGITALIS GLOXINOIDES.

SWEET WILLIAM.

DOUBLE HOLLYHOCKS.

DOUBLE WALLFLOWER.

Page 85—Annual Catalogue for 1891 of Manie's Four-Leaf Clover GUARANTEED SEEDS. Address all Orders to WM. HENRY MAULE, No. 711 Filbert St., Philadelphia, Pa.

85

# EVERLASTINGS

The Everlasting Flowers are justly very popular, not only for their Summer display in the garden, but will retain their beauty for years if cut as soon as they come into full bloom, tied in small bunches, and dried slowly in the shade, with the heads downward to keep the stems straight.

**ACROCLINIUM.**—A beautiful class of everlasting flowers; graceful border plants and valuable for winter bouquets and decorations.
—**Roseum Flore Pleno.** New double rose colored variety, habit tall and branching, flowers large, the best sort yet introduced. 10c.
—**Finest Mixed.** Rose and white. 5c.
**AMMOBIUM.**—A pretty and useful little white flower for making bouquets, summer or winter. Grow about 18 inches high, stiff and angular in appearance, very hardy.
—**Alatum Grandiflorum.** The largest flowering sort, flowers pure white. 5c.
**GLOBE AMARANTHUS.**—Bachelor's Button. A species of Cockscomb, with

XERANTHEMUM.

GLOBE AMARANTHUS.

good-sized blossoms, perfectly round. Start in frame or pot if possible, and transplant to open ground.
—**All Colors Mixed.** 5c.
**HELICHRYSUM.**—Large, full, double flowers, of various colors, from bright yellow to scarlet, shaded and tipped. Peculiarly desirable as dried specimens; exceedingly handsome bouquets may be formed of them for Winter.
—**Dwarf Double Mixed.** All colors. 5c.
—**Tall Double Mixed.** Various shades. 5c.
**RHODANTHE.**—Some care is necessary in starting seeds of the Rhodanthe, but you will be rewarded for your care with an abundance of pretty bell-shaped flowers, which for making up into bouquets in Winter are indispensable. Select light rich soil in a warm and sheltered situation.
—**Finest Mixed.** 10c.
**XERANTHEMUM.**—These are very beautiful, everlasting flowers, highly prized for Winter bouquets.
—**Fine Mixed.** Large double globe-shaped flowers. All colors. 5c.
**EVERLASTINGS.** Finest mixed. All the leading varieties in a single packet. 5c.

RHODANTHE.

## ORNAMENTAL GRASSES

Lovers of Everlastings and those who grow them for Winter decoration, will need a few of the grasses to work up with them, giving a pleasing relief to the brilliancy of their showy companions. Should be gathered when in full bloom, and hung up in a dark, dry place with heads downward to dry.

**AGROSTIS NEBULOSA.**—The most beautiful; fine and feathery. 10c.
**BRIZA MAXIMA.**—Quaking Grass. Large racemes of beautiful, rattling indispensable as a bouquet or design grass. 5c.
**COIX LACHRYMA.**—Job's Tears. 5c.
**ERIANTHUS RAVENNÆ.**—Exquisite white plumes, similar to pampas grass. Unexcelled for designing. 10c.
**EULALIA JAPONICA.**—Striped leaves, very beautiful. 10c.
**GYNERIUM ARGENTEUM.**—Pampas Grass. Magnificent silvery plumes. 10c.
**HORDEUM JUBATUM.**—Squirrel Tail Grass. Fine for bouquets. 5c.
**STIPA PENNATA.**—Feather Grass. Very ornamental. 5c.
**ORNAMENTAL GRASSES.** Finest Mixed. All the above and others in mixture. 10c.

HELICHRYSUM—DWARF DOUBLE.

COIX LACHRYMA.

GYNERIUM ARGENTEUM.

BRIZA MAXIMA.

## ❋ ORNAMENTAL CLIMBERS ❋

One of the most interesting and useful class of garden plants, and this list I believe embraces the most popular and satisfactory varieties. Many a relic, tree-stump, or veranda, otherwise unattractive, can be made beautiful by planting them.
**AMPELOPSIS.**—Japanese Ivy, or Miniature Virginia Creeper. An introduction from Japan which has proven entirely hardy. It grows as rapidly as the old Virginia Creeper, and attains a height of fifty feet. It clings firmly to any wall, tree, etc. The leaves are small on young plants, which at first are of an olive green brown color, changing to bright scarlet in the Autumn.
—Veitchi. 10c.
**ARISTOLOCHIA.**—Dutchman's Pipe. A rapid growing climber with large heart-shaped foliage, and very curious flowers resembling a pipe. 20 feet.
—Sipho. Brownish purple. 10c.
**BALLOON VINE.**—Cardiospermum. A rapid growing, handsome climber, with inflated membranous capsules, from which it derives its name.
—White. 16 feet. 5c.
**CANARY BIRD FLOWER.**—A very attractive, creeper, bearing a neat yellow flower, beautifully fringed. 10 feet. 10c.
**CLEMATIS.**—Rapid growing climbers, fine for arbors and verandas. Soak the seed in water for 24 hours before sowing.
—Flag Mixed. 10c.
**COBÆA.**—A rapid growing climber, bearing an abundance of large bell-shaped flowers. 10c.

—**Scandens.** Rich purple. 13 feet 10c.
**COCCINEA.**—A handsome climber of the Gourd species, with dark, glossy green foliage, snow-white bell-shaped flowers, bearing fruits about 2 inches long which turn to a brilliant carmine. Start seed early in frame or in the house. 10 feet.
—Indica. 10c.
**CONVOLVULUS.**—Morning Glory. A well-known and beautiful free flowering class of climbers, with brilliant and varied colored flowers, growing in almost any situation.
—Major. Very fine mixed. 5c.
**DOLICHOS.**—Hyacinth Bean. A French Hyacinth Bean, with beautiful clusters of purple and white flowers. 15 feet.
—Fine Mixed. 5c.
**GOURD ORNAMENTAL.**—A very useful and ornamental class of rapid-growing climbers. The fruit is of various shapes and colors, some very large and others very small. All are hard-shelled and will keep for years, never decaying.
—Small Varieties Mixed. All sorts. 5c.
—Large Varieties Mixed. All sorts. 5c.
**IPOMEA.**—Cypress Vine. Fern-like foliage and scarlet flowers decidedly beautiful. 15 feet.
—Quamoclit. Bright Scarlet. 5c.
**LOPHOSPERMUM.**—A beautiful climber, with showy flowers of large size, resembling foxglove; foliage soft, velvety texture, shaded with bronze.
—Scandens. Rosy purple. 10c.
**MAURANDIA.**—A beautiful climbing plant for conservatory or trellis-work.
—Finest Mixed Varieties. 10c.
**MOMORDICA.**—Commonly known as Balsam Apple. No

trailing plant can surpass this in striking beauty of fruit and foliage. 12 feet.
—**Balsamina.**—Balsam Apple. Apple-shaped fruit. 5c.
—**Charantia.**—Balsam Pear. Pear-shaped fruit. 5c.
**NASTURTIUM MAJUS.**—Tall Tropæolum. Admirably adapted for rock-work, banks, covering trellises; or rustic-work. 10 feet.
—Spitfire. Brilliant scarlet, very showy. 10c.
—Choice Tall Mixed. 10c.
**SWEET PEAS.**—Lathyrus Odoratus. Beautiful fragrant free flowering plants, thriving in any open situation; blooming all Summer and Autumn if the flowers are cut freely, and the pods picked off as they appear. 6 feet.
—Fine Mixed. All colors shades and markings. 5c. For a select list of beautiful new and rare Sweet Peas—see novelties.
**THUNBERGIA.**—Black Eyed Susan. An ornamental, rapid growing climber. The flowers are very pretty, and are borne profusely during the season. Fine for vases, rustic work or greenhouse decoration. Delights in a light, rich soil. 6 feet.
—Fine Mixed. White, buff and orange. 5c.

REMEMBER THAT FOR $1.00 YOU CAN SELECT FLOWER SEEDS IN PACKETS TO THE AMOUNT OF $1.30; $2.00 TO THE AMOUNT OF $2.75; $3.00 BUYS SEEDS TO THE AMOUNT OF $4.25, ETC.

COBÆA SCANDENS.

BALLOON VINE.

LOPHOSPERMUM—SCANDENS.

SEEDS. Address all Orders to WM. HENRY MAULE, No. 1711 Filbert Street, Philadelphia, Pa., U. S. A.

# CHOICE SELECT SEEDS

## FOR GREENHOUSE and WINDOW-CULTURE

In the following will be found seeds of plants that are adapted to house-culture, and while it requires careful treatment to grow them successfully, it is an interesting study to watch, day by-day, the development of these rare and beautiful plants.

**ABUTILON.**—*Chinese Bell Flower.* Beautiful green-house shrubs of strong growth, and easy cultivation; free flowering, with pretty drooping bell-shaped flowers of various colors, well adapted for Summer flowering in the garden, where they bloom profusely, many having hand some variegated foliage which are quite attractive.
—Choice Hybrids Mixed. 25c.

**AZALEA.**—Charming free flowering shrubby plants, covered with a mass of bloom, thrives best in a mixture of rich loam and sand.
—Indica. Finest mixed varieties. 25c.

**BEGONIA.**—Plant of great value for Summer decoration or window gardening. To secure the best results they should be planted as soon as the ground becomes warm. They are covered the whole Summer with bright and elegant drooping flowers; blooming the first season from seed, if sown in February or March, in a temperature of 60 degrees; for Winter or Spring blooming, sow from august to October. Tubers must be kept from frost in dry sand.
—Tuberous-Rooted. Hybrid Fine Mixed. Handsome single and double varieties. 25c.

**CHRYSANTHEMUM.**—Indicum Japonicum. New Japanese variety, flowers of a peculiar form, and a great variety of colors, shades and markings. 10c.

GLOXINIA.

**GLOXINIA.**—A bulbous-rooted plant, producing in great profusion, during the Summer months, its large bell-shaped flowers, of the richest and most beautiful variety of brilliant colors.
—Choicest Mixed. From finest erect and drooping varieties. 25c.

**HELIOTROPE.**—A half-hardy perennial, flowering during the whole season; its delightful perfume makes it a most desirable bouquet flower.
—Choice Mixed. Many shades. 10c.

**LANTANA.**—Strikingly handsome, producing heads of various colors and changing hues; for pot culture or bedding. 2 to 5 feet.
—Finest Hybrids Mixed. 10c.

**LEMON VERBENA.** Aloysia Citriodora. A green-house deciduous shrub with a very fine perfume and graceful habit, is easily grown from seed, and there is nothing more desirable than its fragrant foliage for making up with bouquets. 10c.

**LINARIA.**—Kenilworth Ivy. A charming, small neat, hardy perennial trailing plant, suitable for baskets, vases, pots and rock-work.
—Cymbalaria. Lavender and purple. 10c.

**OXALIS.**—Popular and attractive; good effect in baskets or rock-work. ½ foot.
—Rosea and Valdiviana Mixed. Pink and yellow. 10c.

**PASSIFLORA.**—Passion Flower. A highly interesting climber, bearing beautiful flowers.
—Cœrulea. Flowers deep blue; very hardy. 10c.

**PRIMULA.**—Chinese Primrose. Most splendid Winter blooming plants; specially adapted to house culture.
—Fimbriata Mixed. Splendid fringed varieties. 35c.

**SMILAX.**—Popular greenhouse climber, leaves deep glossy green; flowers white and fragrant. 10c.

**TORENIA.**—A very fine, new, distinct, tender, annual, a splendid pot plant for vases, hanging-baskets, or for growing out-of-doors.
—Fournieri. Sky-blue flowers, yellow centre. 10c.

CINERARIA—FINEST MIXED LARGE—FLOWERING.

**CALCEOLARIA.**—Highly ornamental, both for conservatory and garden; producing a mass of beautiful pocket-like flowers early in the spring.
—Hybrida Fine Mixed. Superb strain. 35c.

**CENTAUREA.**—*Dusty Miller.* Fine for bedding, vases, hanging-baskets and pots; also extensively used for margins.
—Gymnocarpa. Graceful silver foliage. 10c.
—Candidissimi. Splendid silvery broad leaves. 10c.

**CINERARIA.**—*Cape Asters.* A favorite, attractive, free-flowering plant, blooming during the winter and spring months.
—Finest Mixed. Large flowering varieties. 25c.

**COLEUS.**—A very universal favorite in foliage decorations.
—Fine Mixed. Excellent strain. 25c.

**CYCLAMEN.**—Charming bulbous-rooted plants, with beautiful foliage, and rich colored orchid-like fragrant flowers; favorites for Winter and Spring blooming.
—Persicum. Choice Mixed. Splendid strain. 35c.

**FUCHSIA.**—*Lady's Ear Drop.* A well-known popular greenhouse plant, of easy culture for the house or shady situations in the garden.
—Choice Mixed Hybrids. 25c.

CALCEOLARIA HYBRIDA—FINE MIXED.

**FERNS.**—A well-known and useful ornamental plant for window decoration, baskets, vases, etc.; and shady positions in the garden during the Summer. Seed is slow to germinate and requires some care and attention. Sow in Spring in boxes, with a light covering of soil, keep moist with a covering of fine moss. Thrive best in a peaty and sandy soil.
—Choicest Mixed. A fine collection. 25c.

**GERANIUM.** *Pelargonium.* These well-known garden favorites are as indispensable for in-doors as for out-of-door decoration, and should be extensively cultivated.
—Finest Varieties Mixed. 25c.

**A WILD-FLOWER GARDEN.**—For a number of years past it has been my custom to offer a mixture of flower seeds, which I thing I have appropriately named "A Wild-Flower Garden," containing as it does from 200 to 250 varieties of Annuals, Perennials Everlastings, Ornamental Grasses and Choice Greenhouse Seeds, in one grand mixture. I have received, many flattering testimonials, of the wonderful beauty and most pleasing results obtained from this superb mixture, in fact it is a difficult matter to describe what an endless variety of beautiful flowers can be obtained from my Wild Flower Garden Mixture, which on account of the various seasons of bloom, insures something new every day. Pkt. 10c.; 3 pkts. 25c.; oz. 35c.

PRIMULA—FIMBRIATA.

PASSIFLORA CÆRULEA.

# Summer Flowering Bulbs

### ▲ My Colored Plate Specialties No. 5 ▲

**TIGRIDIAS, Shell Flowers.** Are very easily cultivated, and always sure to bloom in any situation; their large and handsome flowers resembling some of the peculiarly marked tropical shells being greatly admired. I know of no flowering bulb that arouses more interest or pleasure than the Tigridias.

**Grandiflora Red, (No. 1.)** Large glowing crimson, centre variegated with yellow. A handsome sort, and deserves to be largely cultivated.

**Conchiflora Yellow, (No. 2.)** Yellow, spotted crimson.

**Alba White, (No. 3.)** Flowers large pure white, spotted crimson.

**ALL THE ABOVE** 10 cts. each, 3 for 25 cts.; 7 for 50 cts.; per doz., 75 cts. I will send one bulb of each of the 3 colors, for 25 cts., or four of each for 75 cts.

**IRIS KAEMPFERI, (No. 4.)** It is impossible to describe this most handsome species of the beautiful Iris. They are thoroughly hardy and produce their many distinct and showy colored flowers in great profusion, of immense size, some measuring from 7 to 9 inches across. They bloom for a period of from 5 to 7 weeks during June and July, and thrive luxuriantly in a moist situation. Mixed colors, 15 cts. each; 2 for 25 cts.; 5 for 50 cts.; per doz., $1.00.

**CAMASSIA FRASERI, (No. 5.)** A beautiful and vigorous growing bulb, attaining a height of 1 to 3 feet. It bears loose racemes of from twenty to thirty flowers, over two inches across. The color varies from a deep to a pale blue, and is in bloom during the whole summer. It thrives best in a deep rich soil of rather sandy character in a moist situation, but for that matter, will give satisfaction anywhere. A group in flower has a fine effect and is excellent in a cut state, the buds of spikes opening in the house. 15c. each; 4 for 50c.; per doz., $1.25.

**GLADIOLI CERES, (No. 6.)** A most graceful and beautiful Gladioli, producing an enormous spike of handsome flowers of a rich soft pink, shading to an almost pure white on the outer edge of the petals. The individual-blooms are of immense proportions, and is in fact one of the handsomest Gladioli ever introduced. 10 cts. each, 6 for 50 cts.; per doz., 75 cts.

**GLADIOLI BRENCHLEYENSIS, (No. 7.)** This handsome and distinct perfectly hardy Gladioli is without an equal either for size of flowers or its bright and showy colors. The flower stalks are of immense size, while the individual blooms attain most wonderful proportions, the single flower on colored plate giving you some idea of its large size. Its color is also accurately shown, which is a bright cardinal red, with a salmon red centre, lower petals showing a distinct blotch of yellow and a handsome stripe of purplish blue. They are perfectly hardy and will come up from year to year, multiplying to such an enormous extent that from a few bulbs you can secure hundreds in a single year. 10 cts., each; 6 for 50 cts.; per doz., 75 cts.

**CANNA. Ehemanni, (No. 8.)** A most handsome Canna growing about 6 feet high, producing large racemes of bell-shaped flowers, 4 to 5 inches long, drooping like a Fuchsia, and in color a lovely brilliant rosy pink. Its foliage is very striking, reminding one of the luxuriant foliage of the Banana. 15 cts. each. 4 for 50 cts.; $1.25 per doz.

**CANNA. Flaccida, (No. 9.)** An exceeding pretty dwarf Canna only growing about 3 feet high, with large and handsome light green leaves. Its lovely deep canary yellow flowers, spotted and flaked with crimson, are of enormous size, and closely resemble some of the finest Orchids. As a border for a bed of taller sorts has no superior. 15 cts. each; 4 for 50 cts.; $1.25 per doz.

## ONE OF EACH OF THE ABOVE 9 HANDSOME SUMMER FLOWERING BULBS FOR 75 CENTS.

**TUBEROUS-ROOTED BEGONIAS.**—Until a few years ago the wonderful effects the tuberous Begonias produced as a bedding plant were little known, to-day they stand at the head of the list and have deservedly become popular. The dry tubers can be planted at any time when the ground is warm and will produce a wealth of beauty and profusion of bloom all the summer and fall. The flowers embrace many shades and hues, such as Crimson, Pink, White, Yellow, Orange and Scarlet, of enormous size, having measured as high as 4 inches in diameter. The bulbs should be taken up after frost, and kept in a dry, warm place over winter.

**Single Varieties in Mixture,** 15 cts. each; 4 for 50 cts.; per dozen, $1.25.
**Double Varieties in Mixture,** 40 cts. each; 3 for $1.00.

**SUMMER FLOWERING OXALIS.**—For bordering or margining nothing can surpass the Summer Flowering Oxalis. The bulbs when planted about 3 inches apart produce an unbroken row of elegant foliage and pretty flowers, and, as they bloom in a very short time after planting, furnish a neat and attractive border the whole season. No flower is easier grown than the Oxalis and are sure to succeed in all soils and situations. Bulbs planted first of May will flower by the first of June, and produce their beautiful flowers uninterruptedly the whole summer. In the autumn the bulbs can be lifted and stored in a cellar like Gladiolus.

**Dieppi, Pure White.—Lasandria, Fine Rose Pink.** Either sort, 10 cents, per dozen : 25 for 15 cents ; 50 for 25 cents ; 100 for 40 cents.

## Tuberoses

The ever popular Tuberose is so well known, that but little description will be necessary. By many they have been endorsed as the most delicious of all the sweet-scented summer flowering bulbs, and rightly too, for few flowers can equal the Tuberose in fragrance. They produce long spikes of waxy-like pure white flowers, and to those who have never grown this popular favorite would say, in my opinion no flower garden is complete without a few stalks of Tuberoses. My stock of bulbs is very fine this year, will bloom profusely the coming season.

**Excelsior Dwarf Double Pearl.** Do not grow as tall as the Double Italian, but spikes are longer, flowers large, full double and sweet. 8 cents each ; 4 for 25 cents ; 9 for 50 cents ; per dozen, 65 cents.

**Italian or Tall Double.** Spikes 4 feet, flowers not as large or as heavy as the Pearl, but open more perfectly, and a purer white. 8 cents each ; 4 for 25 cents; 9 for 50 cents; per dozen, 65 cents.

**New Variegated Leaved.** Leaves bordered creamy white, flowers single, very large and extremely early, blooming several weeks earlier than other sorts ; very fragrant. 10 cents each ; 3 for 25 cents ; 7 for 50 cents; per dozen, 65 cents.

## Gladiolus

The Gladiolus is one of the most popular and beautiful of the summer flowering bulbs, with tall spikes of flowers, some two feet or more in height. The flowers are of almost every desirable color, blotched and spotted in the most curious manner.

**Lemoine's Hybrid, Half Hardy.** Originated with M. Lemoine of France. For vivid and rich orchid like coloring it has no equal. Very fine mixture, all shades and blotches. 10c. each ; $1 per doz.

**Extra Fine Mixed.** All colors, very choice. 5c. each ; 6 for 25c.; per doz., 40c.

LEMOINE'S HYBRID GLADIOLUS.

EXCELSIOR PEARL TUBEROSES.

88

TIGRIDIAS.
10 CTS. EACH 3 FOR 25 CTS.

IRIS KAEMPFERI.
15 CENTS EACH.

GLADIOLI
10 CENTS EACH OR 6 FOR 50 CTS.

1. TIGRIDIA GRANDIFLORA RED.    4 IRIS KAEMPFERI MIXED COLORS. 7 GLADIOLUS BRENCHLEYENSIS.
2. TIGRIDIA CONCHIFLORA YELLOW. 5 CAMASSIA FRASERI.        8 CANNA EHEMANNI.
3. TIGRIDIA NBA WHITE.

A FEW PHOTO'S
From BRIAR CREST.

W<sup>M</sup> HENRY MAULE,
Philadelphia.

# The Three Gems.

**MILLA BIFLORA.—Mexican Star Flower.**—A most remarkable and handsome summer flowering bulb, succeeding admirably in sunny positions. The flowers are pure waxy-white, with a delicate lemon yellow centre. Each bulb produces from 6 to 8 flowering stalks, the flowers being delightfully fragrant. The cut blooms will last for days in water. 10 cents each; 3 for 25 cents; 7 for 50 cents; 85 cents per doz.

**BESSERA ELEGANS.—Coral Drops.**—Produce unique flower stems about 2 feet high, supporting a dozen or more of beautiful bell-shaped flowers of a rich coral scarlet, with distinct white cup. They bloom shortly after being planted in the open border, oftimes producing a succession of flower stalks, thus blooming until killed by frost. An excellent bouquet flower. 10 cents each; 3 for 25 cents; 7 for 50 cents; 85 cents per doz.

**CYCLOBOTHRA FLAVA.—Golden Shell.**—The habit of this little Golden Gem is truly charming. The flowers are of a rich golden yellow, spotted black and beautifully cupped. The foliage is thin and rush-like. An excellent bouquet flower, lasting a long time in water, in fact a few sprays of each of the Three Gems placed together form a cluster heretofore unseen in the way of flowering bulbs. 10c. each.; 3 for 25c.; 7 for 50c.; doz., 85c.

**APIOS TUBEROSA.—Tuberous Rooted Wistaria.**—A native climber and one of the most beautiful in cultivation. A profuse bloomer, bearing lovely clusters of rich deep purple flowers, with a delicious violet fragrance. It is a wonderfully robust grower, attaining a great height, its vine and dense foliage resembling the common Wistaria. The bulbs are perfectly hardy, needing no protection whatever; they are excellent for food when cooked, being fully equal to a potato. 10 cents each. 3 for 25 cents ; 7 for 50 cents ; 75 cents per doz.

**MONTBRETIAS.**—One of the most desirable and handsome Summer and Autumn blooming bulbs, and are in full glory a month after all the tender plants are killed by frost. Each bulb produces several flower-spikes, some 10 inches long, together with numerous side spikes, making them exceedingly floriferous.

**Crocosmiæflora.**—Has proved entirely hardy, blooms from July until killed by frost. Flowers large, beautifully formed, base of flower bright orange, sprinkled with purple spots. 10 cents each; 3 for 25c.; 7 for 50c.; per doz. 80c.

**Pottsii.**—Flowers bright orange-red of most perfect form and grace, resembling a miniature Gladiolus. 10 cents each, 3 for 25 cts.; 7 for 50 cts.; per doz. 75 cts.

**HYACINTHUS CANDICANS.—The Giant Summer Flowering Cape Hyacinth.**—A new species of Hyacinth. Planted in the Spring, they bloom in August and September. Foliage is extremely effective, resembling the Yucca. Very showy for the centre of a bed, also effective if grown in groups. The flower spikes are from 4 to 5 feet high, bearing from 20 to 30 large bell-shaped, pure white, fragrant blossoms. Strong bulbs produce 2 or 3 and even 4 flower stems during its blooming season. 10c. each; 3 for 25c.; 7 for 50c.; per doz., 75 cents.

**SPIDER LILY. Hymenocallis Caribæa.**—Grandest of evergreen Lilies, bearing many tall flower-spikes, surmounted by 8 to 12 large, white, sweet-scented flowers, blooming for several weeks. They are highly prized by florists for floral designs, on account of their delicacy and delicious odor. The evergreen leaves afford a beautiful ornament during the winter among other plants. They thrive best in a moist situation, and planted out in May will flower in July. Are also desirable for growing in water, placing bulb in a vase or bowl, treating same as the Hyacinth. Also admirably adapted for pot culture, and can be forced into flower in from 6 to 8 weeks' time. Strong Blooming Bulbs, 30c. each; 4 for $1.00.

APIOS TUBEROSUS.

MONTBRETIA CROCOSMIÆFLORA.

SPIDER LILY.

89

**ZEPHYRAN-THUS.**—Zephyr flowers or Fairy Lilies. Habit similar to Amaryllis, easily cultivated, thriving in any good garden soil. Desirable either for open ground or pot culture, producing their handsome, waxy, lily-like flowers freely all Summer. As cut flowers they are unsurpassed, and if placed in a vase in water will remain perfect for days. No lover of flowers should fail to include Zephyranthus in their collection.

**Atamasco.**—Large, beautiful, pure white, waxy-like flowers. 10c. ea.; 3 for 25c.; 90c. per doz.

**Rosea.**—Color clear rosy pink, handsome upright flowers. 15c. each; 4 for 50c.; $1.00 per dozen.

**Sulphurea.**—Fine clear yellow, superb flower. 15c. each; 4 for 50c.; $1.25 per dozen.

**LILIUM AURATUM. The Golden-Rayed Lily of Japan.**—This handsome Lily has deservedly become one of the standard favorites of the flower-garden. Deliciously fragrant, immense blooms, nearly a foot wide when fully expanded, and produced in the greatest profusion, stamps Lilium Auratum as one of the finest. The color and markings of this magnificent Lily surpasses all others; flowers are pure white, spotted with intense chocolate crimson, with a bright golden yellow band running through the centre of each petal. The illustration below is from a photograph of a plant standing about 6 feet high, with over 20 large and perfect flowers fully expanded at one time. My stock of this beautiful Lily this year is better than ever before, and I am prepared to supply my customers with as fine bulbs as can be secured anywhere. Choice, sound bulbs, 25c. each; 5 for $1.10; $2.50 per doz.

*Zephyranthus Atamasco.*

## HAVE YOU noticed those special offers on the back of order sheet?

**THE SPOTTED CALLA LILY. Richardia Alba Maculata.**—This is indeed a magnificent species of the Calla Lily, its glossy dark green leaves dotted with numerous white spots, making its appearance unique. The flowers are pure white with a black centre, and are very beautiful. They grow freely in any ordinary soil either indoors or out. They flower splendidly in the garden, planted in the Spring, and in the fall the bulbs can be dug and kept in the cellar, dry, over winter. As a pot plant, the Spotted Calla Lily is highly recommended. Strong bulbs, 20c. each; 3 for 50c.; 7 for $1.00.

**CALADIUM ESCULENTUM.**—A very effective tropical-like plant suitable either as a single plant on the lawn, masses in beds, or for margins of water. Its very distinct apron-like leaves often attain the length of three feet by twenty inches wide. Bulbs can be stored in dry sand in winter and kept from year to year. Large bulbs, 20c. each; 3 for 50c.; $1.75 per doz.

**FANCY-LEAVED CALADIUMS.**—No plant is more desirable for floral decorations, greenhouse culture or window-boxes than the Fancy-Leaved Caladiums. They produce most elegant large leaves spotted, marked and variegated with white, pink, scarlet, etc. They are among our finest foliage plants, and are always greatly admired. They thrive best in a shady situation, and should be planted in fairly-enriched sandy loam. 30c. each; 4 for $1.00; $2.50 per dozen.

**AMARYLLIS BELLADONNA SPECTABILIS BICOLOR.**—The finest of all the Belladonna Lilies, its handsome and showy flowers being larger than those of the ordinary species. The color of the flowers is white, a delicate carnation at the base, and rose toward the upper part, striped or marbled in bright carmine. The large umbels of this magnificent Amaryllis are beautiful beyond description, a single flower with a little green forming a splendid bouquet. The bulbs thrive best in a light sandy soil, and may be planted rather deep, different from methods observed with other Amaryllis. A strong point in favor of the Amaryllis Belladonna Spectabilis Bicolor is that they are perfectly hardy, needing no protection whatever. I have a good stock of this grand specialty and although the demand will no doubt be enormous, I feel confident that I have enough to meet all orders. 30c. each; 4 for $1.00; $3.00 per doz.

*SPOTTED CALLA LILY.*

*LILIUM AURATUM.*

*CALADIUM ESCULENTUM.*

*AMARYLLIS BELLADONNA SPECTABILIS BICOLOR.*

**Double Tiger Lily**

**IPOMŒA MEXI-CANA.—Tuberous root-ed Morning Glory.—** This beautiful climber has a dark glossy green, clear-cut foliage, somewhat re-sembling a Passion Vine. It forms a root the size of a small Dahlia, which is safely wintered in the cellar and when planted out in the Spring will grow rapidly, and be in flower in a short time. The vine produces its large satiny, violet crimson flowers in clusters, and unlike any of its species, remains open all day long. Good strong bulbs. 20 cents each ; 3 for 50 cents ; 7 for $1.00.

**DOUBLE TIGER LILY.—Tigrinum Flore Pleno.**—This really perfectly double Lily, should be planted in every garden in the land. They are of stately habit, growing from 4 to 6 feet high ; foliage dark green, very long, and bearing an immense number of bright and lovely double orange-red flowers, distinctly spotted with black, accurately shown in illustration. If you have never planted Lilies you should try the Double Tiger Lily ; if you have a collection you should add this one to make it complete. 15 cents each ; 4 for 50 cents ; $1.25 per dozen.

**IPOMŒA MEXICANA.**

**HARDY CYCLA-MEN.**—This handsome species of Cyclamen, has a large and solid bulb that can be planted in a pot of ordinary soil, and will com-mence to bloom almost im-mediately. The flowers which are borne in great profusion, are of monstrous size, and vary in color from pure white to deepest rose and red. The bulbs retain their vitality for years pro-ducing a large number of flowers each succeeding season. In mild localities this Cyclamen is perfectly hardy. Mr. William Rob-inson in the *London Garden* says of this beautiful species: "Nothing can be more agreeable to the lover of hardy plants than en-deavoring to naturalize these charming flowers,

now rarely seen out of the greenhouse. The best position would be among dwarf shrubs, etc., that would afford slight shelter, on banks or sunny spots in copses, or on the rockery in a sunny, warm situation. There is scarcely a country seat in England in which the hardy cyclamens could not be naturalized." I have a fine stock of this handsome Cyclamen, and am prepared to offer them at a very reasonable figure. Good strong bulbs, 25 cents each ; 3 for 60 cents ; 6 for $1.00; $1.75 per dozen.

**MADEIRA, OR MIGNONETTE VINE.**—Also known as Mexican Vine. A beautiful climber, with glossy green leaves and beautiful long racemes of white fragrant flowers, of rapid growth, a few tubers producing vines sufficient to cover one side of a cottage in a single season. Tubers, 8c. each , 4 for 25c.; 65c. per doz.

**LILIUM.—Canadense.**—This is our native bell-shaped Lily, and a very handsome one it is, deserving of a largely increased cultivation. Produces its handsome droop-ing yellow and red flowers on tall erect stems, which are quite handsome and attractive. 15c. each ; 4 for 50c.; $1.25 per doz.

**HARDY CYCLAMEN.**

*Lilium, Canadense.*

**DAHLIA ROOTS** The last two years have brought the Dahlia to the front rank of our Sum-mer Flowering Bulbs, and well they should be there is no flower produces a finer effect for floral decorations, and among florists have become quite popular as a bou-quet flower. Below will be found a select list of new and scarce Double Large flowering sorts, together with the most desirable Pom-pon and Cactus varieties.

Any of these 15 superb Dahlias, 25c. each ; 3 for 65c.; one root of each of the 15 varieties, mak-ing a collection of unsurpassed beauty, $2.75, postpaid.

**LARGE FLOWERING VARIETIES**
**Sunset.** Beautiful yel-low, tipped with crimson.
**Dandy.** Maroon, white-tipped, distinct.
**The Bride.** White-tipped Lilac, very large and handsome.
**Apollyon.** Bright Orange Scarlet, very large and attractive.
**Camelliaflora.** Not so large but perfectly double pure white.
**Golden Crown.** Clear bright yellow.
**Floret.** Hand-some shade of pink.
**Dawn.** Rich cream, perfect bloom.
**Bicolor.** Crimson, striped carmine, fine.
**Modesty.** Beauti-ful shade of lilac, full, large.
**POMPON DAHLIAS.**
**Guiding Star.** Pure white, beautifully shaped petals.
**Little Goldlight.** Hand-some yellow, light and dark shades.
**Maroon Beauty.** Dark velvety maroon, very striking.
**CACTUS DAHLIAS.**
**Constance.** Pure white, very graceful.
**Lord Lyndhurst.** Rich scarlet, shaded maroon.

*Floret Dahlia*

## MAULE'S FLOWERING PLANTS FOR 1891

THE steadily increasing demand for Flowering and Tropical Plants, Orchids, curious Cacti, Small and Ornamental Fruits, etc., has induced me to give more space and attention to this department of my business this season than ever before. You will therefore find the next 20 pages entirely devoted to many new and exceedingly rare plants, quite a number of which are offered this season for the first time. It has been my aim to select only those plants that will give the purchaser the utmost satisfaction, and I know that every one favoring me with an order for plants this year will be more than satisfied with their investment. It will be noticed also, that my prices are very reasonable, considering the quality and size of stock. To my old customers it is unnecessary to say anything in regard to the superior excellence of Maule's Plants, but to the many new readers who will receive my catalogue this year for the first time, I need only say that **Maule's Plants are just as reliable as Maule's Seeds.** More cannot be said, for better seeds than Maule's were never sold, and **stronger, healthier plants than I propose to send my customers the coming season cannot be procured from any one;** at least such has been the verdict of all who have tried them, and I propose this year to increase the good reputation which they now hold in the esteem of all lovers of flowering plant life.

**IPOMŒA PANDURATA, The Hardy Moon Flower.**—This beautiful hardy Ipomœa has proven perfectly hardy as far north as Boston, Mass., and for giving a quick dense shade no other hardy twiner can equal it. Large tubers will make a growth of 25 feet in a single season, and retain their large foliage down to the ground until frost. Although we have called this variety a Moon Flower, it is also by all means a day flower as well, as flowers are open day and night alike. While other vines, such as Wistarias, Bignonia, etc., will not flower until after several years' planting; this from strong tubers will bloom the first year, and such blooms! Imagine from 1,000 to 1,200 flowers, measuring 3¼ to 6 inches across, open on one vine at once; the color being white, shading to pink and purple in the throat, the blooming period extending several months. Prices for sound good size tubers, (not the sl m stems which the vine produces above the tubers which will be offered by some dealers this season, but good, strong bottom tubers). 25 cts. each; 3 for 60 cents.

**CYCAS REVOLUTA, the True Sago Palm.**—Every one who has seen this most magnificent Cycas will admit that no other plant can equal it in grandeur. The numerous leaves produced from the upper part of the stems are used extensively by florists for decoration, and usually sell at $5.00 per pair, and old plants are often sold at $100 to $200 per pair. We have a fine stock of plants, well rooted and established in pots at prices ranging from 75 cts. to $50.00 each; but dry roots we mail at 50c. each. These prices are extremely low.

**ZAMIA INTEGRIFOLIA.**—Similar to the above, with finer foliage, but seldom producing so large a stem, still a very beautiful plant. Price for dry roots reduced to 35 cents each, postpaid.

CYCAS REVOLUTA.

IPOMŒA PANDURATA.

92

I invite your particular attention to the following list of new and rare everblooming Roses. It is a well-known fact that from year to year a large number of new varieties are forced upon the market, many of which are either absolutely worthless or have no distinguishing feature from the old and tried sorts; while this is true, it is also a fact that for many years I have had, now and then, most valuable acquisitions that have stood the test of trial and criticism. In selecting the following list I have aimed at **the cream of newer sorts, which I offer at very low rates, considering their choice character.**

**NEW TEA ROSE, MADAME HOSTE.**—A grand tea rose that will certainly become one of the standard sorts. Color is generally a whitish yellow, with deep buff yellow centre; in cool weather the petals change to a clear ivory white. Every lover of roses is acquainted with the popular Perle des Jardins, and when I state that Mme. Hoste is larger and longer, I feel confident one and all will be anxious to secure it. 25c. ea.; $2.50 doz.

**NEW EVERBLOOMING ROSE, DUCHESS OF ALBANY.**—Also known as the Red La France. I consider this new and handsome rose the grandest introduction for many years, either as a rose for the garden, or to force for cut flowers in winter. The Duchess of Albany is a sport from the well-known La France, and retains all the characteristics of the type, but larger in size, deeper in color and of more wonderful form. The flowers are of a deep even pink, deep enough to warrant its title of Red La France. Very large and full, highly perfumed, and produced in wonderful profusion thrown well up above the foliage upon long and stiff stems. The growth is more robust than the La France, with beautiful light green foliage. 25c. each ; $2.50 doz.

**NEW EVERBLOOMING ROSE, THE GEM.—The Fair Unknown.**—Another handsome rose, blooms of large size, color creamy white, shading to yellow toward the base of the inner petals, the outer petals being occasionally tinged with pink. The gem is a vigorous grower, a profuse bloomer, equally desirable as a pot rose, or in the open ground. 20 cts. each ; $2.00 doz.

**PRINCESS DE SAGAN.**—A new French Rose, noted for its beautiful buds, of the brightest scarlet crimson which can be cut on long stems; flowers medium-sized and fragrant. It is a profuse bloomer, and is sure to gain admirers wherever grown. 20 cents each ; $2.00 doz.

**THE BRIDE.**—The Bride is a pure white rose of large size and most perfect form. The buds are pointed and the ends of the petals are slightly curved back, giving it a most chaste and elegant appearance. A free-flowering rose, either for Summer or Winter. Undoubtedly the finest pure white rose ever introduced. 25 cents each ; $2.50 per dozen.

**AMERICAN BEAUTY.**—This grand rose is a seedling found in the gardens of Mr. Bancroft, the historian, at Washington, D. C., who has, perhaps, the finest collection of roses in this country. American Beauty is a rose of large size, having the ever-blooming qualities of the Tea Rose with the delicious odor of the Damask or Moss Rose, and equally valuable for Winter or Summer flowering. Color a deep brilliant pink, shaded toward centre with rich carmine. 40c. each ; $4 doz.

**CRIMSON EVERBLOOMING ROSE, METEOR.**—A remarkably rich dark velvety crimson rose ; so dark that under certain conditions it is blackish crimson. It is a constant and profuse bloomer, vigorous and healthy growth, with no tendency to mildew. No dark red rose ever before offered will be as useful for Summer cut flowers, being so double that it produces perfect blooms in the hottest weather. 20 cents each ; $2.00 per dozen.

**SOUVENIR DE WOOTTON.**—One of the best monthly roses ever offered, being equally desirable for both Summer and Winter flowering. While a Hybrid Tea Rose, the foliage is of substantial texture, and the grand crimson color, perfectly double, of fine form, and unusually fragrant. Named after Wootton, the summer residence of Mr. George W. Childs, Phila. Pa., 25 cts. each ; $2.50 per doz.

**LUCIOLE.**—A robust grower, and profuse bloomer. The flowers are of large size, full and of good substance, color, bright rose carmine, tinted with yellow. 20 cents each ; $2.00 per dozen.

**MADAME PIERRE GUILLOT.**—A grand rose ; large full globular flowers, with great depth and substance ; color, delicate orange yellow, bordered with fine rosy pink. 30c. each ; $3 per doz.

**ERNEST METZ.**—Fine large full flowers, and beautiful long pointed buds ; color, clear satiny pink. 25 cts. each ; $2.50 per dozen.

**THE QUEEN.**—One of the very best pure white varieties for general planting. A vigorous, healthy grower, and a continuous bloomer. Flowers are large and full. 20 cents each ; $2 per doz.

One strong plant of each of the above 12 handsome Everblooming Roses sent post-paid to any address for $2.25.

PRIMULA OBCONICA.

**PRIMULA OBCONICA.**—A profuse blooming Primrose, bearing on long stems heads containing 10 to 15 flowers. It thrives well in the garden, or in a cool house, and will grow in favor with those desiring plants that will grow easily. The flowers are pure white, shading occasionally to lilac, and have the true Primrose fragrance. It is constantly in bloom and is sometimes called the perpetual blooming Primula. It is in all respects a lovely flower, and as it becomes better known will be appreciated at its true worth. 15c. ea.; 4 for 50c.

**ABUTILON ECLIPSE.**—A new, most beautiful and distinct Abutilon, which is accurately shown in illustration. The leaves are beautifully spotted with golden yellow on a green ground. The flowers are orange yellow, and are produced abundantly. It is an excellent plant for edging foliage beds, and as a basket or vase plant is unsurpassed, while as a specimen in the window or conservatory it has few equals. 20c. each ; 3 for 50c. ; 7 for $1.00.

ABUTILON ECLIPSE.

## POPULAR $1.00 PLANT COLLECTIONS

**I will send any 6 of the following collections for $5, or the whole 10 for $7.50.**

**COLLECTION No. 1.** $1.00 postpaid. Comprises 10 beautiful Begonias, 5 of the best flowering sorts, and 5 Fancy Leaved varieties, each one distinctly labeled, and sent free by mail on receipt of $1.00.

**COLLECTION No. 2.** $1.00 postpaid. Comprises 12 handsome Chrysanthemums, no two alike, each one distinctly labeled, and sent free by mail on receipt of $1.00.

**COLLECTION No. 3.** $1.00 postpaid. Comprises 8 of the prettiest Hardy Climbing Roses, each one distinctly labeled, and sent free by mail on receipt of $1.00.

**COLLECTION No. 4.** $1.00 postpaid. Comprises 15 beautiful Monthly Roses, my selection of the most desirable varieties, each distinctly labeled, and sent free by mail on receipt of $1.00.

**COLLECTION No. 5.** $1.00 postpaid. Comprises 10 Extra Choice Hardy Hybrid Roses, each one distinctly labeled and sent free by mail on receipt of $1.00.

**COLLECTION No. 6.** $1.00 postpaid. Comprises 12 new and rare Plants for house or garden, somewhat of a Surprise Collection, each one distinctly labeled and sent free by mail on receipt of $1.00.

**COLLECTION No. 7.** $1.00 postpaid. Comprises 10 desirable Double Geraniums, each one distinctly labeled and sent free by mail on receipt of $1.00.

**COLLECTION No. 8.** $1.00 postpaid. Comprises 10 beautiful specimens of Hardy Shrubbery, each one distinctly labeled and sent free by mail on receipt of $1.00.

**COLLECTION No. 9.** $1.00 postpaid. Comprises 10 of the most handsome Hardy Climbers, each one distinctly labeled and sent free by mail on receipt of $1.00.

**COLLECTION No. 10.** $1.00 postpaid. Comprises 8 Unique, Fancy-Leaved Geraniums, each one distinctly labeled and sent free by mail for $1.00.

## 9 Handsome Geraniums

**MARCUTEA.**—Remarkable shade of red, blended with maroon and salmon, edged with pink, very large truss, semi-double.

**GOLD FINDER.**—Habit of growth, dwarf and sturdy. Trusses of medium size, bearing large double florets of intense orange scarlet.

**CLIFFORD.**—A valuable sort which is indeed hard to describe. Color a rich dark maroon, with a distinct blending of light purple, shaded with a rich glowing pink, large truss.

**CANDIDISSIMA ALBA PLENA.**—The finest of the double whites; strong, vigorous habit, foliage large and of a deep, rich green, with clearly defined bronze zone in the leaf; flowers pure white, large truss. A good bedder, and for window culture stands without a rival.

**BRUANT. The Giant Geranium.**—This variety can truly be named the Giant Geranium, producing exceptionally large trusses, and borne in immense spherical balls, measuring from 6 to 8 inches in diameter. The leaves are round and neatly zoned, making dense growth, and is without an equal as a bedder. Color of flower a beautiful light vermilion red.

**MARY HILL. Double Pink.**—A fine new pink, semi-double; color a dark shade of pink bordering on red; florets and truss very large and of perfect form.

**S. A. NUTT. Double Scarlet.**—Finest of the double reds; truss very large and full; semi-double; color, deep blood crimson, very free bloomer; in every way desirable.

**GERTRUDE.**—Flowers of a beautiful semi-double form; color, clear bright salmon, centre and outer edges touched with white; shaded carmine; foliage dense, and an excellent bedder.

**NEW VARIEGATED SWEET-SCENTED ROSE GERANIUM, LADY·PLYMOUTH.**—A handsome variegated variety of the sweet-scented Rose Geranium, fragrance same as parent family, leaves bronzy green fringed with creamy white; distinct, beautiful and attractive.

ANY OF THE ABOVE SUPERB GERANIUMS, 20 CENTS EACH; 3 FOR 50 CENTS; $1.75 PER DOZ. ONE PLANT OF EACH SENT POSTPAID TO ANY ADDRESS FOR $1.25.

Geranium Candidissima Alba Plena.

NEW PERPETUAL FLOWERING BEGONIA "DEWDROP."

### THE DEWDROP BEGONIA

I cannot do better than to give the introducer's description of this choice Begonia. "THE DEWDROP BEGONIA is always in bloom, will stand the strong sun during Summer, and it is one of the finest pot plants ever introduced. In the new Begonia Dewdrop we have the best flowering Begonia ever obtained. Its graceful flowers are produced in profusion during the winter months; it can be planted out in the strong sun in the spring, and will be one mass of bloom the entire summer. It will grow and thrive anywhere, and requires no more care than a geranium. It is a dwarf, compact-growing variety; the foliage bright glossy green, with shell-shaped leaves and stems of light crimson. The blooms are produced in clusters of from 6 to 8 florets, which are satiny white with golden-yellow stamens. Planted out in the sun during the summer, the color changes to a delicate shade of pink, with crimson stems, making a beautiful contrast. Unlike other Begonias, it is a profuse bloomer." 20 cts. each; 3 for 50 cts.; 7 for $1.

# Chrysanthemums

**MRS. ALPHEUS HARDY.—The Ostrich Plume Chrysanthemum.** One of the most distinct and handsome Chrysanthemums ever offered. The flowers are pure white, one foot or more in circumference, petals turning gracefully inward, dotted with a peculiar hairy or plumelike growth, the whole resembling a mass of snow white ostrich plumes. The accompanying illustration gives you but a faint idea how really beautiful this Chrysanthemum is, and no one reading this should fail to secure at least one plant, and when in bloom you will behold what it is impossible to describe.

**KIOTO.**—A handsome new incurved variety, flowers of enormous size, with glossy petals, forming into an almost perfect ball of deep chrome yellow ; quite distinct.

**LILIAN BIRD.**—Just think of Chrysanthemum flowers 12 inches in diameter. Such is the characteristics of the Lilian Bird. Beautiful pale flesh color, with long tubular petals of perfect form.

**MRS. CARNEGIE.**—Another very large flowering sort, almost equaling Lilian Bird in size. In color is of the richest deep crimson. This sort was awarded a silver cup valued at $400 by Mrs. Carnegie for the handsomest seedling.

Any of the above handsome Chrysanthemums, 25 cents each, 5 for $1.00 ; $2.00 per doz.

**SPECIAL OFFER.—**I will send one plant of each of the four sorts, free by mail, on receipt of 75 cents.

VIOLET SWANLEY WHITE.

# Two Grand Violets

**SWANLEY WHITE.**—A most beautiful Violet, being pure white, double, and deliciously fragrant. It is a free bloomer, its large, double, white flowers above its glossy, green foliage producing a most wonderful effect. Good strong plants, 15 cents each.

**MARIE LOUISE.**—Deep violet blue, double, fragrant and free-flowering. Should be grown by all interested in the culture of cut flowers on account of its easy forcing qualities. Good strong plants, 15 cents each.

One plant each of these Two Grand Violets, for 25 cents.

Chrysanthemum
Mrs. Alpheus Hardy

**HYDRANGEA PANICULATA GRANDIFLORA.**—A fine hardy shrub, introduced from Japan. It is of bushy and compact growth, attaining a height of several feet ; flowers are white and borne in immense pyramidal panicles more than a foot long ; remains in bloom a long time. Undoubtedly one of the finest hardy shrubs lately introduced. Price, 20 cents each ; 3 for 50 cents.

**HYDRANGEA. Otaksa.**—Unusually large glossy green foliage, strong habit of growth. The flowers are borne well above the foliage, trusses frequently measuring 10 inches across. Color, rich dark pink. It is a profuse bloomer and although not hardy, still deserves to be largely cultivated. Price, 20 cents each ; 3 for 50 cents.

**HELIOTROPE. Roi des Noirs.**—A beautiful new Heliotrope, that when better known is sure to become a favorite. The flowers are of a dark violet purple, with clear white eye. The foliage is unlike any other variety, being pointed, and dark green in color. It is an abundant bloomer, and of rich fragrance, and is desirable either for Summer decoration or Winter flowering. 20 cents each ; 3 for 50 cents.

Hydrangea Paniculata Grandiflora

½
NATURAL
SIZE

Heliotrope
Roi des Noirs

## MY COLORED PLATE SPECIALTIES No. 6.

**CLERODENDRON BALFOURI.**—Much ado has been made over certain climbers of late, but scarcely any can compare with this, which I now offer for the first time. In the small space allowed on colored plate there is but little chance to show its beauty, which is unique. No other plant in cultivation displays such colors of creamy-white and scarlet, and such profuse flowering. I can assure you that young plants are often entirely covered with bloom. When only a foot high as many as 20 to 30 flowers often can be counted, and this of course increases as the plants become old. I have in mind an engraving published in an English Horticultural paper, showing a plant with more than 400 flower bunches. As it requires no care to grow, everyone can be sure of perfect success and a beautiful effect with but little trouble. It thrives in a rich soil and may be planted out in Summer. Price, 25 cents each; 3 for 60 cents.

**CLERODENDRON FRAGRANS.**—This is entirely distinct from the above, being of dwarf shrubby growth, and bearing large double white flowers of the most delicious fragrance. Price, 30 cents each; 3 for 50 cents.

One plant of each of the above Two Handsome Clerodendrons sent free by mail on receipt of 45 cents; 2 of each for 75 cents.

**BRYOPHYLLUM CALYCINUM. Sprouting Leaf.**—Imagine the Leaf of a plant suspended by a thread in the air and having little plants growing from the notches. Take the same leaf and place it in a saucer filled with moist earth, moss, or any other material, and a colony of vigorous plants will soon cover it; but that is not all this interesting plant from India will do for us, as, after making a rapid, strong, vigorous growth, it will reward us with a most elegant panicle of flowers, most curious and interesting, resembling, first, a bunch of grapes, then later, burst and complete the flower. Remain on the plant for many weeks, and always delight whoever sees them. Should be grown by every one as a beautiful foliage plant and curiosity. Flowers in colored plate are only about ⅓ natural size. 25c. each for strong plants; 3 for 60c.; 6 for $1.

**THE EVERBLOOMING OXALIS, GOLDEN STAR. Oxalis Ortgiesi.**—There is not another Oxalis in cultivation that can compare with this new variety from the Andes of Peru. To begin with, it blooms the whole year round, its bright golden star-like flowers covering the plant in profusion Winter or Summer, in-doors or out. Next we must admire its very peculiar foliage—fish-tail like—dark olive-green above, and purple below, affording a most pleasing contrast; even the leaf stalks, which are bright red, add beauty to the whole. Were this a plant of difficult culture, it would command the highest price, but, fortunately, it can be grown by every one and everywhere; and whoever buys three or four plants can soon propagate enough from cuttings to have a large bed of them in the garden, or for filling window boxes. I have put this plant on my colored plate, as I wish all my customers to appreciate its beauty. Price, 25 cents each; 3 for 50 cents; 5 for $1.00.

**PLUMBAGO CAPENSIS. Sky-blue.**—No plant that I know of will be as much appreciated after a few months' trial as this. It is undoubtedly the most prolific bloomer that can be had. As soon as one truss fades a dozen are ready to take its place. Neither is there another plant known bearing flowers of such a peculiar blue. Grown in a large pot or tub it will soon form a large mass which will be constantly in bloom if pinched back; and, if desired as a climber for porches or trellises, it only needs to be left alone. We can recommend it highly where flowers are in demand. Price, 20 cents each; 3 for 50 cents.

**PLUMBAGO COCCINEA SUPERBA. Superb Scarlet Flowering.**—Similar in every respect to the above, except in the color of the flower, but not quite so free a bloomer. Price, 20 cents each; 3 for 50 cents.

**PLUMBAGO CAPENSIS ALBA.**—A white flowered sort, dwarf compact; free bloomer; free grower. Price, 20 cents each; 3 for 50 cents.

**A FINE COMBINATION.**—The Red, White, and the Blue Plumbago planted together in one pot, are universally admired when in bloom, appearing, as they do, as if the various colors grew on one and the same plant. These, our national colors, harmonize beautifully. Try it, and you will be pleased. One plant of each variety for 50 cents; 3 of each, $1.25.

**STAR-FISH FLOWER. Stapelia Variegata.**—This is a very peculiar plant, indeed, and when in flower attracts a great deal of attention. Scarcely any one will believe that its flowers are not artificial. They are large, often three inches across, of a peculiar texture, and almost a work of art, appearing like embossed or stamped leather, the color being yellow with maroon markings. Unlike any other Stapelias, this one grows with the greatest freedom, the smallest branch, if put in soil soon making a large plant. For hanging baskets or large jars it is very suitable, as it is of the drooping habit. The sight of one flower would well repay you, but a strong plant will often produce twelve to twenty at one time. Price, 25 cents each; 3 for 50 cents.

**THE RAINBOW CACTUS. Echinocereus Candicans.**—No Cactus has ever created such a sensation. Last year thousands upon thousands were sold, and that at very high prices. Two years ago single specimens were eagerly bought up at $2 to $5 each. Every one who sees it, wants it. It is a most magnificent plant, thickly covered with spines, ringing from cream color to deep crimson. The great beauty of the plant, combined with the large size of the flowers, which often measure 5 inches in diameter, combine to make it the most desirable Cactus in cultivation. The colors are well-portrayed in my colored plate, but it is impossible, of course, to reproduce their satiny lustre and brilliancy, which must be seen to be appreciated. Some may question the accuracy of the number of blooms on the one plant, but I have the photograph of the original, bearing 13 flowers. It requires absolutely no care, as it will grow for months without watering, and blooms as well. I need not say more to recommend it. Price, 40c. each for large plants; extra large plants, 60c; still larger, $1, postpaid.

"THE QUEEN" THE GRANDEST CACTUS KNOWN

COPYRIGHTED BY R. BLANC 1890

MY special offer on colored plate opposite includes one plant each of Clerodendron Balfouri, Bryophyllum Calycinum, Oxalis, Golden Star, Plumbago Capensis, Star-Fish Flower and the Rainbow Cactus.

**THESE 6 BEAUTIFUL PLANTS FREE BY MAIL ON RECEIPT OF $1.25.**

## THE QUEEN CACTUS
### Phyllocactus Latifrons.

THIS is undoubtedly the **Grandest** of all the **Cacti**, and one that should be grown by every person in the land. Indeed, if any one was to ask me for only one cactus, this is the one that I would recommend. As a pot plant, it often blooms when only one year old, and unlike many other Cacti, it will do so at various times throughout the season, beginning from April until way into October. It will also grow well in the shade, an advantage not possessed by any other Cacti. The flowers are a wonder indeed, frequently **measuring 30 inches in circumference**, and composed of hundreds of delicate petals, pure white within and clear yellow on the outside. The center of the flower is gracefully encircled by waxy-like filaments which seem to be in motion all the time. The delicious odor of the flowers pervades a whole room. Wherever it blooms crowds flock to see it. To prove what a grand plant it makes I give an illustration copied faithfully from a photograph (made by flash light) of a plant which is in the possession of a Germantown fancier. This plant has had, more than 50 flowers open at one time, and consid'ble more than one hundred in a season. It must be remembered also that the flowers open at about sunset, and it is wonderful to see them expand gradually, which they do in about a half hour. It can be grown in any kind of soil and requires no special treatment, whatever. Having grown a large stock I can offer very fine plants at 35 cents each postpaid; larger plants from $1 to $5.

This and the Rainbow Cactus are the best Cacti to grow for blooming, being entirely distinct. I will mail one good plant of each, to same address, 60c.

96

Annual Catalogue for 1891 of Maule's Henry Leaf Clover GUARANTEED SEEDS. Address all Orders to WM. HENRY MAULE, No. 1711 Filbert Street, Philadelphia, Pa. U. S. A.

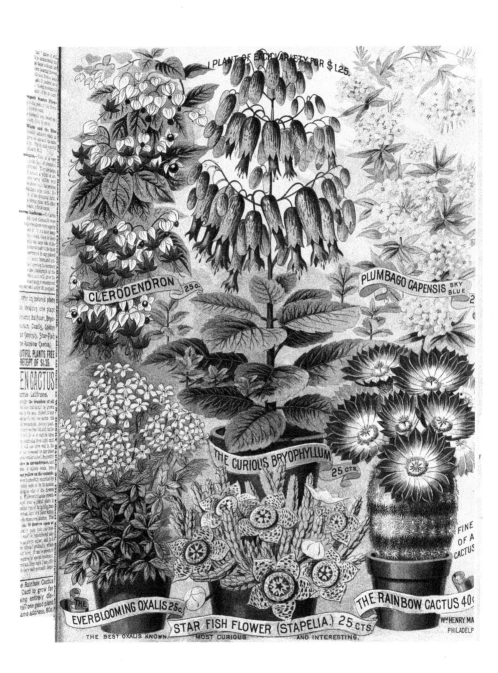

1 PLANT OF EACH VARIETY FOR $1.25.

CLERODENDRON 25c.

PLUMBAGO CAPENSIS SKY BLUE

THE CURIOUS BRYOPHYLLUM 25 CTS.

EVERBLOOMING OXALIS 25c.

THE BEST OXALIS KNOWN

STAR FISH FLOWER (STAPELIA.) 25 CTS.

MOST CURIOUS    AND INTERESTING.

THE RAINBOW CACTUS 40c

FINE OF A CACTUS

Wm HENRY MA
PHILADELP

# THE GREAT JAPANESE WINEBERRY.

We quote as follows from the description of the introducer of this wonderful new fruit : " Prof. Gregson, of the Japanese Imperial Agricultural College, while traveling among the mountains of Japan for rest and recreation, came upon this berry growing in a wild state. Its exceeding lusciousness and beauty prompted him to dry some of the berries and send the seed of them to relatives in this country, with the information that if it succeeded, it would prove the most valuable berry novelty ever introduced. It belongs to the raspberry family ; is a strong, vigorous grower, attaining the usual height of a raspberry, and is perfectly hardy in all positions without protection. It is in fact more hardy and vigorous than any raspberry or blackberry. It stands alike the cold of Northern winters and heat of Southern summers, without the slightest degree of injury. Its leaves are of the darkest green outside, and silvery white underneath. The young shoots and branches are covered with a reddish-brown hair or moss. The fruit is borne in large clusters, often 75 to 100 berries in a bunch. These berries are from the time of formation and bloom until they ripen enclosed in a "burr," which is formed by the calyx covering them entirely. When ripe the burr opens, exhibiting a large berry of the brightest, light glossy scarlet, or sherry wine color. The burrs and stems are covered with a heavy reddish moss, like a moss rose bud. Our plate but poorly represents the beauty of a cluster of fruit and burrs. The flavor of the fruit is entirely different from any other berry, being very sprightly, sweet and juicy, having no disagreeable sour, but a delicate and luscious flavor peculiar to itself, and superior to other berries. It is very juicy and makes the finest quality of wine. It commences to ripen early in July and continues in bearing for a long time. It is the most prolific berry known, the bushes being literally covered with its luscious fruit. It is propagated from the tips like cap raspberries and dewberries, and can be increased rapidly."

Strong, well-rooted plants, $1.00 each ; 6 for $5.00. Plants not quite so large, 50 cts. each; 6 for $2.50.

Wm HENRY MAULE

PHILADELPHIA.

STECHER LITH CO ROCHESTER N.Y

# FUCHSIAS

**Mrs. E. G. Hill.** Undoubtedly the largest double pure white Fuchsia ever offered. It surpasses that popular sort, the Storm King, from the fact that the habit of growth is quite erect, being a clean, upright, stocky, grower, and a very prolific bloomer. Flowers very large and double, the corolla is a beautiful, satiny white, the sepals are well reflexed, and of a beautiful, bright, scarlet, pink. Introduced by M. Victor Lemoine, of France, and is unequaled. 20 cts. each; 3 for 50 cts.; 7 for $1.00.

**Weeping Beauty.**—While we have offered this elegant sort for several seasons, yet the demand is unabated. Its habit is pyramidal, sending up a straight centre stock, the lower branches extending well out, shortening as they come near the top; this gives to the plant a most unique and striking appearance; the foliage is a rich bronze-green, and flowers of immense size; the corolla opens a rich deep purple, changing to blood-red, while sepals are fiery crimson. 20 cents each; 3 for 50 cents; 7 for $1.00.

**PHENOMENAL.**—Without doubt the largest flowering Fuchsia ever offered, the corolla measuring 2 inches across; very full and double, of a beautiful azure violet, flaked with red. 20c. each; 3 for 50c.; 7 for $1.00.

FUCHSIA.
MRS. E. G. HILL.

## THE SIX HANDSOMEST CARNATIONS

**Duke of Orange.**—A fine shade of creamy yellow, slightly variegated red, flowers large, and plant of strong and robust habit.

**Portia.**—The most intense bright scarlet; strong habit of growth; flowers borne on long foot-stalks; good size and very free-flowering. One of the very best crimsons.

**Lamborn.**—Compact grower, flowers pure waxy white, grown on long stems, very large floret; unsurpassed by any in perfection of bloom.

**Grace Wilder.**—Undoubtedly the handsomest pink Carnation ever introduced. The color is a brilliant peach rose, very large and finely fringed.

**Chester Pride.**—White ground, delicately variegated pink, flowers of immense size, and habit unexcelled. A most beautiful variety.

**Seavan.**—A distinct dark blood crimson; flowers large and of fine form, a strong and robust grower, sure to please.

Any of the above Carnations, 20 cents each; 3 for 50 cents; 7 for $1.00.

**SPECIAL OFFER: One each of above 6 truly handsome Carnations, free by mail, for 75 cts.**

## TWO BEAUTIFUL HARDY CLIMBING ROSES

**Mary Washington.**—In this lovely Rose our first President took special delight and named it in honor of his mother, Mary Washington. The flowers are of large size, pure white, perfectly double, deliciously fragrant, and a very profuse bloomer. 25 cents each; 3 for 60 cents.

**The Climbing General Jacqueminot.**—Another handsome climbing Rose, deserving of extended cultivation. Color, deep crimson, full and double, and bloom most profusely. 25 cents each. 3 for 60 cents.

**One plant of each of these two Climbing Roses sent postpaid on receipt of 40 cents.**

PORTIA CARNATION.

**NEW GOLDEN LEMON THYME.**—This handsome and wonderful Thyme is perfectly hardy, spreading itself and growing as rapidly as the old variety of Thyme. The leaves are curiously edged and variegated with golden yellow, increasing in brilliancy of color as the Autumn approaches, giving the appearance of a bed of gold. Its usefulness as an edging or border plant has no superior, and if properly pruned during the summer season will produce a most charming effect in the fall months. As a basket plant for in or out-door decorations it is also desirable. Its fragrance is most delightful resembling the sweet Lemon Verbena, while the fragrance of the old Thyme is still apparent. In addition to its highly ornamental qualities, it is equally desirable for culinary purposes as the old Thyme. 20 cents each; 3 for 50 cents; 7 for $1.00, postpaid.

**HOLT'S MAMMOTH SAGE.**—After having thoroughly grown and tested this valuable variety for several years, we can recommend it most highly. The illustration shows leaf of average size. The plants are very strong-growing, the first season attaining one foot in height, and spreading so that a single plant covers a **circular space three feet in diameter.** The leaves are borne well above the soil, keeping them clean; they are very large and of **unusual substance**, strong in flavor and of superior quality. **A single plant of Holt's Mammoth will yield more than a dozen plants of the common Sage.** It is perfectly hardy, even in New England, and attains still larger growth the second season. It rarely flowers, and **never runs to seed.** Price: 3 plants for 25 cents; 7 for 50 cents, or 15 plants for $1.00.

**One plant each of New Golden Thyme and Holt's Mammoth Sage sent postpaid for 25 cents; 2 plants of each for 40 cents; 5 plants of each for $1.00.**

NEW GOLDEN LEMON THYME

HOLT'S MAMMOTH SAGE

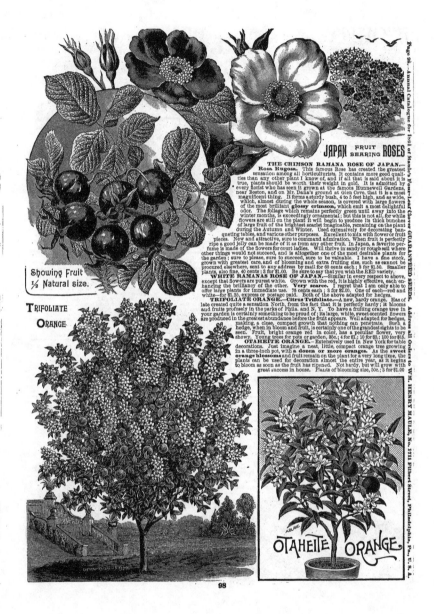

## JAPAN FRUIT BEARING ROSES

**THE CRIMSON RAMANA ROSE OF JAPAN.—Rosa Rugosa.** This famous Rose has created the greatest sensation among all horticulturists. It contains more good qualities than any other plant I know of, and if all that is said about it is true, plants should be worth their weight in gold. It is admitted by every florist who has seen it grown at the famous Hunnewell Gardens, near Boston, and on Mr. Dana's ground at Glen Cove, that it is a most magnificent thing. It forms a sturdy bush, 4 to 5 feet high, and as wide, which, almost during the whole season, is covered with large flowers of the most brilliant **glossy crimson**, which emit a most delightful odor. The foliage which remains perfectly green until away into the winter months, is exceedingly ornamental; but this is not all, for while flowers are still on the plant it will begin to produce its thick bunches of large fruit of the brightest scarlet imaginable, remaining on the plant during the Autumn and Winter. Used extensively for decorating banqueting tables, and various other purposes. Excellent to mix with flower or fruit pieces. New and attractive, sure to command admiration. When fruit is perfectly ripe a good jelly can be made of it as from any other fruit. In Japan, a favorite perfume is made of the flowers for court ladies. Will thrive in sandy or rough soil where other things would not succeed, and is altogether one of the most desirable plants for the garden; sure to please, sure to succeed, sure to be valuable. I have a fine stock, grown with greatest care, and of blooming and extra fruiting size, such as cannot be procured elsewhere, sent to any address by mail for 60 cents each; 3 for $1.50. Smaller plants, also fine, 40 cents; 3 for $1.00. Be sure to say that you wish the RED variety.

**WHITE RAMANAS ROSE OF JAPAN.**—Similar in every respect to above, except that flowers are purest white. Grown with the red, it is highly effective, each enhancing the brilliancy of the other. **Very scarce.** I regret that I am only able to offer large plants for immediate use. 75 cents each; 3 for $2.00. One of each—red and white—for $1.25, express or postage paid. Both of the above adapted for hedges.

**TRIFOLIATE ORANGE.—Citrus Trifoliate.**—A new, hardy orange. Has of late created quite a sensation North, from the fact that it is perfectly hardy; it blooms and fruits profusely in the parks of Phila. and N. Y. To have a fruiting orange tree in your garden is certainly something to be proud of; its large, white, sweet-scented flowers are produced in the greatest abundance before the fruit appears. Well adapted for hedges, making, a close, compact growth that nothing can penetrate. Such a hedge, when in bloom and fruit, is certainly one of the grandest sights to be seen. Fruit, bright orange red in color, has a peculiar flower, very showy. Young trees for pots or garden, 35c.; 4 for $1.; 10 for $2.; 100 for $15.

**OTAHEITE ORANGE.**—Extensively used in New York for table decorations. Just imagine a neat, little, compact orange tree growing in a three-inch pot, with **a dozen or more oranges.** As the **sweet orange blossoms** and fruit remain on the plant for a very long time, the plants can be used for decoration almost the entire year, as it begins to bloom as soon as the fruit has ripened. Not hardy, but will grow with great success in house. Plants of blooming size, 50c.; 3 for $1.00

Showing Fruit ½ Natural size.

TRIFOLIATE ORANGE.

OTAHEITE ORANGE.

**"FOAM FLOWER" (Tiarella Cordifolia.)**—"It is a strange fact that while many plants of doubtful value are widely distributed in gardens, some real treasures for no apparent reason, are overlooked. Such has been the fate of the lovely Foam Flower, which, though perfectly hardy and of rapid increase, flourishing anywhere, is only now becoming known. It is a plant of great beauty of leaf and flowers. The starry blossoms are creamy white, and the buds tinged with pink. A mass of them seen a few yards off, appearing like a wreath of foam. The young leaves are of a tender green, daintily spotted and veined deep red, while the older ones are of a rich red-bronze." I copy the above from The Garden. What more need I say in praise of this beautiful plant? Price 25 cents each ; 3 for 50 cents ; 7 for $1.00.

**THE DOUBLE PINK MORNING GLORY.—(Calystegia Pubescens Fl. Plena.)**—When first seen, the flowers of this handsome twining plant are certain to be taken

FOAM FLOWER.

for appearance. In reality it is a **double pink** Morning Glory, and so perfectly hardy that where once established, it will soon cover arbors, trellises and balconies. Useful as a cut-flower, and another of those good plants that have been too much neglected. Try it and you will be delighted. Price, 20 cents each ; 3 for 50 cents ; 7 for $1.00.

**JAPANESE AZALEA.**–Azalea Mollis.—This is a new species of low growth, with very showy flowers, measuring two to three inches across, embracing all shades of white, yellow, orange and red, and commencing to bloom even before the leaves appear. Old specimens are so densely covered with flowers, that they almost seem artificial. Their perfect hardiness make them the most desirable of all the species. Excellent also for forcing in bloom in the house. I can furnish 3-year-old plants at the very low price of 30 cents each ; 2 for 50 cents ; 5 for $1.00. Older ones, 50 cents, 75 cents and $1.00 each. Not a single one of my customers should omit this from their order.

**HIBISCUS MUTABILIS Fl. Pl.—Mexican Rose or Cotton Rose.**—One of the most curious of the genus. The large double flowers are **pure white in the morning**, changing to **pink** at noon, and by night are a uniform **light-red**; and as the flowers last for nearly half the next day, the contrast between them and the newly opened white ones is very striking. After the plant is done blooming in November, it should be cut back nearly to the ground ; this keeps the plant in a compact form, and the flowers are larger and better. It is one of the most interesting plants that I offer. 25 cents each ; 3 for 50 cents ; 7 for $1.00.

**CISSUS INCISA.**—A beautiful tropical species, a native of the extreme south-western coast of Florida. Leaves compound (three leaflets), evergreen ; a rapid grower, sending down long air roots ; a curious and interesting vine. 20 cents each ; 3 for 50 cents.

THE DOUBLE PINK MORNING GLORY.

The U. S. Mail brings Maule's Seeds, plants, etc., to every one's door, or rather post-office, into whose hands this book may come ; and as I always guarantee safe arrival, my customers, whether in Maine or California, run absolutely no risk whatever.

**"TURKEY'S BEARD."—"Xerophyllum Asphodeloides.—**The aspect of this tuberous-rooted plant is very interesting and beautiful. It forms a spreading tuft of grassy leaves when well grown, and bears a flower stem 2 to 4 feet high, terminated by a compact raceme of numerous white blossoms. Only recently introduced by plantsmen. Large plants. 20c each ; 3 for 50c.

**ST. BRUNO'S LILY.—(Anthericum Liliastrum.)**—One of the very best hardy perennial plants in cultivation, producing an enormous number of pure white sweet-scented Lily-like flowers, very early in the Spring, easily forced in pots, and useful for cutting. It will succeed in every garden, and increase very rapidly. Price, 20 cents each ; 3 for 50 cents ; 7 for $1.00.

**SCARLET BUTTERFLY. Asclepias Tuberosa.**—Hardy plant bearing close compact umbrels of brilliant **orange-colored** flowers on stems 2 feet high. One of the showiest of our autumnal flowers. 15 cents each ; 3 for 25 cents ; 5 for 50 cents.

W. W. Rohrman, P. M. Paisano, Texas. My flower plants, also the strawberries arrived to-day, and was surprised upon opening them, they looked as if they had been packed to-day, they were so fresh. I am very thankful for the prompt attention my small orders receive.

TURKEY'S BEARD.

ST. BRUNO'S LILY.

One plant of each of the above 8 unique varieties for $1.25 postpaid.

A flower spike—Sanseviera Zelanica.

**GASTERIA MACULATA.**

**GASTERIA MACULATA.**—This plant is so entirely distinct from the Sanseviera that it should not be omitted from your list. The leaves, which are arranged in the shape of a fan, are thick and fleshy, regularly spotted with white dots. It will grow for everybody, and produce tall spikes of flowers, each of which is a jewel in itself; colors being orange, flesh, green and yellow. 35 cents each; 3 for 90 cents.

**AMARYLLIS EQUESTRE.**—A truly grand Amaryllis, producing freely, clusters of very large flowers of the most satiny, orange scarlet with a white stripe through centre of petals. Superior in every respect to many of the highest price Amaryllises. They always give satisfaction, for their flowers are simply grand. Large blooming bulbs, 30 cents each; 2 for 50 cents.

**SANSEVIERA ZELANICA.**

**SANSEVIERA ZELANICA.**—This singular plant is eminently adapted for use in parlors, vestibules, and other decorative purposes, as its leaves remain in a perfect state for years. These leaves grow to a length of 3 to 4 feet, and are beautifully striped crosswise with white variegations on dark green ground. It will grow equally well in sun or shade, and while it loves plenty of water, it will also thrive for months without it. Its use for all ornamental purposes is therefore apparent. It bears a spike densely crowded with large, creamy white flowers of exquisite appearance. I can especially recommend this plant as a great acquisition. Price 20 cts. each; extra large plants by express, 75 cts.

**AMARYLLIS FORMOSISSIMA.—"Jacobean Lily."**—Few Amaryllis can be sold cheap. Of this variety, however, we have purchased an enormous stock, owing to its good, free blooming quality, and the beauty of its dark red, velvety flowers. A pot of it, when in flower, is sure to elicit the greatest admiration from all who see it. Of the easiest growth by the most inexperienced. Price, 20 cents each.

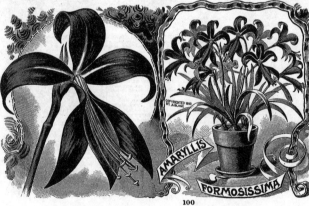

BEAR IN MIND that all my prices on Bulbs and Plants, include delivery free by mail, at your nearest post-office. I also guarantee safe arrival in all cases. If they reach you in poor condition, I always replace the damaged plants free of charge.

## THE WAX PLANT,

**Hoya Carnosa.**—The old-fashioned wax plant is again in great demand, and no wonder indeed, as it is one of the few plants that withstand with impunity the dry air of living rooms. It will improve from year to year, and produce its waxy-like clusters of sweet-scented flowers in great profusion. No one should be without it. Price, 20 cents each; 3 for 50 cts.; 7 for $1.00.

**Variegated Leaved.** —A finely variegated leaved form of the above at 40 cents each; 3 for $1.00.

Mrs. E.O. Wannamaker, Orangeburg, S. C.: "My flowers reached me looking almost as well as those I had growing. Accept many thanks for the extras. Seeds to hand also; you kindly sent me several extra packets which are all good."

Mrs. A. M. Park, Greenwood, Neb.: "My cuttings came to hand to-day, fresh, and nice. I am very much pleased with them, and there were so many of them."

### MARBLED LEAF.

**MARBLED LEAF, Goodyera Pubescens.**—A most beautiful, perfectly hardy plant, with broad, rich, dark, velvety green leaves, elegantly striped with white. It bears white flowers with a lemon yellow blotch on the lip, which is curiously twisted and contorted; spikes numerous, remaining long in perfection. Splendidly adapted for growing in pans or pots of peaty soil. At the low price we quote them, every one should try this beautiful novelty. 20c. ea.; 3 for 50c.; 12 for $1.50.

### Three Unique Climbers

**ANTIGONON LEPTOPUS.**— The Rosa de Montana of Mexico. An elegant climber that should be more widely distributed; ordinarily hardy here, but when killed by frost springs up again with renewed vigor, and in a very short time covers anything given to run on. During the entire summer and fall it is covered with rose-colored flowers, produced on long racemes in greatest abundance. Roots tuberous, grow to a large size. 20 cents each; 3 for 50 cents.

**POTHOS AUREA.**—A beautiful aroid climber, with heart-shaped leaves marked and spotted green and yellow in very large blotches. Easily grown on a wall or trellis, to which it will cling by the long roots that are thrown out all along the stem. Finest variegated leaved climber I know of. 25c. each ; 5 for $1.

**ECHITES PALUDOSA.**—A class of plants so very much neglected, probably because they are practically unknown in this country, although cultivated to some extent in Europe. All are climbers, beautiful in flower and leaf, and well adapted to out-door culture north. Flowers white, tinged with pink, very delicate and beautiful; requires plenty of water. 30c. ea.; 4 for $1.

### MEXICAN AIR PLANT.

**MEXICAN AIR PLANT, Tillandsia Utriculata.**— A very interesting plant which can be grown in any living room. It can be fastened on a piece of wood, a branch of a tree, or even suspended in the air, simply tying a little moss around the roots; grown in this way it is very attractive. Leaves are of beautiful silvery green, and gracefully recurved. Flower spikes of most brilliant colors, yellow, vermilion, and purple; remain on the plant for many weeks. Price, 15 cts. each; 2 for 25 cts.; extra large plants, 50 cts.

**BUTTERFLY ORCHID, Epidendrum Venosum.**—This splendid Orchid is one of the very best. Every one knows the beauty and value of a good orchid, but on account of the extravagant price few people are able to possess one. Here is an opportunity for getting one of the best and easiest growing sorts for only 35 cents. All that is necessary to grow it successfully is to secure the plant and a little moss bunched around the roots, to a piece of board or bark, a treatment similar to the Mexican Air Plant above, and suspend it in a window or conservatory. Keep the moss wet and the plant free from dust and you will have a unique and beautiful object. It blooms freely, producing large panicles of gay flowers which keep perfect a long time. The flowers are composed of several colors; delicate butterfly-like. Strong plants of blooming size, 35 cts. each; 4 for $1.

**PURPLE BUTTERFLY ORCHID.**—Another variety of Orchid with much larger and distinct flowers flaked with purple spots on lower lip. Foliage droops elegantly, just the reverse of E. Venosum. A much rarer sort, hence price is higher. 50 cts.; 3 for $1.

### WAX PLANT.

### AFRICAN SNAKE PALM, or RED CALLA, Amorphophallus Rivieri.—"Snake Palm,"

"Devil's Tongue," and other curious names are given by the few who have possessed this wonderful aroid, probably for the reason that the stem supporting the large palm-like foliage is so distinctly marbled with large blotches of pink, grey, dark green, and various other colors. Strong tubers will send up a most curious flower, often attaining the length of three feet on a stalk two or three feet high, resembling a gigantic Calla, only dark red in color. A fine plant for the lawn or for growing in pots. Price, 25 cts. each, up to $1.00 for extra large roots.

**AFRICAN SNAKE PALM.**

**BUTTERFLY ORCHID.**

101

**MANETTIA VINE**

MANETTIA VINE FLOWERS—NATURAL SIZE.

**THE MANETTIA VINE.**—Much has been said in favor of this very graceful climber, but not too much, indeed, for it has proved to be one of our best plants for Summer blooming. When only 2 or 3 inches high its bright **coral red flowers** tipped with **deep canary yellow** begin to appear. They are of a peculiar waxy texture appearing almost artificial, and therefore remain fresh for a long time. When in full bloom the plants are **a gorgeous sight,** the bright green foliage enhancing the brilliancy of the flowers. As a pot plant in the house or for planting out, it will prove a great acquisition. Price, 25 cents each ; 3 for 60 cents.

**RANUNCULUS.—Fair Maids of France.**—It is scarcely necessary to speak of the beauties of this gem, with its neat dressy flowers sporting every **color of the rainbow.** The double sort, which I offer, forms a dense tuft, profusely laden all Summer with blooms. Being of easy culture, I can greatly recommend them. Dry roots, 10c.; 3 for 25c.; 15 for $1.00.

Ranunculus. Fair Maids of France. Flowers ¼ size.

**MALAYAN JESSAMINE.—Rhynchospermum Jasminoides.**—Now that climbers are so in vogue, I am pleased to be able to offer this very rare sort, knowing that it will delight every purchaser. To be able to have the **most delicate, sweet-scented and pure white,** waxy-like flowers in profusion almost the whole year round, and dark evergreen foliage to set them off to advantage, is something that cannot be had from other plants. For florists nothing could be more useful, as it blooms more profusely in Winter than at any other time, making it a most desirable house plant. The vine will live a life-time, and form **specimens as shown in cut,** which was executed accurately from a plant shown at an exhibition. Price, 30 cents each ; 2 for 50 cents.

**SWEET SAXIFRAGE.—Saxifraga Granulata. Fl. Pl.**—Why this lovely little plant has not been taken up by other dealers we cannot tell, as it certainly is very handsome and useful for Summer blooming, completely covering its neat foliage with large **pure white flowers,** as large as those shown in illustration, which shows a plant, and flowers above natural size. They are very useful for cutting, as they remain fresh for a long time. When once planted they can be left to themselves and will increase rapidly. Will grow in any waste place, rockwork, etc., or in pots as well. Awarded first-class certificate in England. The bulbs, though small, will bloom freely. Having many thousands, I can offer them at 3 for 10c.; 10 for 25c.; 25 for 50c.

**THE BLACKBERRY LILY. Pardanthus**—Leopard Flower and other names have been given to Pardanthus, a genus of very curious plants from China and Japan, bearing on stalks, 3 to 4

MALAYAN JESSAMINE.

SWEET SAXIFRAGE, CUT ABOVE SHOWING NATURAL SIZE OF FLOWERS; CUT BELOW THE PLANT.

inches high, large flowers of the richest golden yellow and orange, elegantly spotted with purple and crimson, which always attracts attention, no matter where grown. When the flowers have faded they are succeeded by shiny black berries, which can hardly be distinguished from the blackberry. I have a remarkable strain, more vigorous than usually seen, and producing larger flowers. A single plant will produce a quantity of bloom. Perfectly hardy. 15 cents each ; 4 for 50 cents.

PARDANTHUS THE BLACKBERRY LILY

**BRUGMANSIA.**—An old plant, offered under many names, but one which cannot be sufficiently praised. The striking beauty of specimens bearing from 20 to 50 flowers **often a foot long,** of a creamy white color, and highly sweet-scented, is something seldom to be forgotten. It makes a magnificent lawn plant, which can be wintered in a cellar or be kept growing during winter, when flowers will be had during holidays. It can be relied upon to thrive and bloom freely, and when it once has flowered, no one will ever part with it. In fact, it is one of the plants that you cannot do without, if you have a garden or greenhouse. By mail, 25 cents each; extra large, by express, $1 to $2. **A double flowered** variety of above, still more desirable, equally as large, 40 cts, ea.

## BRUGMANSIA

**HEDYCHIUM CORONARIUM.—The Ginger or Butterfly Lily.**—A new and very desirable plant, either for open ground or pot culture; it is constantly in bloom. Here in the open ground it is in flower from July to October. It prefers a moist, partially shaded situation, where it will form large dense clumps three to four feet high. Flowers are borne in large clusters, terminal on every stalk, and resemble very much a *large white butterfly;* pure white and very fragrant. 30 cents each; 4 for $1.00.
**HAMELIA PATENS.**—A West Indian plant, and why it has not become better known is a mystery. It is deserving of a prominent place in the open ground, and in the greenhouses north during winter. Flowers in cymes, of a bright orange color, and freely produced nearly all summer. The foliage of this plant is very handsome, being of olive-green above, very lustrous; the under-side of the leaves are deep wine-color; as a foliage plant alone it deserves cultivation. It is offered for the first time. 30c. each; 4 for $1.
**ALOCASIA.—Gigantea.**—Splendid aroid plants, with large dark green foliage, veined, and variegated with lighter shades; of easy culture, preferring moist ground and partial shade. Will grow to a large size if favorably situated. 25 cents to $1.00 each.

John M. Daniels, Columbia, S. C.: "I want to say briefly that my last order for seeds, etc., is received, and am much pleased with same; but want to add that the collection of berries, etc., is growing finely, and not one failed to root and grow. The Gregg berry has a flower-bud upon it—a sprout but four inches long. No one need go anywhere else for anything in the seed or plant line but to your house, and shall always recommend Maule's seeds and plants to everybody. I sincerely thank you for your unwavering promptness and courtesy, as well as generous liberality in dealing.

**PERUVIAN LILIES.—Alstroemeria.** If you wish to make a magnificent show of flowers, try a few of these South American Lilies so rare in our gardens. Plant them a foot deep in a sunny situation, protect in winter with dry leaves, and your labors will be rewarded with a splendid display of Orchid-like flowers in various colors, from May until November. I have several distinct varieties. viz., bright **orange,** rosy-white, orange and red, red and green. My choice of varieties, 25 cts; 3 distinct sorts 50 cts.
**BIGNONIA GRANDIFLORA.—Procox. Large Early Trumpet Flower.** The value of the ordinary Trumpet Creeper is well known, but this variety eclipses it in every way. To begin with, its flowers are nearly double the size: their color is of the most intense orange scarlet, and they are produced on plants only one year old, something that cannot be expected from the older sorts. Planted at the foot of a tree this vine will soon cover its branches completely, and daily smother it with its large bell-shaped flowers and delicate, graceful foliage. The subject illustrated herewith, and which was engraved from a photograph, only gives a slight idea of the effect produced. The

LEWISIA REDIVIVA.

plant can of course be used for many other purposes, such as covering walls, arbors, trellises, and porches. Grown as a pot-plant, a fine, sturdy bush can be made of it by cutting down, thus enabling the plant to spread itself. At a late Horticultural Show such a plant was exhibited, and excited a great deal of comment. Price, 30 cents each; 4 for $1.00.
**LEWISIA REDIVIVA.**—A most remarkable and beautiful rock-plant, of dwarf growth, which, for the size of the plant, bear very large flowers of a pleasing pink, and of decidedly handsome appearance. The roots are succulent, and possess the power of retaining life under the most unfavorable conditions. It should be grown in sunshine and be kept high and dry. It is also good for growing in pots. Very interesting. 20 cents each; 3 for 50 cents.
**LIATRIS SPICATA.—Kansas Gay Feather.**—These plants, which are so highly appreciated in Europe, and of which so much has been said of late, should be found in every garden. L. Spicata is one of the handsomest and nearest in growth, bearing a spike 2 feet high, of **violet-purple flowers,** retaining their wonderful beauty for a long time and will produce quite a mass of bloom. Price, 15 cents; 3 for 50 cents.
**LIATRIS PYCNOSTACHIA.**—Is by far the handsomest, bearing very dense spikes of purple flowers, so close and compact as to resemble a round bush: as shown on the left of our illustration. Price, 20 cents; 3 for 50 cents.

## BIGNONIA GRANDIFLORA.

One plant of each of the above 2 handsome Liatris sent free by mail on receipt of 30 cents.

LIATRIS

W. O. Walker, Carrtuck C. H., N. C.: "I received my seeds some time ago. Accept my thanks for the many extras. The plants came all in good order. Every one thought them the plants and nicely packed."

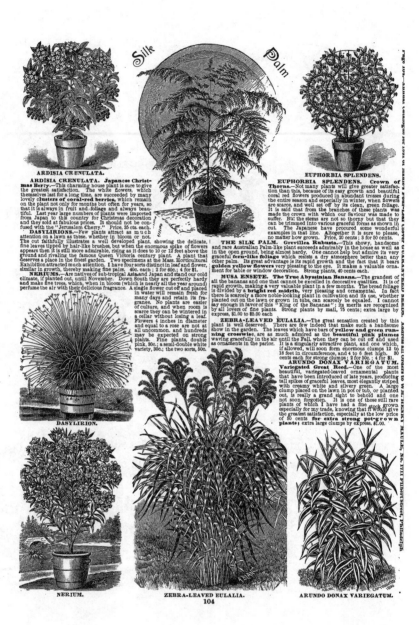

## ARDISIA CRENULATA.

**ARDISIA CRENULATA. Japanese Christmas Berry.**—This charming house plant is sure to give the greatest satisfaction. The white flowers, which themselves last for a long time, are succeeded by many lovely **clusters of coral-red berries**, which remain on the plant not only for months but often for years, so that it is always in fruit and foliage and always beautiful. Last year large numbers of plants were imported from Japan to this country for Christmas decoration and they sold at fabulous prices. It should not be confused with the "Jerusalem Cherry." Price, 35 cts. each.

**DASYLIRIONS.**—Few plants attract as much attention on a lawn as these, whether in bloom or not. The cut faithfully illustrates a well developed plant, showing the delicate, fine leaves tipped by hair-like brushes, but when the enormous spike of flowers appears then it is still more admirable, rising as it does to 10 or 12 feet above the ground and rivaling the famous Queen Victoria century plant. A plant that deserves a place in the finest garden. Two specimens at the Mass. Horticultural Exhibition attracted much attention. I have four sorts distinct in leaf and flower, similar in growth, thereby making fine pairs. 40c. each ; 2 for 60c.; 4 for $1.

**NERIUMS.**—Are natives of sub-tropical Asia and Japan and stand our cold climate, if planted out, until November. Down South they are perfectly hardy and make fine trees, which, when in bloom (which is nearly all the year around) perfume the air with their delicious fragrance. A single flower cut off and placed in water will remain fresh for many days and retain its fragrance. No plants are easier of culture, and when room is scarce they can be wintered in a cellar without losing a leaf. Flowers 4 inches in diameter and equal to a rose are not at all uncommon, and hundreds may be expected on strong plants. Fine plants, double pink, 30c.; a semi-double white variety, 30c.; the two sorts, 50c.

**DASYLIRION.**

**NERIUM.**

## EUPHORBIA SPLENDENS.

**EUPHORBIA SPLENDENS. Crown of Thorns.**—Not many plants will give greater satisfaction than this, because of its easy growth and beautiful coral red flowers produced in abundant trusses during the entire season and especially in winter, when flowers are scarce and well set off by its clean, green foliage. It is said that from the branches of these plants was made the crown with which our Saviour was made to suffer. But the stems are not so thorny but that they can be trimmed into various graceful forms as shown in cut. The Japanese have procured some wonderful examples in that line. Altogether it is sure to please, no matter how grown. Price, 20 cents ; 3 for 50 cents.

**THE SILK PALM. Grevillea Robusta.**—This showy, handsome and rare Australian Palm-like plant succeeds admirably in the house as well as in the open ground, being almost hardy. One cannot help but admire its very graceful **fern-like foliage** which resists a dry atmosphere better than any other palm. Its great advantage is its rapid growth and the fact that it bears **golden yellow flowers** very pleasing to the eye. It makes a valuable ornament for table or window decoration. Strong plants, 40 cents each.

**MUSA ENSETE. The True Abyssinian Banana.**—The grandest of all the bananas and one that cannot be excelled in decorative qualities. It is of rapid growth, making a very valuable plant in a few months. The broad foliage is divided by a **bright red midrib**, very pleasing and ornamental. In fact there is scarcely a more noble-looking plant in cultivation and its use, whether planted out on the lawn or grown in tubs, can scarcely be equaled. I cannot say enough in favor of this "King of the Bananas"; its merits are recognized by all lovers of fine plants. Strong plants by mail, 75 cents; extra large by express, $1.00 to $5.00 each

**ZEBRA-LEAVED EULALIA.**—The great sensation created by this plant is well deserved. There are few indeed that make such a handsome show in the garden. The leaves which have bars of **yellow and green running crosswise**, are as much admired as the **beautiful pink plumes** waving gracefully in the air until the Fall, when they can be cut off and used as ornaments in the parlor. It is a singularly attractive plant, and one which, if allowed, will soon form enormous clumps 12 to 18 feet in circumference, and 4 to 6 feet high. 30 cents each for strong clumps ; 2 for 50c. ; 4 for $1.

**ARUNDO DONAX VARIEGATUM. Variegated Great Reed.**—One of the most beautiful, variegated-leaved ornamental plants that have been introduced of late years, producing tall spikes of graceful leaves, most elegantly striped with creamy white and silvery green. A large clump placed on the lawn in pot or tub, or planted out, is really a grand sight to behold and one not soon forgotten. It is one of those still rare plants of which I have had a fine stock grown especially for my trade, knowing that it would give the greatest satisfaction, especially at the low price of 50 cents **for extra strong pot-grown plants;** extra large clumps by express, $1.00.

**ZEBRA-LEAVED EULALIA.**

**ARUNDO DONAX VARIEGATUM.**

## CRINUMS.

**CRINUM KIRKY.**—This magnificent bulb, which often attains the size of 6 to 8 inches, produces flowers of the greatest beauty. Usually two flower stalks of dark purplish color are sent up at the same time, each bearing a large umbel composed of a dozen or more **enormous lily-like flowers** of the greatest beauty and fragrance. The petals are broad, and pure white, with a deep reddish purple stripe through the centre. A plant which always creates a sensation when it blooms, which it does with the greatest freedom. Extra large bulbs are usually sold at $3 to $5. My price is $1; 3 for $2.

**CRINUM AMERICANUM.**—In every way this rivals the above in stateliness and grandeur. Like it, nothing can approach it as a pot plant, and where beauty of flowers are concerned, it is by some preferred, being pure white, waxy-like and fragrant, and producing fully as many, if not more flowers. I mail strong flowering bulbs at 50 cents each; 3 for $1.00.

**CRINUM CAPENSE.**—Rose, sweet scented, one of the finest Crinums; hardy, with slight protection. Producing many flower stalks, 3½ to 4 feet high, and crowded with 10 to 15 blooms. Excellent soft, 40 cents.

**PANCRATIUM MARITIMUM.**—Hardy, with protection, bearing large white 'lily-like flowers on long stalks. Quite distinct from any of the above. Very desirable. 25 cents each.

**LILIUM LEOPOLDI.**—Most splendid form of lily, in the style of Tigrinum, but far superior. Color, orange, elegantly spotted with dark purple. 15 cents each; 4 for 50 cents.

**HABRANTHUS ANDERSONII.**—A charming bulb, producing in early Spring a number of erect flowers; of a coppery color shading to red, exceedingly pretty. 15c.; 4 for 50c.

**ANIZANTHUS BICOLOR.**—Scarce bulbous plants from Cape of Good Hope, with flower spikes overtopping the foliage, bearing numerous bright-colored flowers. In the variety being scarlet and black a quite uncommon combination. sure to surprise you. 20 cts. each; 3 for 50 cts.

## PEACOCK FLOWER.

**Morea Pavonia.**—Perhaps one of the most distinct flowers in cultivation. The petals are pure white, with a distinct black eye surrounded with blue, which is again shaded with purple. It is a very free bloomer, perfectly hardy and one of the attractions of English gardens. 15c. each; 4 for 50c.

## GAY QUEEN.

Named **Phaedranassa**, alluding to the beauty of the flower. A bulbous plant, almost new here, bearing immense clusters of **showy flowers**, 2 to 4 inches long, of various colors quite distinct from any other bulb. Beautiful foliage; elegant as a pot plant or for the open ground and much admired.

**P. Chloracea.**—Flowers **purplish rose**, tipped with green, fine. 20 cts. each; 3 for 50 cents.
**P. Gloriosa.**—Scarlet, yellow and green. 20 cents each.
**P. Viridiflora.**—Green and yellow flowers. Exquisite. 20c
The three varieties to one address for **50 cts.**

Peacock Flower.

GAY QUEEN.

## Special Offer

I will furnish the entire collection of bulbs mentioned on this page, 20 in all, for $4; regular price $5.45; any four priced at 15 cts. each, for 50 cts; any three priced 20 cts. each, for 50 cts; any three priced 25 cents each, for 60 cts., all post-paid.

106

## MOUNTAIN ROSE.

**Antigonon Leptopus.**—Rosa de Montana is the favorite name of the Mexicans for this cheerful climber, which is almost hardy here and certainly so with protection. The flowers are **deep rose colored,** in long clusters and in such profusion that there is scarcely a leaf to be seen. Endorsed by the best authorities. **ROOTS,** 20 cents each; 3 for 50 cents.

**ALBUCA.**—Fine large bulbs succeeding admirably everywhere. They bear long spikes of **star-like flowers** that are very pleasing; in color yellow and white. 20 cents each; 3 for 50 cents.

**GOLDEN HOMERIA.**—Fine summer-flowering bulbs, the blooms of which are **orange red and yellow,** very showy and enduring, soon forming large clumps. A great acquisition. 20 cents each; 3 for 50 cents.

**THE WHITE IRIS, Iris Florentina.**—Pure, white and beautiful. The true Florentina Iris, so much praised in Italy. Of easiest growth. 15 cents each; 4 for 50 cents.

**SPRING SATIN FLOWER, Sisyrinchium.**—A beautiful early Spring flower, produced on long spikes. In color they are a pale blue, very pleasing to the eye. Charming subject for growing in pots or in the garden. 15 cents each; 4 for 50 cents.

**CLIDANTHUS FRAGRANS.**—Very ornamental half hardy bulbs from Brazil, the leaves of which appear after the flowers, which are **yellow** in color and exceedingly fragrant. One of the rarest plants in this country and which I offer as a novelty. 25 cents each.

**FURCRAEA GIGEANTEA.**—Bulbous plants, growing to an enormous size, and producing rosettes of forty to fifty **immense leaves** and flowers, scapes 15 to 20 feet high; furnished with hundreds of large flowers, which are milky white inside and greenish on the back. Most noble specimen plant. Can be out back in Winter and kept in cellar. Certain to please. 40 cents each; 3 for $1.00.

**RED-FLOWERED ZINZIBER.**—I accidentally came across what is believed to be something entirely new in this line, to wit: a **Red-Flowering Ginger** plant. It bears a large panicle of scarlet flowers, like the well-known French Cannas, but lasting actually three weeks in full perfection. The roots of this plant are valuable for preserving, being the same as the Ginger of commerce; a fine foliage plant as well. Fine roots, 25 cents; 3 for 50 cents.

## VARIEGATED GLADWIN.

An ornamental plant of the very greatest value, and highly appreciated in England, where it is used for choicest decorations. Its leaves, as will be seen in cut, resemble those of the Pandanus, being variegated with **white and green stripes**. The flowers are of a pleasing blue, and freely produced; and that is not all, for they are succeeded by large capsules which burst open when ripe and expose a number of **bright red seeds** as large as peas, which can be used for many purposes. The plant is perfectly hardy and easily grown by any one. I anticipate a heavy demand for them at the low price of 25 cts.; 3 for 50 cts.; extra strong roots, 50 cts.

VARIEGATED GLADWIN

## True Rose of Jericho,

great satisfaction I have imported a number of these curiosities from Syria. They are the true and only **Resurrection Plant** mentioned in the Bible, and although actually dead, have a strange faculty of **opening and spreading** out their dried-up leaves and branches when placed in water, and closing up again when dried. My cut, made direct from photograph, shows plant open and closed. This is an attractive article of ornament for the table, mantel-piece or window, and will retain its peculiar properties for twenty-five to fifty years. You will certainly enjoy it, and want more when you see it. Price, 20 cts. each ; 3 for 50 cts.

THE "**MEXICAN RESURRECTION PLANT**," entirely distinct from the above, but also interesting. 15 cents ; 2 for 25 cents.

**ANDROMEDA MARIANA.**—The Ethiopsan princess "Andromeda," after whom this handsome native shrub was named, might well have been proud of her namesake, for no artist could do justice to its beauty as seen growing in its native haunts. Snow is white, but the whiteness of its flowers excel it. Their sweet fragrance and general appearance have also caused them to be named the "Lily of the Valley." It should have a place in every garden. Strong plants, 25 cents ; 3 for 60 cents.

**VARIEGATED-LEAVED HYDRANGEA.**—Imagine a plant similar to the famous H. Paniculata, but with foliage edged with a **broad pure white margin.** One of our finest exhibition specimens. 30 cents each.

**VARIEGATED-LEAVED AGERATUM.**—A Mexican species with **light purplish blue flowers,** but entirely distinct from any other having leaves beautifully marked and **splashed with white.** 30 cents each.

**FITTONIA.**—Pretty plants of dwarf growth, suitable for in-doors. The leaves are closely veined with a bright pink mosaic like net-work, very rare. 30 cents each.

**MARANTA.**—The arrowroot plant of the South, forms large bunches of **bright green** foliage surmounted by panicles of white flowers, extremely interesting and handsome. 15 cents each ; 4 for 50 cents.

**DWARF POMEGRANATE.**—Remarkable for their magnificent and perfectly double flowers, as large as Pæonies; much admired also for the fruit which is produced on single flowered sorts. 25 cents each.

**ARISTOLOCHIAS.**—No plants attract greater attention when in bloom than these. Some have flowers one and two feet in length, resembling as described "a flying eagle," "a boat," "a duck," "a Dutchman's pipe," etc. Having only recently obtained my stock, I could not find room for full description in my catalogue. They are all curious. Three sorts, 30 cents each.

### SILVER-STRIPED PEPEROMIA.

## Silver-Striped Peperomia.

So thick and waxy-like are the leaves of this parlor gem that almost every one takes it for an artificial plant. The color along the veins is bright green, the intervening space being a metallic white. The whole leaf has the appearance of being powdered with silver. As an ornament for a dinner table or for parlor windows it is excellent as it requires but little light and stands much ill-usage. It improves from year to year. The small spikes of white flowers are also interesting. Price, 35 cents each, 4 for $1.00.

**PRIDE OF ASIA, (Melia Floribunda.)**—Few plants are as handsome as this in general habit of growth. It forms the neatest little tree-like plant imaginable, growing in a solid mass, almost like a ball, of dark green delicately cut foliage, remaining on the plant all Winter. Its flowers which are produced on long spikes, are of a beautiful purple and so fragrant that they pervade the air for quite a distance. As a pot plant, it is a little beauty. 25 cents each, 3 for 60 cents.

**PASSION FLOWERS, (Passiflora.)**—Every one should grow these magnificent flowering climbing plants, the flowers of which are so beautiful. The petals, which are blue without, are lilac with purple and white within, and spread themselves out in a flattened manner, with a row of filaments arranged around an inner circle. The flower was named "for passion" by the early missionaries, who in their religious zeal imagined they saw emblems of the crucifixion, the crown of thorns, nails, hammer, etc., in the various parts of the curious blossoms. 25 cents each 3 for 60 cents.

**DAY BLOOMING JESSAMINE.**—This variety is very similar to the Night Blooming Jessamite, but far superior in every respect. In the first inc. the panicles of flowers are as a deal longer, often the size of trusses of lilac, and they are of the purest white. Of course it is as fragrant as the old-fashioned sort so well renowned, but as it blooms in the day time, it is much more desirable. This plant is new North, and might well be called Florida Lilac. 25 cents each, 3 for 60 cents.

**CLIMBING CACTUS.**—Undoubtedly the most beautiful climbing foliage plant in cultivation. One that will delight you with the many different colors displayed on the leaves, each one being a picture in itself. White color, purple, gray, pink and green are well blotched and spotted in a graceful manner, and the leaves are heavy and embossed as if they were artificially made. A rapid grower in a warm place. A most beautiful plant. 20 cents each, 3 for 60 cents.

**CLIMBING HYDRANGEA.**—This exceedingly rare Hydrangea was introduced from Japan. It is a handsome, rapid growing plant, clinging with tenacity to any tree or building by which it may be planted, and attains a height of 50 feet. The flowers, resembling those of shrubby Hydrangea, remain in bloom a long time. Many good words are said for it. Perfectly hardy. 25 cents each ; 3 for 60 cents.

**LARGE PANICLED WISTARIA, (Wistaria Multijuga.)**—One of the greatest novelties introduced of late, and over which French floriculturists are going wild. It was introduced from the Imperial Garden of Pekin, and resembles the well-known Wistaria in habit, but bearing clusters of flowers measuring 20 to 40 inches in length, undoubtedly one of the grandest plants known. 30 cents each ; 2 for 50 cents ; 4 plants for $1.00.

**ARUM ITALICUM.**—Hardy perennial handsome Calla-like leaves veined yellow, handsome waxy-like flowers. 20c. ; 3 for 50c.

**TRADESCANTIA DISCOLOR.**—Fine plants with long erect leaves, blood red underneath and green on face. The red showing well makes a fine contrast. Boat shaped flowers. 15 cents ; 4 for 50 cents.

**ALLAMANDA HENDERSONI.**—Gorgeous plants, the flowers of which are a grand sight, being sometimes 6 inches in diameter and of the finest golden yellow, edged and shaded to crimson. Elegant foliage. Rapid grower. 25 cents ; 3 for 60 cents.

**AGAVES, (Century Plants).**—I call particular attention to my collection of highly decorative plants of which I have 25 distinct varieties at all prices. They for splendid objects for lawns, decorating, and are of easy growth, requiring very little care. Desirable for porches, parlors, halls, etc. Price, 50c. each ; 3 for $1.00.

**YUCCA ALOEFOLIA VARIEGATA.**—Leaves stripped with white and pink ; makes elegant specimens form the lawn in Summer, and for parlor or hall during Winter ; rare in this country, and always admired by everyone that sees it. The plant endures dry air and dust very well, and is fine for house culture. $1.00 each.

### CLETHRA ALNIFOLIA.

## Clethra Alnifolia.

This beautiful sweet scented flowering shrub is far less often seen than its beauty warrants. No one could fail to admire it. The leaves are of a deep green and the spreading panicles of white, bell-shaped flowers borne at the ends of the shoots, are produced in the greatest abundance. It is often called the "Bee Plant," because bees are attracted to it by the delicious odor of the flowers. It comes in bloom July and Aug. when few flowers can be had, and, as it is of dwarf growth, can be used for many purposes. Perfectly hardy. 25c. each ; 3 for 60c.

**FARFUGIUM GRANDE.**—(See cut.) Highly decorative plant with round leaves as large as tea saucers ; of a **dark green color,** freely blotched with yellow. A great acquisition of easiest culture. 30c. each.

**CATALPA, Japanese Hybrid.**—As an ornamental or useful tree Japanese Hybrid Catalpa is of great value, being one of the most rapid growers of all hardy trees, and one of the most beautiful. From the smallest sprouts it will grow in four or five years to a large size. The foliage is dense, large, and luxuriant, deep, glowing green. It is a most profuse bloomer, being literally loaded with flowers, and remaining in bloom several weeks. The flowers are white, with small purple dots, and a touch of yellow around the throat. They have a very pleasant and delicate fragrance, and a tree in bloom not only presents a magnificent spectacle to the eye, but also fills the air for quite a distance with its agreeable odor. Small trees planted in village lots grow, without cultivation, in five years, to be 25 ft. high and 24 in. in circumference at two feet from the ground. I believe the Japanese Hybrid is destined, when known, to take a prominent place in the very front rank of trees for timber as well as ornamental plantations. In rapidity of growth it rivals the most luxuriant trees of temperate climate ; while its hardiness has been demonstrated by its standing unlimited 25° or more below zero. Price of vigorous, well-rooted trees, by mail post-paid, 15 cts. each ; 4 for 50 cts.; 10 for $1.; 25 for $2.; 100 for $6.

## Worthy and Desirable Fruits

IN order that my customers may be supplied with the most valuable fruits, I have carefully prepared a SELECT LIST of varieties comprising those that have been thoroughly tested in all parts of the country, and proven adapted to a variety of soils and climates, as well as the novelties of recent introduction, which, by their many points of excellence, give promise of superiority, so that any article from the list may be ordered with confidence of success.

Thrifty, well-rooted trees and plants, of medium size, receive less shock in transplanting, suffer less in transportation, start off more promptly, make better growth, and in many ways are more desirable than larger stock.

Of most varieties such trees and plants can be selected and sent safely *by mail*, post-paid, at prices affixed, though some others are such vigorous growers as to become too large for mailing and will be sent by express at same rates at purchaser's expense.

### Pears

JAPAN GOLDEN RUSSET.—This variety was accidentally found in an importation of Japanese trees and plants. Its rampant growth, with dark glossy brown wood and large luxurious foliage, was so distinct from anything with which we were familiar, that we were at once impressed with its wondrous vigor and beauty and anxiously awaited its fruiting, feeling assured that if such a healthy growing tree should produce a desirable fruit, it would be gladly received by all fruit and fruit tree growers as well as for ornamental purposes; nor did we have long to wait, for remarkable as it appeared in vigor and beauty it was none the less remarkable in fruiting, and at two years of age was heavily laden with the beautiful GOLDEN RUSSET PEARS, which were found to be crisp, juicy, sweet, pleasant and unsurpassed for canning or preserving. The JAPAN GOLDEN RUSSET tree has continued to bear enormously EVERY YEAR, having no off years. The past season, when all varieties failed, Kieffer not excepted, THE JAPAN GOLDEN RUSSET produced its usual heavy crop, showing it is not affected by the sudden changes of heat and cold. Its bearing propensities are so great that the fruit hangs in great masses and clusters, and consequently, if not thinned, the tree will not increase rapidly in size, and is therefore nicely adapted to small plots or can be planted closely. The abundance of thick, tough, leathery leaves of THE JAPAN GOLDEN RUSSET enables it to endure great heat and drought and will particularly adapt it to dry, hot climates and parched, sandy soils where the European varieties cannot exist. It also matures its wood so perfectly that it would require very intense cold to injure it. Nor has it ever been affected by blight or insect enemies of any kind. It also makes a remarkably handsome Lawn Tree and will become a profitable market variety, as well as desirable for family use. The leaves are large and velvety, measuring 6 to 8 inches in length by 3 to 4 in width and of dark green color until fall, when they become a beautiful bronze, changing to a brilliant crimson, and with their branches bending under their load of GOLDEN RUSSET PEARS, it is a thing of beauty indeed. The fruit is of a handsome uniform, perfect pear or apple shape, so that it has been suggested that it may be a hybrid between the Apple and the Pear, of good size, 8 to 10 inches around and becoming a beautiful golden russet color. Ripening in September. **Price, mail or express, $1.00 each; 3 for $2.00.**

**BARTLETT.**—Large, yellow, juicy, excellent, heavy bearer, reliable everywhere, August.

**LE CONTE.**—Large, smooth, greenish yellow, handsome, rampant grower, early and prolific bearer. September.

**KIEFFER.**—Large, showy, rich, golden yellow, with red cheek; very handsome, excellent for canning, vigorous grower and very productive. October.

**LAWRENCE.**—Medium size, canary yellow, very productive, delicious quality, and good keeper. November and December.

Price by mail or express, any of the last four, 40c. each, or 3, your choice, for $1.

### Apples

The following five varieties have proven hardy, vigorous and productive, and will succeed in all sections. They cover the entire season, from early to late. Price, by mail or express, 25c. ea.; $2.50 doz.

**YELLOW TRANSPARENT.**—The earliest apple known; large, rich, transparent, handsome, yellow, juicy, excellent.

**RED BEITIGHEIMER.**—A German variety, very large, and of beautiful, purple, crimson red; excellent quality. Tree vigorous, productive; ripens in Autumn.

**RED CIDER.**—Strong grower, immensely productive; bright red, good quality. Fall and Winter.

**DICKINSON.**—Large, deep red, juicy, mild sub-acid; good, abundant and annual bearer. December to March.

**DELAWARE WINTER.**—Vigorous and productive; large, bright red, sub-acid, rich and good. December to July.

**SPECIAL No. 1.**—For $1.00 I will send by mail or express one tree each, of the above five varieties of apples.

108

## Japan Plums

Plums of this strain have given a renewed interest to Plum culture. Their hardiness, rapid growth, freedom from insects, early bearing, great and uniform productiveness render the industry one that can be engaged in with pleasure and certainty of success.

**KELSEY.**—Very large fine yellow, overspread with rich crimson, with delicate bloom, flesh firm, melting, rich and juicy. Remarkably small pit. Tree a vigorous grower, enormously productive, and fruit a good shipper. Late and very valuable.

**SATSUMA BLOOD.**—A fine, large plum of oriental class—as large as Kelsey and five to six weeks earlier. Flesh solid and blood-red throughout; juicy, fine quality; pit very small; tree a strong grower, hardy and productive.

**ABUNDANCE.**—Medium size, dark red, delicious.

**OGON.**—Early, yellow, large, delicious; bears young, and enormously.

**GOLDEN BEAUTY.**—A native sort; an annual, certain and enormous bearer of medium-sized handsome golden-yellow plums, good quality, excellent for cooking. Late curculio or other insects have no effect on the skin.

Any one planting the above varieties will be sure to have plums and an abundance of them. All the above by mail or express, 50 cents each; 3 for $1.00.

WHY NOT MAKE UP YOUR ORDER TWO OR THREE WEEKS AHEAD OF TIME THIS YEAR AND THUS AVOID THE RUSH AT THE PLANTING SEASON.

## Downing ❋ Everbearing ❋ Mulberry

Makes a handsome lawn tree, producing berries at 4 to 5 years of age, that ripen early in the season and continue all Summer. The foliage is valuable for silkworms, and the fruit excellent for chickens as well as a fine table dessert. The late Henry Ward Beecher said, he regarded it as an indispensable addition to every fruit garden and that he would rather have one Downing Mulberry tree than a Strawberry bed. Price by mail or express, 50 cents each.

## ELEAGNUS ❋ LONGIPES

A valuable New Fruit as well as a magnificent · Ornamental · Shrub from Japan

Perfectly hardy. **Free from disease and INSECT VERMIN** of all kinds. Very attractive, in bloom in May, after which, until late in Fall it is clothed in luxuriant green foliage; silvery underside and producing in profusion handsome bright red berries, which make delicious sauce.

This fruit has been grown and highly prized in an amateur way for a number of years; but not until the past season has its real value as a garden or market fruit been recognized. We anticipate for this rare and valuable addition to our list of choice fruits, an immense demand as soon as its great merits become known to the public. Below we give extracts from William Falconer in the *Rural New Yorker*:

"The shrub ELEAGNUS LONGIPES is one of my special favorites. I have grown it for years, and the longer I know it the better I like it. It is a native of Japan, and belongs to the Olive family of plants, and is perfectly hardy. As a garden shrub it grows to a height of five feet or more, is bushy and broad, and thrifty plants begin to fruit when two to three years old. The leaves are oval, oblong green above, silvery beneath, and last in good condition all Summer long, and are never disfigured by insect vermin. The flowers are small, silvery yellow and borne in great abundance and in full bloom about the 8th to 10th of May. The fruit is oval, very fleshy and juicy, bright red and drooping on slender pedicles on the underside of the twigs, and borne in immense profusion. It is ripe about July 4th to 10th. We use the fruit for sauce as one would cranberries, and a delicious sauce it makes, especially for children; indeed I like it so well that I have planted it in our fruit garden as a standard crop as one would currants." Price, by mail or express, 50 cents each; 3 for $1.00.

## Peach

Wonderful

## Peaches

**MT. ROSE.**—The largest early peach, white with red cheek, excellent, productive and reliable. Price, by mail or express, 15 cents each.

**GLOBE.**—Very large, yellow, with red cheek; delicious, vigorous and productive. Price, by mail or express, 20 cents each; 6 for $1.00.

**WONDERFUL.**—The most valuable late yellow peach yet introduced. As large as Globe, as late or later than Smock, remarkable grower, enormous bearer, so as to require braces and props to support the heavy crop of fruit. Many specimens measure ten to eleven inches around and weigh as many ounces. Rich golden yellow with red cheek, very handsome, flesh yellow, rich, high flavored and delicious, free stone, excellent for canning, a good keeper and good shipper. Price, by mail or express, 25 cents each; 5 for $1.00.

**FORD'S LATE WHITE.**—A handsome late white Peach, very sweet and delicious, large size and very productive. Price, by mail or express, 20 cents each; 6 for $1.00.

ELEAGNUS LONGIPES

# NUTS & NUT-TREES

NUT CULTURE is an industry that until recently has received but little attention. The large returns from individual trees, and immense profits from established orchards, have stimulated the interest and our foremost enterprising fruit growers are planting nut trees largely for market purposes; and others who enjoy the nuts during the Winter are realising that in order to have an abundant supply, it is only necessary to plant the trees, as hardy varieties are now grown that succeed in all sections of the United States.

A Kentuckian, who has 200 chestnut trees and about 300 walnut and butternut trees says: "His income from them year by year, is larger than that of any farmer cultivating 300 acres of ground." He sells his crop on the trees for cash, and the only expense is for taxes.

A gentleman in Georgia, Mr. H. C. Daniels, has a Pecan tree which bears annually from ten to fifteen bushels of nuts, which sell readily at wholesale for $4.00 to $5.00 per bushel. An orchard of Pecans set 30 feet apart each way, requiring 48 trees to the acre, at above rates, would give handsome returns.

Don Bernard Guirado of California, owns an English walnut orchard, which he reports, yields him a net profit of $15,000.00 every year. As the orchard contains 100 acres, this is at the rate, year in and year out, of $150.00 from each acre.

L. H. Burke has a 40-acre orchard near Riviera, which, although not in full bearing last year, gave him a return of almost $6,000.00. These figures show that the English walnut is a good tree to plant in California, and they are now being grown successfully over a large scope of the country.

The Chestnut is also very valuable, not only for timber purposes, but for market. Of the improved varieties of large nuts, two to three bushels per tree is but an ordinary yield, and as they come to bearing at two to three years of age, or as young as a peach tree, and the nuts sell at 25 to 40 cents per quart, the profits must be very gratifying and the business pleasant and popular. When the culinary uses of the Chestnut are more generally appreciated in this country, as they are in Europe, the demand for those of large size will be immense. European cooks know how to utilize them in a number of ways.

**THE JAPAN MAMMOTH SWEET CHESTNUT.** —Is among the most valuable recent introductions from Japan. It is quite distinct from the European varieties, being hardier, and the nuts are of a superior flavor and sweetness. The leaf is long and narrow like a peach leaf, of dark green color, making an ornamental lawn tree. Comes to bearing at two to three years of age, and while yet in the nursery grows 3 to 4 feet high. They are heavily laden with nuts of enormous size, measuring 4 to 6 inches around, and ranging from 3 to 7 in a bur. Their early bearing and great productiveness of such enormous nuts are the wonder and admiration of all who see them. They are dwarf in habit, and can be planted closer together. No fruit garden is complete without a **Japan Mammoth Sweet Chestnut.** By mail or express, 50 cents each. $5.00 per dozen.

**SPANISH CHESTNUT.**—Is a handsome round-headed, spreading tree of rapid growth, and produces an abundance of large nuts of good quality, that sell readily at high prices. Valuable for ornament and fruit. A gentleman of our acquaintance realizes an average of $50.00 a year from the sale of nuts from two trees of **Spanish Chestnuts.** Price by mail or express, 40 cents each. $4.00 per dozen.

**AMERICAN.**—The well-known chestnut of the forest, of rapid upright growth. A handsome shade tree. The nuts are unsurpassed for sweetness and delicacy of flavor. Price, mail or express, 30 cents each. $3.00 per dozen.

**THE ENGLISH WALNUT, or MADEIRA NUT,**—Is a handsome growing tree, with light green foliage and silvery-white bark, very ornamental. Nuts large, thin-shelled, sweet, delicious, and sell readily at high prices in market. Price, mail or express, 50 cents each; $5.00 per dozen.

**THE BUTTERNUT.**—Is a rapid growing tree, with long tropical looking foliage. Begins to bear quite young, and produces enormously. Nuts long, kernel very sweet and delicate flavor. A very desirable tree. Price, mail or express, 35 cents each. $3.50 per dozen.

**THE PECAN.**—Is a beautiful symmetrical and very rapid growing tree with luxuriant, light green foliage, which it retains until late in the Fall, rendering it a very conspicuous and attractive shade tree, producing in great abundance oblong, smooth, thin-shelled nuts with sweet and delicious kernels. The nuts are very desirable for family use, or valuable for market. Price, mail or express, 35 cents each. $3.50 per dozen.

**THE FILBERT** or Hazelnut is of the easiest culture. Dwarf, hardy, abundant yielders, and comes to bearing very young. Price, mail or express, 25 cents each. $2.50 per dozen.

JAPAN MAMMOTH, SWEET CHESTNUT TREE, FOUR YEARS OLD PRODUCING SIX QUARTS OF MAMMOTH NUTS.

# SOMETHING NEW
## JAPAN WALNUT
### JUGLANS      SIEBOLDIANA

This species is found growing wild in the mountains of Northern Japan, and is without doubt as hardy as an oak. The leaves are of immense size, and of a charming shade of green. The long, pendant male catkins, as well as the clusters of female flowers crowned with purple stigmas, add further beauty to this remarkable tree. The wood appears to be similar to that of the common walnut, although a little less veined. The nuts, which are produced in extreme abundance, grow in clusters of fifteen and even twenty, have a shell thicker than the English walnut, but not as thick as the black walnut, very much resembling Pecan nuts. The meat is sweet, of the very best quality, flavor like Butternut, but less oily and much superior. The trees grow with great vigor, assuming a very handsome form, and need no pruning; mature early, bear young, and are more regular and productive than the English walnut. The species is of easy culture, reproducing itself perfectly by seed, and grows with great vigor. Having an abundance of fibrous roots, it transplants as safely as an apple tree. $1.00 each ; 3 for $2.00.

**SPECIAL NO. 2.** ONE TREE EACH OF THE ABOVE EIGHT VALUABLE NUTS MAKING A DESIRABLE AND PROFITABLE COLLECTION, BY MAIL OR EXPRESS FOR $2.50.

> WHAT BETTER ILLUSTRATES THE MAGNITUDE OF THE BUSINESS ANNUALLY DONE IN MAULE'S SEEDS, PLANTS, ETC., THAN THIS CATALOGUE ITSELF?

FILBERT.

American Chestnut.

SPANISH CHESTNUT.      PECAN NUT.

English Walnut or Madeira Nut.

BUTTERNUT.

110

# SMALL FRUITS.

## Strawberries

At dozen rates will be mailed free; at 100 rates, add 25 cents per hundred to cover additional expenses, postage, etc.

**GANDY.**—The latest of all Strawberries, and of such vigorous growth as to produce a crop of fruit the first season planted and hence has become known as the First Season Strawberry. Fruit large, firm and attractive. Price by mail, 80 cts. per doz.; by express, $1.00 per 100; $5.00 per 1000.

**MICHEL'S EARLY.**—Strong grower, good foliage, very productive, good quality. By mail, 35 cts. per doz.; express, $1.00 per 100; $5.00 per 1000.

**BUBACH, P.**—Strong grower, healthy foliage, very large, fine color, very productive, good quality. Early. By mail, 35c. per doz.; ex., $1 per 100; $5 per 1000.

**BOMBA.**—Good grower, prolific, large, firm, rich, dark red throughout, best for canning. Price by mail, 35c. per doz.; express, $1.00 per 100; $5.00 per 1000.

**PINE-APPLE.**—Strong grower, productive of very large bright red berries of excellent quality. By mail, 50c. per doz.; by express, $1 per 100; $5 per 1000.

**SHARPLESS.**—Strong grower, large irregular shaped berries of rich flavor. One of the best. By mail, 35c. per doz.; by express, $1 per 100; $5 per 1000.

**SPECIAL No. 3.**—By mail, ½ doz. each of the above 6 varieties for $1.00.

## Currants

**CRANDALL.** A new black currant growing 6 to 8 feet in height and in tree form, and absolutely proof against currant worm and other insects; enormously prolific; no other small fruit approaches it in productiveness; generally produces fruit the first season planted; berries very large, ¾ in. in diameter. For all culinary purposes, either for pies or sauce, green or ripe, and for jelly or jam when ripe, it has no superior. Price by mail, 30 cts. each; 4 for $1.00.

**WHITE GRAPE.**—The largest and best white currant; strong grower and very productive, bunch large and long; berry large, handsome, translucent white. Price, by mail, $1.00 per dozen; by express, $5.00 per 100.

**CHERRY.**The most popular red currant; very productive; bright red berries, excellent for wine or jelly. Price, by mail, $1 per doz.; by ex., $5 per 100.

## Black- and Raspberries

will be mailed at dozen rates free of postage. By mail at 100 rates if 40 cts. per 100 be added.

**CUTHBERT, Rasp.**—Red, large, excellent, strong grower, hardy and late. Price by mail, 75 cts. per doz.; by ex., $2 per 100; $15 per 1000.

**GOLDEN QUEEN, Rasp.**—Yellow, large, delicious, very rich, strong grower, very hardy. Price by mail, $1 per doz.; by ex., $6 per 100; $20 per 1000.

**PIONEER, Black Rasp.**—Very early, very productive, hardy, rich, good quality. Price by mail, 75c. per doz.; by express, $2.50 per 100; $20 per 1000.

**EARLY HARVEST BLACKBERRY.**—Is the earliest known; blackberry, enormously productive, valuable for early market. Price by mail, 75 cts. per doz.; by express, $2.00 per 100; $15.00 per 1000.

**WILSON, Jr.**—The largest known blackberry; very productive and good quality. Price by mail, 75 cts. per doz.; by express, $2.00 per 100; $15.00 per 1000.

**LUCRETIA DEWBERRY.**—Very large, very early, very productive, very hardy, very good quality. Mail, 75c. per doz.; exp. $2 per 100; $15 per 1000.

**SPECIAL No. 4.**—By mail, 3 plants each of the above 6 varieties for $1.00.

## Gooseberries

**INDUSTRY.**—Very large, rich dark red, and of delicious quality. An English variety that resists the mildew, and succeeds admirably in the U. S. Mail, 25c. each; $2.50 per doz.; by ex., $18 per 100.

**DOWNING.**—An American variety, very large size and excellent quality. Strong grower, very productive, and free from mildew. Price, by mail, 15 cents each; $1.50 per dozen; by express, $8.00 per 100.

**SPECIAL No. 5.**—Three plants each of the above 2 valuable varieties of gooseberries and 3 plants each of the 3 currants in opp. column for $2 postpaid.

## Grapes

I have carefully selected the following varieties as being entirely hardy, vigorous, healthy growers, free from mildew and adapted to all sections of the country or city, and as there is no fruit more easily and quickly grown, there is no reason why persons having but a few feet of vacant ground should not have an abundant supply.

**CONCORD. Black.** So popular and well-known as to need no description. Succeeds everywhere. Price, mail or express, 25c. each; $2.50 per doz.

**MOORE'S EARLY. Black.** Seedling of Concord and nearly 2 weeks earlier, strong vigorous grower and free from rot and mildew; fruit very large and very good quality. Price, by mail or express, 25 cents each; $2.50 per dozen.

**NIAGARA. White.** Hardy, strong grower, very productive, bunch large, showy and good quality. The best white grape. Price, by mail or express, 25 cents each; $2.50 per dozen.

**POCKLINGTON. White.** Seedling of Concord; tough leathery foliage; free from mildew; very large, sweet and delicious, with slight trace of native aroma. Price, by mail or express, 25 cents each; $2.50 per doz.

**WYOMING. Red.** A grape very much resembling the Delaware in size, color, appearance, etc., though of stronger and healthier vine; succeeds everywhere; very early. Price, by mail or express, 25 cents each; $2.50 per dozen.

**WOODRUFF. Red.** Another seedling of Concord, strong grower; bunch and berries large, attractive and good. By mail or ex., 30c. each; $3.50 per doz.

SPECIAL No. 6.
ONE OF EACH OF
THE ABOVE SIX
GRAPE VINES FOR
$1.00.

111

# ☀ THOROUGHBRED PIGS ☀

Page 112.—Annual Catalogue for 1891 of Maule's Four-Leaf Clover GUARANTEED SEEDS. Address all Orders to WM. HENRY MAULE, No. 1711 Filbert Street, Philadelphia, Pa., U.S.A.

My stock has always been and will always be my best advertisement. Few, if any, in the live-stock business, shipping as largely as I do, spend so little in advertising. A pair of pigs, a sheep, or a trio of chickens sent into a neighborhood, is at once a standing advertisement of the superior excellence of my stock, bringing me frequently any number of other orders, so that I have not only made shipments to all parts of the United States, but also exported a large number of animals to the West Indies, Europe, etc.

## ☀ CHESTER WHITES ☀

**This most profitable breed** originated in Chester Co., this State, not 40 miles from our office. Order direct and obtain the genuine; by placing your order at once you insure the pick of hundreds of as Fine Pigs as can be found in America. We consider ourselves Headquarters for the Best Specimens of this Breed. It will repay you to read the following short summary of their merits:

**CHESTER WHITES** are invaluable on account of their large size—they readily weighing 200 to 225 pounds at five to six months old, 400 to 500 pounds at twelve or fourteen months, 1000 pounds even, not being an unusual weight attained by well-

The genuine Chester White, such as we ship, have the following prominent characteristics: head very short and broad between the eyes; ears, medium, and projecting forward; neck, short and thick; joints, large and full; body, lengthy, deep and "well-ribbed out," giving ample room for large, sound lungs; back, broad and very straight; hams, large full and deep, with fine bones; legs, short and well set under the body; of sufficient strength for bearing the heavy weight; hair, perfectly white; skin, fine and thin; tail, neat and small in proportion to size of body. The accompanying cut of the fine pair "King of Chester County" and "Chester County Model of Perfection," is drawn from life by an artist visiting the farm for that purpose. Price: Single pigs 2 to 3 months old, $12.50; pair, boar and sow, not akin, $20.00; trio, 1 boar and 2 sows, not akin, $29.00.

fattened old porkers. Fine forms; ready fattening qualities—as they can be fattened for market at any age, and may be fed to any reasonable weight desired; good bacon, flesh rating as A 1; docility and prolificness. They are gentle, quiet and easily kept. They are not liable to mange as some prejudiced breeders, or those who have "axes to grind" on other grindstones, so positively state. Chester Whites are also a well and thoroughly established breed, with well defined characteristics to which they breed very true—as true as the Berkshires or Poland Chinas.

There is no doubt that the fame and good name of Chester Whites has suffered considerably by the shipments of certain unprincipled dealers; men, such as will be found in every business, who would buy up worthless mongrels, whose only pretense to the genuine was their white color and perhaps looped ears, and palm them off for the "Genuine Chester Whites." There are as poor hogs in Chester County as anywhere in America, and we have sol the pure stock of Chester Whites in this very county at FANCY PRICES. We have shipped our pigs to almost every State in the Union, and everywhere they prove the very best sort of an advertisement, procuring for our firm numbers of new customers. We have no superior, if any equal, in our shipments of this profitable breed.

## GUARANTEE
I guarantee all stock shipped to be strictly first-class, and as represented, also that they shall arrive at destination in good order.

BOXING, ETC.—I box comfortably, but at the same time as lightly as possible, deliver on board cars in this city, put trough for feed and water in box, and supply feed for journey free of charge. Customers must pay transportation charges.

ALL ORDERS WILL BE FILLED IN ROTATION AS RECEIVED.

## NOTE
I CAN FURNISH OLDER PIGS OF ANY OF THESE BREEDS, AND WILL CHEERFULLY SUBMIT PRICES ON APPLICATION.

## POLAND CHINAS
I claim for Poland Chinas that for early fattening qualities and continued growth, they are second only to Chester Whites. They will readily fatten into pork at nine to ten months, when they will weigh 300 to 325 pounds. As perfected to-day, the Poland China is, beyond doubt, entitled to a position as a very valuable breed, specially suited to roughing it on the Western plains. We have in them a breed thoroughly established, of fixed characteristics, of fine style and unquestioned good qualities, which can be relied upon for the production of a progeny of like qualities and character. The Poland Chinas are the most popular and numerous breed of swine in the Western States, being found in large quantities, bred more or less pure, in almost every section of the West and North-West. Price: Single pig, 2 to 3 months old, $15.00; pair, boar and sow, not akin, $25.00; trio, 1 boar and 2 sows, not akin, $35.00.

## SMALL YORKSHIRES
Have united in them a great many superior qualities that recommend them to all. They fatten easily at an early age; meat is very fine in texture and quality. They grow to a size that is very desirable for family or packers' use. Careful experiments show them to waste less in dressing than any other breed. I offer a most excellent strain of this breed and send certified pedigree with each pig shipped. Price: Single pig, 2 to 3 months old, $15.00; pair, boar and sow, not akin, $25.00; trio, 1 boar and 2 sows, not akin, $35.00.

**JERSEY RED.**

## JERSEY REDS
The Reds have been bred in New Jersey upwards of fifty years, consequently are thoroughly established, breeding in all cases remarkably true. The most important qualities for which they are esteemed are—first, unusually heavy weights attained at small cost. Second, hardy constitutions. Third, good breeding and fattening qualities. Fourth, their exemption from the mange. They are of one solid red color throughout. When full grown they are of a dark but very red color, and perfectly free from white. They have short snout; small head in proportion to size of body; loop ears. They should have a long, deep, and rangy body, and rather coarse bone; hair, inclining to bristles on the back. They will weigh at twelve months, 300 to 400 lbs., and at eighteen to twenty months, 450 to 700 lbs. I ship extra choice specimens of this breed, and all pigs shipped are guaranteed pure bred and first-class; in every particular. Price: Single pig, 2 to 3 months old, $10.00; pair, boar and sow, not akin, $18.00. trio, 1 boar and 2 sows, not akin, $26.00.

## BERKSHIRES
I have for many years made this breed a specialty, and consider that I ship specimens that are unsurpassed. With every pig sent out from my establishment goes a certified pedigree which is short and direct to importation. I will give some of the esteemed qualities of this breed. Sows are very prolific and good sucklers. They at all times breed remarkably true in color, markings, etc. They are unusually hardy, with high vital powers, shifting well for themselves. Our pigs are very strong, active and grow well. They may be fattened and marketed at any age. Their flesh is of the very highest quality. They are less liable to disease than other breeds. Price: Single pig, 2 to 3 months old, $15.00; pair, boar and sow, not akin, $25.00; trio, 1 boar and 2 sows, not akin, $35.00.

**BERKSHIRE.**

*HAVE YOU READ the Special Announcement for 1891 on back of ORDER SHEET enclosed with this Catalogue ?*

# THOROUGHBRED POULTRY AND EGGS FOR HATCHING

I have spared no expense to have the finest stock of each breed, and keep several distinct yards of each breed, so that we can send out stock not akin. The prices quoted, which are my very lowest, are for first-class breeding fowls, from the very best strains and properly mated.

**EGGS FOR HATCHING** I guarantee all eggs fresh, and true to name. I can ship eggs by express only, and use the utmost care in packing, but cannot guarantee any number to hatch, as this depends on causes over which I have no control. I have frequently forwarded eggs from 1000 to 3000 miles, and had 12 out of 13 hatch out a chick.

**ROSE COMBED BROWN AND WHITE LEGHORNS.**—Similar to the single combed, except that they have a rose comb. Price, Brown or White, single male, $4; pair, $7; trio, 1 cockerel and 2 pullets, $10. Eggs, $2 per 13.

**WHITE-CRESTED BLACK POLISH.**—Excellent layers and of fine quality for the table. These fowls attract a good deal of attention, and for an ornamental fowl for park or lawn, I can highly recommend them. Price, single male, $4; pair, $7; trio, 1 cockerel and 2 pullets, $10. Eggs, $2.50 per 13.

**BUFF COCHINS.**—They thrive well in the smallest yards, and are most excellent Winter layers. Price, single male, $4.00; pair, $7.00; trio, 1 cockerel and 2 pullets, $10.00. Eggs, $2.50 per 13.

**WHITE COCHINS.**—Very hardy, and make excellent broilers. Mature early, good Winter layers. Price of both fowls and eggs, same as Buff Cochins.

**PARTRIDGE COCHINS.**—Attractive appearance and large size. Price of both fowls and eggs, same as Buff Cochins.

**WHITE PLYMOUTH ROCKS.**—Have all the good points that make the Plymouth Rock such a favorite, but have a pure white plumage. They are very prolific layers and make excellent mothers, a most profitable breed for either the farmer or fancier. Price, single male, $4.50; pair, $8.00; trio, 1 cockerel and 2 pullets, $11.00. Eggs, $2.50 per 13.

**BARRED PLYMOUTH ROCKS.**—For general purposes, may be justly entitled the "Farmer's Fowl." They are very hardy, most excellent layers, and one of the very best market fowls. Price, single male, $3.50; pair, $6.50; trio, 1 cockerel and 2 pullets, $9.00. Eggs, $2.00 per 13.

**LIGHT OR DARK BRAHMAS.**—No breed makes larger or better broilers, at 8 to 10 weeks, than the Brahmas. Very docile and easily enclosed by a low fence. Price for either Light or Dark Brahmas, single male, $4.00; pair, $7.00; trio, 1 cockerel and 2 pullets, $10.00. Eggs, $2.00 per 13.

**BROWN AND WHITE LEGHORNS.—Single Comb.**—They mature very early, and make good table fowls. Price, either Brown or White, single male, $4.00; pair, $7.00; trio, 1 cockerel and 2 pullets, $10. Eggs, $2 per 13.

**WHITE-FACED BLACK SPANISH.**—One of the handsomest fowls, and also one of the best layers. Price, single male, $4.00; pair, $7.00; trio, 1 cockerel and 2 pullets, $10.00. Eggs, $2.50 per 13.

**BLACK HAMBURGS.**—Are non-setters, and for layers are hard to surpass. Price, single male, $4.00; pair, $7.00; trio, 1 cockerel and 2 pullets, $10.00. Eggs, $2.50 per 13.

**HOUDANS.**—Are prolific layers of large rich eggs. Price, single male, $4.00; pair, $7.00; trio, 1 cockerel and 2 pullets, $10.00. Eggs $2.50 per 13.

**BLACK-BREASTED RED GAME.**—Are most excellent table fowls, prolific layers; good foragers and when desired can bear the closest confinement. Price, single male, $4.50; pair $8.00; trio, 1 cockerel and 2 pullets, $11.50. Eggs, $2.50 per 13.

**MAMMOTH BRONZE TURKEYS.**—They are good layers, and are the most profitable breed for market. Gobblers 2 years old will often weigh 30 to 40 pounds. Price, single gobbler, $7.00; pair, $10.00; trio, 1 gobbler and 2 hens, $14.00. Eggs, $6.00 per 18.

## INDIAN GAMES.

### THE BEST GENERAL PURPOSE FOWL EVER KNOWN

**INDIAN GAMES.**—They are the quickest growing chick from the shell up to 10 or 12 weeks of any breed, large or small. At 12 weeks old have seen males that weigh 3 to 4 lbs. each. This wonderful growth is accounted for by the fact that they grow a very short feather, thus the nourishment required by other breeds to grow feathers is used by the Indian Games to produce flesh. They lay large eggs and are the equal of the well-known Plymouth Rock for laying qualities. The flesh is of the finest quality, juicy and tender. They are easily cared for, and are, without doubt, the fowl for those who want quick growth, good size, good laying and eating qualities and beauty in appearance. In general appearance they are powerful and broad; plumage short and cannot be too hard and close; carriage upright, back sloping downward toward the tail; color of cock a green glossy-black with brown or crimson markings. Hen ground color, chestnut brown with beautiful lacing of green, glossy black; legs in both sexes yellow or orange. Hens, when full grown, weigh seven to eight pounds and cocks nine to eleven pounds. **Fanciers and others starting in this breed in 1891 will make more money out of Indian Games than all other breeds combined.** I offer eggs from birds imported direct Rock for laying qualities. The finest quality, juicy and tender. They are easily cared for, and are, without doubt, the fowl for those who want quick growth, good size, good laying and eating qualities and beauty in appearance. I offer eggs from birds imported direct from the largest and best breeders in England at $8.00 per 13; $15.00 per 26. I also can furnish eggs from yards of home-bred birds, bred last year from the best imported stock, $6 per 13; $11 per 26.

**DERBYSHIRE RED CAPS.**—This breed although well-known in England is comparatively new in the U. S. From my experience with them the last three or four years I can heartily recommend them as most excellent layers and also first-class table fowls. They are fast becoming a favorite in this country; they are beautifully marked and in color are a red or rich brown and black. Full grown birds will weigh from 6 to 7 lbs. for cock and 5 to 6 for hen. They are non-setters and make a most excellent egg producing sort. Eggs I offer my customers are from birds bred direct from imported stock. $3 per 13; $5.50 per 26.

## POULTRY MARKER

This little instrument is for marking young and old chickens and all kinds of fowl. Invaluable to breeders and farmers, as markings will enable them to recognize their own fowl at a glance. Thus, 15 figures can be made into 225 different combinations and can be increased by marking skin of wing. An advantage for young chicks, as eggs are marked from different breeds and as soon as hatched are marked, thus enabling you to tell their age and every detail. Made in two sizes, nickel-plated, steel cutter and spring, small and neat to carry in vestpocket. Price, 40 cents, postpaid.

### WHITE WYANDOTTE.

**WHITE WYANDOTTES.**—Similar to Silver Laced in plumage which is a pure white. Price, single male, $4.50; pair, $8.00; trio, 1 cockerel and 2 pullets, $11.50. Eggs, $2.50 per 13.

**SILVER LACED WYANDOTTES.**—Unusually hardy, most excellent layers, good mothers. Single male, $4.00; pair, $7.00; trio, 1 cockerel and 2 pullets, $10.00. Eggs, $2.00 per 13.

### BLACK MINORCA.

**BLACK MINORCAS.**—Grow to a good size and are one of, if not the most prolific layers. Eggs very large, weighing from 2 to 3 ounces each. Price, single male, $5.00; pair, $9.00; trio, 1 cockerel and 2 pullets, $13.00. Eggs, $2.50 per 13.

**WHITE MINORCAS.**—Similar to the Black, except in plumage. Price same as the Black.

### PEKIN DUCKS.

### LANGSHANS.

**BLACK LANGSHANS.**—They attain early maturity and grow to a large size. Good layers all the year round. Price, single male, $4.00; pair, $7.00; trio, 1 cockerel and 2 pullets, $10.00. Eggs, $2.50 per 13.

**PEKIN DUCKS.**—They are without doubt the best laying duck known. Price, single drake, $3.50; pair, $6.00; trio, 1 drake and 2 ducks, $9.00. Eggs, $2.00 per 13.

113

# Tobacco and Sulphur Insecticide AND Fertilizer

It will destroy Rose Bugs, Lice, Cut Worms, Vine Bugs, Tomato Worms, Currant Worms, Cabbage Lice and Parasites of all descriptions. Should be applied when the foliage is wet. This powder is the most complete fertilizer for plants and vines. Mix thoroughly with earth in pots, or in the hill, one part powder to five parts earth. Easy of application, and will not burn or injure the plants. Wherever you may use this fertilizer, you will find the foliage of a dark green color, and a healthy vigorous growth. It is of great value for hot-house purposes, nurseries, etc. There are no weed seeds in it. Earth-worms will not live where it is used. Price, trial package, ½ lb., 25 cts.; 2 lbs., 75 cts.; by mail, postpaid.

## Galvanized Steel Wire Netting

PIGEON HOUSES, POULTRY YARDS, LAWN FENCES, AND TRELLISES

Put up in bales, 150 ft. long. This netting is the best grade, made of No. 19 steel wire, 2 in. mesh, double twist and thoroughly galvanized. The 1 ft. wide is extensively used for training vines over porches, up posts, etc., and is far preferable to twine. I offer this netting in bales of 150 lineal feet only. Price, by ex. or freight, at expense of purchaser:

| WIDTH. | SQUARE FEET, PER BALE. | PRICE, PER BALE. |
|---|---|---|
| 12 in. | 150 | $1.15 |
| 18 " | 225 | 1.75 |
| 24 " | 300 | 2.25 |
| 36 " | 450 | 3.50 |
| 48 " | 600 | 4.50 |
| 60 " | 750 | 5.75 |
| 72 " | 900 | 6.75 |

GALVANIZED STEEL WIRE NETTING.

## FOR ALL KINDS OF POULTRY

## IMPERIAL EGG FOOD

WILL MAKE YOUR HENS LAY

Thousands of letters from all parts of the country have been received testifying to its remarkable properties in improving the condition of our domestic fowls and increasing their egg production. It keeps fowls in best condition, and makes poultry the most profitable stock on the farm. It is estimated that one-half the chicks and turkeys annually hatched die before reaching maturity. When the Imperial Egg Food is fed according to directions, sick and drooping chicks will never be seen. It supplies all the needed material for forming bone, muscle, and feathers, and by its gentle tonic effect, strengthens the digestive organs, and lays the foundation for vigorous, healthy, and therefore profitable fowls. They will also be fitted for market a month earlier

## THE Weed Slayer

PRICE, $2.00 BY EXPRESS

THE WEED SLAYER.—I feel confident in offering my customers this tool, that they will find it very superior for use in the garden among Onions, Turnips, Corn, Potatoes, Strawberries, etc.; also very useful for weeding among flowers and in gravel walks. It is very light, weighing but 7 lbs., is strongly made of the best steel and iron, is adjustable to any height of person; cuts from ½ to 1¾ in. under ground and 7 in. wide. Price, packed $2.00 to be shipped by express or freight at expense of purchaser.

### A FEW TESTIMONIALS.

"Will pay for itself every day."—Rural New Yorker.
"Is splendid, worth the price."—Elmira Husbandman.
"The Weed Slayer is equal to five hoes in a garden or field."—Battle Creek Times.
"There is some pleasure and profit in raising Onions now."—J. L. Elmandorf.
"The Weed Slayer is just the thing for cutting Strawberry runners."—A. W. Hovey.
"The Weed Slayer keeps the grass from my gravel walks, and is good cheese."—C. M. Petrie.
"Is the thing for orange cultivation."—D. Pauling.

LANG'S HAND WEEDER.—One of the best weeders made, a band passing over the fingers gives perfect use of the hand for pulling weeds without laying down the tool. Price, postpaid, 30 cents each.

HOSE MENDERS.—Cheap and useful. Each Doz.
Hickman's, ⅜ inch, postpaid ............ 20  $2.00
White Metal, ⅜ " ............ 25  2.50
Woodman, ⅜ " ............ 10  1.00

GARDEN REEL.—Of great use in every garden. $1.10, by express ............ 75

"GEM" HOSE NOZZLE.—This nozzle will throw either a stream or spray. Postpaid, $1.00 each.

GLASS CUTTER AND GLAZING TOOL.—A handy article. Postpaid, 15 cents each.

PRUNING KNIVES.—Saynor's, the finest English. Postpaid, $1.00 and $1.25 each.

PUDDING KNIVES.—Saynor's, the finest English. Postpaid, $1.25 each.

HAND PRUNING SHEARS.—Made of best material, keep sharp a long time, and have great cutting power. Postpaid, $1.25 each.

NEW TREE POLE PRUNER.—Hood and blade operated with a rope; blade is thrown back by a steel spring. Can be screwed on any pole. Postpaid, $2.25 each.

LANG'S WEEDER.
HOSE MENDERS.
GARDEN REEL.
"GEM" HOSE NOZZLE.
GLASS CUTTER.

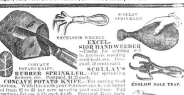

115

Joseph Meehan, the celebrated horticulturist, in the Thanksgiving Number of *The Practical Farmer*, writes as follows concerning " Briar Crest:"

FOR many years Philadelphia was the chief seat of horticulture in this country. The fact that some of the earliest botanists and horticulturists made their home there and founded gardens in which to grow the treasures they collected, gave it prominence from the start. Other cities have since followed in its wake, and have beautiful gardens, but it is safe to say that the love for trees and plants which distinguished it of yore, has in no way declined. Of course, as the city grew it pushed large gardens further and further away from it, so that to-day the best examples of good gardening are found some miles out along the numerous lines of railroads leading to it. The main line of the Pennsylvania Railroad, has been noted for a long time for the beautiful places along it, even as far out as Frazer. It was my good fortune to visit in the early part of September the home of Wm. Henry Maule, one of Philadelphia's prominent seed merchants. His grounds are situated about one mile from Villa Nova, and are easily reached by a well macadamized road. At this place Mr. Maule passes what time he has left after fulfilling the many calls from home which his active business career exacts from him. A more beautiful site does not exist. The fine mansion occupies the summit of a rapidly rising stretch of ground. Mr. Maule is one of many who believe in the beauty of a broad expanse of lawn, and almost seventeen acres have to be cut every week with the lawn mower. The most of the fine old trees, native to the place, have been left, when not interfering with the beauty of the whole. Some fine specimens of the sweet chestnut, shellbark hickory and red cedar, appear to great advantage in the foreground. An immense white oak is quite a feature of the place. In girth it cannot be less than twelve feet in circumference. Its spread of branches overlaps a spring-house, from which water is forced to supply the dwelling. Under the large trees named have been planted Azaleas, Rhododendrons and similar hardy plants, which, though thriving well enough in the sun, are the better for shade, because their flowers last longer when not exposed to the sun. Flower beds everywhere look well this year, and those on his place were no exception. The larger and more prominent ones filled with leaf and flowering plants, such as seem indispensable whe e bright display is required, were at their very best. Great care in arranging the colors to obtain the best contrasts were evident, while the plants themselves were in the best condition. A large rock-work of white flint near the entrance to the mansion was filled with Crotons, Palms and various other tropical plants, which seem better suited than any others when near artificial work of any kind. Beside the fence along the public road which skirts the place, there extends a wide border, certainly more than 500 feet long, planted with hardy shrubs and herbaceous plants. While formed to add attraction to the place, it is also for the purpose of testing the many kinds, to see which are the best for general cultivation. Among the many hundreds of kinds were noticed: Exochorda Grandiflora, Pavia Parviflora, variegated Althæa, Spiræa Thunbergi, and many of the more common, yet indispensable shrubs for home adornment. The Dahlias in this border were an especial feature. Mr. Maule has a fancy for them, and rightly thinks them something every garden should contain; and he has a fine collection. A well-rounded flower is the type of perfection in a dahlia, and the many of this description showed the collection to be a very good one. There are several specimens of the Japan Catalpa here; while a rapid grower, it does not make such a large tree as the ordinary sort, and flowering earlier, it will be desirable or where a large tree is not wanted. At some distance from the house, yet not so far but what its beauty is in sight, are the trial-grounds for flowers, fruits and vegetables. The time of our visit seemed most opportune for witnessing a fine display. The immense field of flowers was a dazzling sight. Petunias, double and single, Zinnias, Cosmos Hybridus, Cockscomb, Alyssum, the various sorts of Dianthus, Phlox, Verbena, Convolvulus and every flower bee ling test was there. A very pretty flower is the Convolvulus Minor, tricolor, which was in full flower. A strain of Phlox, called Star of Quedlinburg, is well worthy of mention. The petals run out to narrow points forming a many-pointed flower of singular beauty. There are many colors of them, just as there are of the common Phlox Drummondii, of which we took this to be a variety.

A Nasturtium, called Cloth of Gold, prove an excellent one for edgings to beds which require something of a greenish yellow color for contrast, which is what the foliage of this sort is. It flowers but seldom, so that the foliage alone is counted on for effect. Gladioli, Tuberoses, Cannas, the various sorts of Flowering Sage and similar plants, all come in for a share of testing on this place. It would certainly be within the truth to say that not less than a million plants were in bloom at the time of our visit. The manner of testing the kinds is carried out on a systematic basis. An office is attached to the trial gardens, in which books are kept, in which everything relating to the plant on trial is minutely recorded. It may be a new flower from Texas, a vegetable from Italy, a fruit from Persia, are we noticed all these names on the record books. The name and address of the person from whom the seed came is put down, the date of sowing, flowering, fruiting and so on, the percentage of good seeds and the comparative value of the article alongside other well-known kinds, are all recorded. All parts of the globe seemed to have contributed something to this trial garden, even the name of far-off Smyrna appearing on the book. Books of this kind should be kept by every gardener as well as by the seedsman who supplies the seeds. In the vegetable trial-ground we noticed a new beet, called Market Gardener's Beet, which is claimed to be the best medium half-long kind, tender at all stages of growth. This shou d be a decided acquisit on, as nowadays gardeners make a late sowing, especially to get something tender for late Fall. The Bush Lima Bean, which the late Peter Henderson did so much to bring into notice, was here loaded down with pods. Tomatoes of all kinds were on trial, to prove which are the earliest and the best. The fruit garden was past its best at the time: raspberries, blackberries, strawberries and similar sorts being past their season. The Niagara grape here, as elsewhere, has proved to be

the best white one out. The Lady and even the old Martha are perhaps sweeter—too sweet to suit many tastes—but for general good qualities, Niagara proves the best of all. Climbing up the walls of the lodge at the entrance gates were a large number of Japan Ivy plants, Ampelopsis Veitchii, some of them in full vigor of fresh, green growth, while others were already showing the beginning of their bright Autumn colors. The common English Ivy was at home as a companion to it. If it would not mind the sun in Winter it would be largely used, but when it freezes hard at night and then gets the rays of a hot sun on it at noon, it is too much for it. Near these vines were Moon Flowers in rampant growth, covering a trellis, a position it is well suited for. To a lover of flowers a visit to these beautiful grounds will give unusual pleasure.

## The Flowers at " Briar Crest."

WE recently paid a visit to "Briar Crest," located on the Gulf road, about one mile and a half from Bryn Mawr, and the beautiful country-seat of Mr. Wm. Henry Maule. It has been several years since the writer visited this place, and from the moment he entered through the gate of the main entrance he became enchanted.

The lawn connected with "Briar Crest" contains about 17 acres. Much care has been given to this lawn, which is dotted all over with handsome beds of flowers and tropical plants. On the main lawn we find a bed designed in shape of a ten-point star. This bed is composed of Geraniums and Coleus. It contains 500 Pilot Geraniums, 1200 Golden Bedder Coleus. It is certainly very handsome. At the lower entrance there is a pear-shaped bed of Verschaffelti Coleus. One of the most interesting features that met our view was a tropical bed composed of fine grasses and all kinds of tropical plants. Another bed which deserves special mention is one in the shape of a crescent.

A bed at the main entrance, about 25 feet in diameter, containing 4800 plants, and composed of Echeveria and Alternanthera, with a Yucca in the centre, is very attractive. Opposite there is a large bed of Hydrangeas with a border of Geraniums, and Cloth of Gold Nasturtiums, mixed with Gladioli of various colors. Opposite the green-houses there is a large Mexican Cactus, about six feet high, surrounded by a six-pointed star of Alternanthera and Echeveria. To the left of the lodge there is a beautiful scroll, fifty feet in length. In the background, the coach house is almost hidden with Cannas and Dahlias. Another bed on the main drive which is certainly very handsomely designed in the shape of a heart, consists of Alternanthera, Coleus and Cacti, numbering over 2000 plants. On one side of this is a leaf of bright yellow Coleus, with dark border. On the other side is a spray of leaves composed of Alternantheras of old-gold color, with red stripes representing the rib of the leaves.

The Rookery near the entrance to the mansion is certainly a very artistic piece of work. It is at least 10 feet high, and over 100 feet in circumference. It is made up of very fine specimens of Crotons, tropical plants and palms, surrounded by a border of dark colors. The rocks are of white flint.

On the west side of the mansion there is an oval-shaped bed of mixed bright colors, which shows very prominently. All over the lawn can be found beds of unique design, each vieing with the other for supremacy. The lawn is kept in excellent condition, and has always the appearance of a velvet carpet. There have been planted recently about 1700 ornamental trees and shrubbery, which have added to the beauty and other portions of the lawn. A raised border containing 1800 smaller plants has been set out along the shrubbery, and adds very materially to the effect.

There are two large green-houses located near the main entrance. In the Winter all the choice plants and flowers are stored in these, and it must be an interesting sight to visit them when the chilling blasts have stripped all outside of its loveliness and beauty. The entire length of the lawn on the Spring Mill road has been planted with flowers of every description.—*Bryn Mawr News.*

CPSIA information can be obtained
at www.ICGtesting.com
Printed in the USA
BVHW041450150219
540385BV00008B/75/P

9 780265 842850